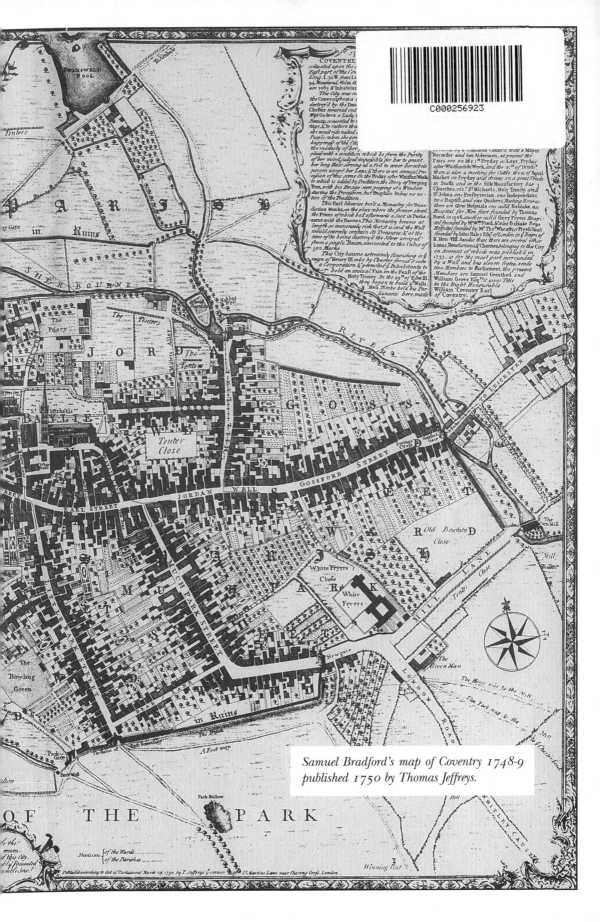

Samuel Bradford's map of Coventry 1748-9 published 1750 by Thomas Jeffreys.

A History of
Coventry

Looking from Cross Cheaping into Broadgate circa 1750 (19th-century engraving by George Webster).

A HISTORY OF

COVENTRY

DAVID MCGRORY

Phillimore

2003

Published by
PHILLIMORE & CO. LTD
Shopwyke Manor Barn, Chichester, West Sussex, England

ISBN 1 86077 264 1

Printed and bound in Great Britain by
MPG BOOKS LTD
Bodmin, Cornwall

For my Heather with love

CONTENTS

LIST OF ILLUSTRATIONS

Frontispiece: Coventry Cross

Acknowledgements

Many thanks to the British Museum, British Library and the Public Record Office for their help. Also many thanks for the continuing help of Coventry City Libraries, Local Studies Section and Coventry City Archives, and particular thanks to Simon Thraves of Phillimore for his hard work in the production of the book. I would also like to thank all of Coventry's previous antiquarians and historians over the centuries who have all contributed in some way to this work. The sources for this work have been gathered over many years and are too numerous to name.

Most illustrations are from my own collection, but those I would like to thank for illustrations are Coventry City Council, Coventry Libraries, Local Studies, *Coventry Evening Telegraph*, Midland Air Museum, John Ashby, Margaret Rylatt, Barry Denton, Les Fannon, Albert Peck, Cliff Barlow, Trevor Pring, Frank Scotland, Joseph York, Roy Baron, Jane Railton, Neil Cowley, Roger Bailey, David Morgan, Kathleen and Susan Spragg and Craig Taylor.

One

BEGINNINGS

PREHISTORY

Warwickshire's earliest known rock deposit lies north of Coventry in the Nuneaton area. It dates to the Pre-Cambrian period and consists of volcanic ash laid down some 600 million years ago. In the Cambrian period the land was swamped by a sea, which began to recede in the Devonian era (408 - 360 million years ago), the north of the county becoming river deltas. The rock laid down in this period is well known in Coventry and the county as the traditional building material, old red sandstone.

In the Carboniferous period (360 - 286 million years ago) Coventry lay within an area of deltaic mudflats and swamp forest, thick with trees and ferns. The crushed remnants of this once great forest were burned in local fires as coal, mined from the 17th century at such places as Wyken, Walsgrave, Binley and Keresley.

As the Carboniferous moved into the Permian period the swamp forest disappeared. The Coventry area was peaceful compared with the north of the county, which suffered from earthquakes. Paddling about in the warm waters of the local lagoons were creatures such as the carnivorous, armour-plated amphibian, Dasyceps bucklandi. This species was local to Warwickshire. In the age of the dinosaur, the whole of the county was covered by a warm shallow sea teeming with life such as fish, ammonites, belamites and dinosaurs, such as the long-necked, four-paddled Plesiosaur and the dolphin-like Ichthyosaur. Fine examples of both have been unearthed in the south of the county, and 'a fine head, much compressed, and a large jaw with teeth' of a Mastodontosaurus was found in Keuper beds in Coventry.

Sixty-five million years ago the sea retreated and the area became temperate, interrupted by three glacial periods and a period dominated by a sub-tropical climate. In the centre of Coventry, on the old Alvis site on the Holyhead Road, a hippopotamus skull was unearthed some years ago. During the glacial period Coventry and part of Warwickshire was covered by Glacial Lake Harrison,[1] the ice from which helped form the landscape we see today.

Just outside Coventry lies the small village of Bubbenhall, where in recent years evidence has been found of early man. At the site of Waverly Wood Quarry archaeologists have unearthed flaked tools and enormous hand axes which were once wielded by Homo Erectus. These have been amino-acid dated and found to be 500,000 years old.[2] Animal remains show that their owners were following the great herds as they migrated across ancient Warwickshire. The site is one of the oldest known in England. Another ancient site on the outskirts of the city is Baginton, where finds from the Lower Palaeolithic have been made,[3] such as a rare quartzite hand axe and flint implements, as well as microliths dating back to the Mesolithic period. These have also been found on the northern edge of the city at what appears to be a seasonal camp on Corley Rocks, Corley. As far back as 1935 there were 23 known sites around Coventry which had turned up worked flint tools.[4] It is also worth noting three worked flints, consisting of a possible arrowhead, a scraper and possible flint knife, found during excavations at the Charterhouse. All the tools were found out of context, which indicates early prehistoric passage, probably along the river through Coventry centre.[5]

Another ancient site, this time within the present city boundary, is the area occupied by Gibbet Hill and part of Warwick University. The area appears to have had almost continuous occupation since the Neolithic period. Amongst the many local finds are stone axes made at the 'axe factory' at Craig Llwyd in North Wales.[6] Recently Iron-Age roundhouses were discovered here. In 1968 a stone butted axe made in the Penzance region was found in the Allesley/Eastern Green area, and an axe made in the Lake District was found at Corley, which leads some experts to believe the Coventry district lay on a prehistoric trade route. A comptonite hammer-axe made in the Griff area near Nuneaton was found in 1968 in a garden in Greendale Road, only one and a half miles from the Penzance axe.[7]

The Neolithic peoples were the first to introduce agriculture, living in settled communities and not following the herds. Wherever they lived can usually be found burial mounds. Few are known in the Coventry area, but sources do tell of lost undated mounds,[8] such as the Giants Grave which could once be found in Hillfields and two undated tumuli in the grounds of Coombe Abbey.[9] This mound could date to the Bronze Age, however, like the two round barrows recorded at Baginton. These were built by the 'Beaker People', one of whose clay 'beakers' was destroyed in the Coventry Reference Library on 14 November 1940. Likewise, the 'Brandon Barrow' in the Brandon area on the edge of the city was destroyed when the branch railway station was built. At Walsgrave-on-Sow in 1882 a finely polished greenstone socketed axe-head was found,[10] which could date from the Mesolithic to the early Bronze Age.

The camp at Corley Rocks was excavated in 1923 and is believed to have been occasionally occupied from the Neolithic to the Roman period. It has been suggested in the past that Barrs Hill in Radford was at some point a prehistoric camp. Clues to this lie in the pre-16th-century local name of Medelborowe or 'middle-borough', borough or burgh signifying a fortified place. It has also been noted that in prints of the area made in the 18th century terracing can be seen on the hillside. This may have been made in the Civil War period, when the area

1   *The only known picture of a tumuli and standing stone in the Coventry area, Coombe Abbey,*
1729.

was occupied for a short time as an 'outer' fortification of the city, but the old ditch fortifications could simply have been re-dug. The *Proceedings of the Warwickshire Naturalist and Archaeological Society* of 1904, in a report on prehistoric covered ways, notes the following: 'Barrs Hill, Coventry, 200 yards, down to Radford Brook. This way has long been filled up.' The sunken track ran down the hill towards Middleborough Road and was wide enough to take one man and one animal walking side by side, in the tradition of all such ancient fort tracks, so that people could use them unseen by enemies, or to escape or outflank attackers. It cannot be linked to any Civil War fortification for it runs not towards the city but away from it. The existence of the track adds weight to the belief that the hill was indeed a prehistoric fortification.

Very little from the Celtic/Bronze-Age period has been found around Coventry, though enough to suggest the passage of people through the area. Broadgate Hill, its original name unknown, is surrounded by a massive ditch which the Saxons called the 'Hyrsum Ditch', the ditch of obedience, which stretches from above Earl Street around the hill-top probably down to Pool Meadow; this lower end was probably the 'rather wide stagnant ditch' mentioned in 1910 in the *Coventry Standard*.[11] It may have formed a barrier to keep people out, or it may have been created to demark a sacred site. It may, of course, date to the later Saxon period and be some sort of town ditch or part of a burh, a fortified enclosure. The Hyrsum has been archaeologically dated to the 12th century, by odd pottery fragments, but it bears a Saxon name and may have been re-dug because of silting in the 12th century, probably during the war between Stephen and Matilda.

On and around Broadgate Hill, the centre of this enclosure, odd finds have been made, such as a hollowed-out log boat and coracle paddle. The valley formed by Broadgate and Barrs Hill was originally a huge lake, which fluctuated in size according to the seasons, known as the Bablake or 'Babbu-lacu'. A remnant was known in the 14th century as the 'Babylake'. An explanation for the name is that it was a stream (some have suggested 'lacu' means stream) associated with someone called Babban, i.e. Babban's stream. This seems unlikely considering that what filled the valley was a large lake stretching from beyond Queen Victoria Road to Market Way to Pool Meadow. This lake has in places left up to thirty feet of silt. When the Woolworth store was being constructed in the early 1950s it was noted that hundreds of oak piles protuded from the lake bed. No proper excavation was done on the site so we can only guess at their possible origins. Much of this ground was still undeveloped as late as 1807.[12]

During the rebuilding of Broadgate in 1947 a workman unearthed a Bronze-Age axe-head, which was displayed but later disappeared. However, a photograph[13] of objects found in Broadgate showed various items from different periods, amongst them the coracle paddle and axe, as well as a socketed and looped palstave dating from between 850 and 650 B.C. A second axe-head of the same type was found in a field at Canley amongst spoil taken from Broadgate during the same excavations. As late as the 1960s the find was dismissed as an unrecorded axe-head blasted a considerable distance from a 'former museum, bombed during the war, [which] stood near this area'.[14] The museum referred to, John Shelton's Benedictine Museum in Little Park Street, was created long after the last bombs fell. Shelton had saved his collection of artefacts from his home, which was burned but not blown up. It seems clear that this second axe originated in Broadgate. Now, one axe could be a casual loss, but two is unlikely. A founder's hoard of damaged implements for re-smelting is also unlikely, as the axes were intact, which leaves the possibility of deliberate burial as an offering on a sacred hilltop, a practice not uncommon in the period we are dealing with. Sadly, during the period when Broadgate was being dug up much evidence of Coventry's early history was destroyed.

There was a third Bronze-Age axe-head from Coventry in the Staunton Collection, said to have been used in the old Coventry Pageants or found on the site of one of the pageant houses. Another axe-head found on Whitley Aerodrome in 1928 has been dated to 1500 B.C.,[15] and a Gallo-Belgic gold stater dating from 57 to 45 B.C. was found in a garden in Beake Avenue, Radford. *West Midlands Archaeology* (35, 1992) reported the discovery of the end link of a decorative bronze bridle bit, dating from the late 1st century B.C. to the early 1st century A.D., found by a metal detectorist in the Coundon area.

During the period known as the Iron Age, Warwickshire lay in the borderlands of the Coritani, to the north-east, the Cornovii in the west and the Iceni in the east. Celtic names survive in local rivers such as the 'Abhain', for Avon, 'Leamh' for Leam, and Sowe, known by the Celts as the 'Samhadh'. The main watercourses running into the centre of Coventry are the Radford Brook and the Sherbourne. The Radford Brook has lost its original name but the

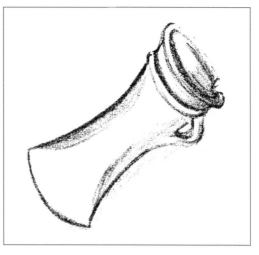

2   *Prehistoric axe-head found in Broadgate in 1947. (Drawing by David McGrory)*

Sherbourne derives from the Anglo-Saxon and is translated 'shere-bourne', meaning 'clear stream'. It does, however, appear to have an older name, the 'Cune'. The ancient Cune/Sherebourne passes through Coundon (Cunehealm), giving the Celtic settlement its name.

The word 'cune' (sometimes spelt 'couen' or 'couaen') can be found in Couaentree, the earliest spelling of Coventry in Edward the Confessor's charter confirming the foundation of Coventry monastery.[16] This has been suggested by many historians as the origin of the Coventry place-name, the 'treabh' element indicating a farmed village on the Cune. The word 'cune' can also be linked to a meeting place of two water sources, such as at Cound near Shrewsbury, where the 'Cound' meets the Severn. Mildenhall in Wiltshire, where the Og meets the Kennet, was known in Romano-British times as Cunetio.[17] It is notable that the Celtic god Condatis gave his name to watersmeets and confluences. Coventry itself had its own meeting place of the waters: the Cune/Sherbourne flowed into the Radford Brook (possibly known as the Cunnet) at the bottom of present-day Trinity Street, where the Mill Dam was. Both watercourses would have fed the great Bablake. The name Cune seems to have been known locally until at least the 16th century and appears to have two meanings in the Celtic language, either 'hound' or, from 'kuno', 'the exalted holy river'. The Anglo-Saxon 'shere-bourne' can be interpreted as sacred or pure river, and it is known that the Celts considered many rivers sacred, especially those, like the Cune/Sherbourne, rising from the earth.

Other former suggestions for 'Coventre' are the 'convent town' or the 'covenant tree', indicating a tree by which a covenant or pact was made between two Danish warriors. Both these have long since been dismissed, a place-name expert in the late 1890s, after many years of confusion, deriving the city's name from a word used in a copy of the Anglo-Saxon Chronicle dated about 1060. 'Cofantreo'[18] is used only once and is translated, ignoring the 'n', as the tree of Cofa. But there appears to be no known Anglo-Saxon personal name 'Cofa', the nearest being 'Cufa'.[19] And 'cofa' is only ever used as part of another word, to mean 'heart'. The Anglo-Saxon pronunciation of the word 'Cofantreo' would be Covantreo, the Saxon 'v' always being written as an 'f', another example being 'Beferburna' pronounced Beverburna, the Bever stream. If Cofa did not exist, and the actual word is 'Cofan'/'Cofen', pronounced Covan/Coven, we have a known Early English word meaning a cave, valley or cell.[20] The site of old Coventry lay on the side of a valley which has a tradition of a cave in its hillside. In the *Oxford Dictionary of English Place Names*, 'Coven' is said to mean a valley among the hills, again fitting for Coventry's location.

ROMAN COVENTRY

There is no firm evidence that in Roman times a settlement existed on the site we now know as Coventry, but there are enough artefacts to prove that if the Romans didn't live here permanently they certainly knew the area.

Traditionally, Julius Agricola passed through Coventry, built a marching camp on Barrs Hill and called the nearby settlement 'Coventina'. Barrs Hill did bear marks of undated fortification, and Roman coins and pottery dating from the reign of Tiberius (A.D.14) to the 4th century have in the past been found upon the hill. Also, at the base of Barrs Hill, Shelton unearthed a wooden causeway 15 feet across built on oak piles driven into the bed of the Babbu-lacu. He declared the work Roman, and to corroborate his theory he also found Roman horseshoes on the bankside near to present Well Street. The structure suggests trained builders, and Agricola's Legio XX (which left Britain A.D.87) are known to have passed through the area. They were engineers and quite capable of constructing a causeway. During building they would have camped on the high ground above the valley, i.e. Barrs or Broadgate Hill.

As for Coventina, there is a shrine dedicated to this Romano-Celtic goddess at the legionary fort at Crawborough in Yorkshire. The goddess, who is part of a water cult, was normally shown naked or semi-naked pouring water from an urn and holding a plant. In the 19th century a 'medal' was found during building work in New Buildings, said to have on one side a woman pouring water from a jug and on the other a naked woman with a plant between her feet. The fact that the medal, now lost, bore a nude woman suggests it was Roman rather than later. At Crawborough, the shrine to the goddess consisted of a decorated altar before a walled pool in which offerings were made. One such pool existed at the bottom of Cox Street and was known as Hob's Hole. Hob, of course, is a name connected with the devil, so the previously sacred paved pool became the devil's hole in Christian times.

In the Sherbourne in Cox Street, near to the hole, Shelton excavated the original riverbed and found 'a coin of Emperor Galinus (A.D. 253-88), a bronze ring, jet ring, toilet set for nails and ears, surgeons needles, pottery, iron handles, bronze for beating out, shears, etc'.[21] These were sent to the British Museum and the smaller objects were identified as 'the contents of a Roman lady's satchel'. This find is significant inasmuch as it shows Coventry lay not in a wilderness familiar only to legionaries but on an established route which Roman women travelled along.

It is thought that two Roman routes met at Coventry, one or both of which may be of prehistoric origin. One of these began from Mancetter (Manduessedum) by the Roman Watling Street (A5). Mancetter was the site of a Roman settlement and legionary fort, and the site of the 'Field of Chariots' where Boudicca's revolt against Roman rule was crushed in A.D.61. It is believed that the horses captured after this event were trained by the Romans in the rare horse-gyrus at the Lunt, Baginton. The road passes Caldecote Hill, Caldecote being a name regularly found on Roman roads, then the Roman pottery kilns at Hartshill, and the Roman camp at Camp Hill. It emerges on the other side of Nuneaton at Caldwell as the present-day B4113. Here we have again the occurrence of 'Cald', which is thought to have indicated some sort of Roman roadside shelter. The road continues through Griff, where stone axes were made, possibly indicating a pre-Roman route, and Bedworth, site of Roman finds and a Roman trackway noted in 1793, and into Coventry through Longford, another name linked with Roman roads.[22]

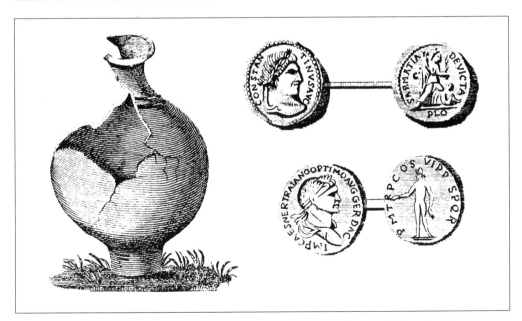

3 *Half of the Roman hoard found in Foleshill.* (Gentleman's Magazine)

The road then continues either along the course of the present Foleshill Road or joins a secondary route following that of the Stoney Stanton Road. Near the bottom of this route in 1792 a large and significant Roman find was made. It was reported in the *Coventry Mercury*:

> On the 17th of December last, was discovered in a meadow at Foleshill, belonging to Mr. Jos. Whiting of that place, in digging a trench, about two feet below the surface, an earthen pot, containing upwards of 1,800 Roman copper coins, principally of the Emperors Constantine, Constans, Constantius and Magentius; most of which remain in the possession of Mr. Whiting, for the inspection of the curious. And on Sunday last, in continuing the same trench, he found another earthen jug, containing a greater quantity of larger coin; but the latter are in greater preservation.[23]

In the *Gentleman's Magazine* of 1793, a correspondent signing himself 'Explorator' added that a 'second pot was much broken when discovered, but appears from the fragments to resemble the former, only is smaller; the coins, though said to be better preserved, and larger, were precisely the same sorts, &c., as those first discovered.'[24] This intriguing hoard of over 4,000 coins was found at Bullester Fields Farm and adds weight to the evidence that a Roman road ran through the site of present-day Coventry.

The track then cut in a westerly direction across the edge of Barrs Hill, in the direction of either Bishop Street or Cook Street and Silver Street, to the lake edge and the site of Shelton's hippo-sandals and causeway. By this site ancient pillars 'of great strength and size' were also unearthed, and in 1796 another now forgotten object, an alabaster statuette of a warrior wearing a laurel crown was found. The figure was reported as being 'considerably below the surface of Bishop Street and near to the Free School there'. The statuette, now lost, was believed to be Roman.

The Warwickshire Natural History and Archaeological Society reported (1868) that in 1820, near the bottom of Broadgate Hill, underneath a medieval cellar, was unearthed an 'old pavement, said to be Roman'. This continued up to the top of Broadgate Hill, for it was here that the *Gentleman's Magazine* of 1793 reports:

> In the last summer the street in Coventry, called Broadgate, was opened to a depth of 5 or 6 feet, when a regular pavement was discovered, and upon that pavement, a coin of Nero in middle brass ...[25]

This find has been dismissed because it is known that a pavement was laid in Broadgate in medieval times, but other finds were made in the area. Shelton unearthed a stone trackway behind the Burges in the 1930s, and around the mid-19th century, workmen unearthed a 10-inch-high marble statue of Mars while digging behind Cross Cheaping. The statue shows one of the legions' most favoured gods leaning against a shield and holding a wheatsheaf in his dual role as god of war and of agriculture. In Cross Cheaping, in the direction of the

Broadgate track, a Roman 'pavement' was discovered at the end of the 19th century.[26] The coin of Nero was not the only one to be found on Broadgate Hill. Nineteenth-century historian William G. Fretton wrote, 'I have several Roman coins found in this locality'.[27] In the Municipal Exhibition at the Drill Hall in 1945, wooden water pipes, found in Broadgate and believed to be Roman, were exhibited.

Other finds from the Coventry district include a possible villa or farmstead site unearthed during the building of the Showcase Cinema in Walsgrave.[28] The area lies below Mount Pleasant, another place-name linked to Roman sites. During a recent dig (1999) in Gosford Street a Roman fibulae brooch was unearthed. A third-century Roman coin, an antoninianus probably of Constantius or Constantine, was unearthed during excavations in Much Park Street in 1970-4.[29] Roman pottery was unearthed in Spon Street in 1976 and coins of emperors such as Antoninus Pius, Gordian, Maximian, Julian and others have been found in Keresley, Radford, Coundon, Whoberley and Stoke. In 1912 a Roman pot in coarse grey-ware was unearthed in Broad Lane. Fragments of Roman pottery were discovered in nearby Broomfield Road,[30] and more Roman pottery was found near Centaur Road.

The Lunt Roman Fort, already mentioned, was first set up, it is thought, at the time of the Boudiccan revolt as a legionary headquarters and then a training camp for captured Iceni horses. It was built on a spur of land overlooking the River Sowe. Its name originally meant 'wooded slope'. Roman occupation at Baginton was unknown until 1928, when Edwards and Shotton discovered two rubbish pits which contained pottery. By 1959 the Roman site was believed to have consisted of a farm or villa.[31] But this was to change when excavations began in 1960 and defensive ditches were unearthed, quickly followed by evidence of a large fort. A settlement appears to have been built up around it, stretching towards the present airport.

The fort continued to grow until A.D.80 when it was abandoned, probably because Julius Agricola needed the troops for his northern campaign. The legions returned in the reign of Galinus (A.D.253-88)[32] and rebuilt a fortification, and the present gateway and ditches date from this period. The gate was dated by a coin of Galinus found in a post-hole. The coin was believed to have been lost, but it is more likely that the gate builders deliberately placed it in the post-hole as a protective offering. A piece of late third-century Wappenbury grey-ware was also unearthed from a ditch.[33]

The gyrus (circular training ring) from the first fort, which has been re-constructed, is unparalleled in western Europe. It measures some 107 feet around and the 'archaeological evidence strongly suggests'[34] that it is a cavalry training ring. Here horses could be conditioned for battle by men positioned around the ring striking their swords against their shields. The sounds mimicked those of battle. The original fort also contained granaries (*horrea*), headquarters (*principia*),

4   *The rare gyrus at the Lunt Fort, Baginton. (Margaret Rylatt/Coventry City Council)*

commander's house (*praetorium*), workshops (*fabrica*), stables and barracks (in the Praetentura). The fort may have originated as a training camp for captured horse, but up until A.D.80 it probably developed as a specialist training centre for elite cavalry such as the *cohors equitata*.

SAXON COVENTRY AND OSBURGA

After the fall of Roman Britain the Romano-British population absorbed Anglo-Saxon immigrants who were well established in the area by the mid-sixth century. The famed Baginton Bowl, a large bronze and silver, enamelled and jewelled bowl, was unearthed at a large burial ground. Many fresh settlements sprang up, as the word 'ley' for 'forest clearing' testifies. These include Keresley, Allesley, Henley, Whitley, Binley, Canley, and Whoberley. Others now lost include Shortley, Bissesley and Pinley.

As for the central settlement in Coventry, we can only make assumptions. No buildings have been found, although this does not mean they did not exist. Dugdale believed the earliest settlement lay on Barrs Hill. Later historians mention that undated coins and old stonework were unearthed here, and tradition tells us that the missionary St Chad passed through the area (there was a St Chad's Well in Stoke) and built a small chapel on Barrs Hill. It is true that Barrs Hill was once the home of a church dedicated to St Nicholas, a dedication which points to an early building. By the Dissolution this chapel had grown into a large church, consisting of a central chancel with towers and spires on both ends, which fact was later remembered in the field names of 'big' and 'little spire field.'

Central England at this time was not a Christian place; it was not until 655 that the heathen king of Mercia, Penda, was killed in battle. His son Paeda, who became a Christian, succeeded him. A year later he was succeeded by Wulphere (656-75), who in 661 allowed the first baptisms in Hwiccia (south Mercia). Although some of the Saxon nobility adopted the faith and allowed the construction of churches, Christianity was less widespread among the rural population. Various edicts throughout the Saxon and into the medieval period outlawed the veneration of trees, rocks and springs.

Osburga (commonly known as Osburg), meaning 'divine fortress', was one of the famed sisters of the Saxon monastic house at Barking. An obscure figure, she is mentioned only once in her lifetime by St Aldhelm, Bishop of Sherborne (died 709). His book *De laudibus virginitatis*, written around 675, was dedicated to the 'Sisterhood of Barking' and records that Osburga and the other sisters of the house left Barking to establish monastic settlements elsewhere. Tradition, the later existence of St Osburg's Pool and the fact that her relics lay in Coventry strongly suggest that Osburga came to Coventry as abbess around the year 700. An anonymous 14th-century manuscript in the Bodleian Library also informs us that, 'In ancient times on the bank of the river called by the inhabitants Sherbourne, which flows right through the city of Coventry, there was formerly a monastery of maidens dedicated to God.'[35]

The monastery would most likely have been a double house holding both monks and nuns and ruled over by an abbess. This was the norm during the seventh and eighth centuries, the church in this period having no wish for seclusion since the suppression of paganism could not be conducted from behind closed doors. Many Christian churches were built directly upon pre-Christian sacred sites, which may explain why Osburga decided to build upon Broadgate Hill. After her death the house was dedicated in her name and her relics displayed in a reliquary on a large crossbeam.

5   *A Benedictine abbess and nun (19th-century engraving).*

6   *Reconstruction of a seventh/eighth-century Saxon church with relic beam (19th-century engraving).*

The monastic house continued to serve the local area through troubled times. In the year 829 Ecgbryth 'overcame the Mercian kingdom', and in 910 the land of the Mercians was 'ravaged'. Archaeologist Mick Aston has suggested that monasticism was 'virtually extinguished' in this period. But most of the Danes that settled in England were massacred on St Brice's Day, 13 November 1002, including those in Coventry, and for some time afterwards Coventry became famous for its Hock Tuesday play, which acted out the massacre. Sixteenth-century historian Robert Laneham says of the play that it was 'wont to be play'd in the citie yearly'.

When Alfred the Great had forced the Danes to agree to the 'Peace of Wedmore' in 878, which confined them to the Danelaw, an area north of Watling Street, it was said that 'much of Mercia was practically in ruins, cities and monasteries had to be rebuilt'. Reminders of the Danes in this area, probably infiltration from the Danelaw, are place-names such as 'Biggin' (Stoke), which is Danish for house, and Keresley, which means 'Kaerers clearing'. Another relic dating to around this period is an axe believed to be Danish in style.

It is recorded in the Anglo-Saxon Chronicles of the year 1016, that 'In this year came Cnut with his host, and with him ealdorman Eadric, and crossed the Thames into Mercia at Cricklade, and then during the season of Christmas turned into Warwickshire, and harried and burned and slew all that they found.' This Danish army was led through the county by one who knew it well, Edric Streona, known to history as Edric the Traitor or Grasper. Cnut took the land by force and was crowned king of all except Wessex. John Rous, the 15th-century priest and antiquarian who lived at the hermitage at Guys Cliff, must have had access to ancient documents for he wrote of the destruction of the Hom Hill fortress at Stoneleigh and added, 'even the Abbey of Nuns at Coventry is destroyed, of which in times past the Virgin St Osburg was the Abbess'.[36] The Danes probably burned down St Osburga's, but some of her bones and her skull survived and were later re-housed in new reliquaries.

By all accounts Cnut ruled well. At the Council of Oxford

7 *Cnut presents a cross to a newly restored church (19th-century engraving).*

in 1018 he agreed to rule under 'one God' and to avoid 'heathen practices'. He grew remorseful for the blood he had shed and the destruction he had caused in taking the throne, and in 1026 he went to Rome. From here in April 1027 he wrote a letter to his people, saying amongst other things that 'I have vowed to God himself, henceforth to reform my life in all things ... and with God's assistance, to rectify anything hitherto unjustly done.'[37] Amongst these rectifications was the rebuilding of many religious houses that his army had previously destroyed. William of Malmesbury says that, 'He repaired throughout England, the monasteries which had been partly injured and partly destroyed by the military incursions of himself or his father; he built churches in all the places he had fought.' The 16th-century antiquarian John Leland, quoting old sources, states that the site of Coventry Priory was formerly the place where 'Kynge Canute the Dane made [a] howse of nunes. Leofrike, Erle of the Marches, turnyd it in Kyng Edward the Confessor's dayes into a howes of monkes.'

The house of nuns that Cnut 'made' must refer to the rebuilding or restoration of St Osburga's. A piece of local red sandstone, decorated with a squirrel in a tree or vine, unearthed in Palmer Lane in 1934 was until quite recently believed to be a piece of a cross but has now been identified as a door jamb which may have formed part of the entrance to the church itself. Another relic of Osburga was found during the excavations of the west entrance of Coventry Priory in 1868, when a letter appeared in the *Coventry Herald* stating, 'Sir, it gives me intense gratitude to behold with my own eyes ... the very seal of Coventry's

8   *The west entrance to Coventry Priory in the 1950s. The columns were originally painted red and white.*

ancient Minister, now in the possession of Mr Hinds, the druggist of Far Gosford Street. It is fine cut-stone … the usual size of a conventual Abbey Seal, with the rude figure of St. Osburg upon it, standing up with a Crozier in her left hand … Mr. Odell, a kind Magistrate of this city, informed me that this sacred relic, which has St. Osburg's name upon it and figure, was found amidst the rubbish while it was being carted away from the excavations then being made for the present Blue Coat School.'[38]

St Osburga's 'restored' church would obviously have housed the relics of Osburga herself. Cnut also gave to the 'church of Coventry' another important relic, namely the arm of St Augustine of Hippo, 'the Great Doctor'. It appears that in 1022 he ordered Archbishop Aethelnoth to purchase the arm in Pavia for a 100 talents of silver and one talent of gold. The relic was presented to the rebuilt/restored church and Cnut was a step nearer to heaven; such a gift 'would gain him many friends and prayers'.[39]

Leland and Sir William Dugdale both state that Leofric created the house in the reign of Edward the Confessor and the date of foundation fits this, 1043 being the year that Edward was crowned. But the 1043 date belongs to a confirmation charter and not the original. It is likely, however, that this confirmation was produced around the same time as the dedication. Dugdale quotes a manuscript written by a later prior, Galfridus (1216-36), who categorically states that Archbishop Edsie performed the ceremony on 4 October 1043 in the presence of Abbot Leofwine (no other abbots are recorded before him) and 24 monks, and this foundation was also confirmed by a papal *bulla*, although it later proved to be a forgery. It could be a complete fabrication or the replacement for a lost document.

Recent (1999-2001) archaeological excavations on the site of St Mary's Priory have produced a spectacular find under the north chancel, near No. 7 Priory

Row. Stone and skeletal remains *in situ* suggest that St Osburga's stood on this site. The curved stonework discovered could reflect the fact that many seventh- and eighth-century Saxon churches had semi-circular apses, even though it is facing north. During the dig a large enclosing ditch was unearthed which had been filled in in the 12th century and may be a defensive or boundary enclosure in the manner of other Saxon churches such as South Elmham in Suffolk. It may, however, date from the fortification of the monastery in the early 12th century by Earl Marmion.

Many early Saxon churches were enclosed or added to in later periods, and the fact that Leland suggests that Leofric turned the house of nuns into a house of monks may infer the swallowing up or extending of the old church with a rebuilding and refoundation under the Benedictine rule. Certainly the monastery of St Mary was also dedicated to St Osburga. The site already had a river and pool, and springs such as the one which fed the Priory's main water source, the Broad Well, also existed.

LEOFRIC, GODIVA AND AELFGAR

Leofric, Earl of Mercia, or, to give him his original title, Leofric, 'hlaford Myrcena' (Lord of the Mercians), was the son of Leofwine, ealdorman of the Hwicce (south Mercia) in 997.[40] Leofwine retained the title even after Cnut had executed his eldest son (Leofric's brother), Northman. Leofric was created Earl of Mercia by Cnut around 1026. His family gained their aristocratic status despite Cnut's policy of replacing Danish earls with Saxons.

Florence of Worcester records that Cnut treated Leofric with 'great kindness' and Ingnulphus adds that the King 'greatly loved Earl Leofric'. Leofric was also a friend and confidant of Edward the Confessor, supporting his right to the throne against the other great earl, the powerful Godwin. The tradition of Leofric as the 'grim' lord, a heartless tyrant who forced his wife to shame herself, is nonsense, and in his lifetime Leofric was considered a great man, a diplomat and a saint. He was extremely religious and attended mass twice a day.

It was expected in this time that all great men should use their wealth to build new churches and bestow land and other gifts upon them. Leofric founded (or re-founded) the great church in Coventry, and supported it with lands, and other churches across his great lordship from Evesham to Croyland in Lincolnshire. Other sides to his character were as soldier and peacemaker. When a revolt began in Worcester which threatened the stability of the throne, it is said Leofric nearly razed the town to the ground. As for the peacemaker, 'It is difficult to tell of the distress and all the marching and the camping, and destruction of men and of horses, which all the English army endured until Leofric the Earl came thither, and Harold the Earl and Bishop Alder, and made a reconciliation there between them.'[41]

The man many considered an uncanonised saint, who had seen miraculous visions and raised Harold I, Harthacnut and Edward the Confessor to the throne, died in 1057 at his hall at Kings Bromley, Staffordshire. The Anglo-Saxon Chronicle informs us that, 'In this same year, on 30 October, earl Leofric passed away. He was very wise in all matters, both religious and secular, that benefited all this nation.' He was brought from his hall in Staffordshire to be buried in great pomp at Coventry at his church of St Mary. Roger de Hoveden wrote that, 'Leofric, that praiseworthy Earl of happy memory, son of Duke Leofwine, departed this life … and was honourably buried at Coventry.' William of Malmesbury adds that Leofric's body came with a huge donation of gold and silver and was lain within one of the porches of the church.

Godiva, whose name was really Godgifu, meaning 'Gods Gift', was the sister of Thorold, Sheriff of Lincolnshire. A charter concerning Croyland Abbey, quoted in the Chronicles of Ingnulphus, now believed to have been written in the 14th century, is our only source connecting Godgifu to Thorold, and its claims are not necessarily fabrications. The charter refers to Aelfgar as Leofric's eldest son, which implies that he and Godiva had more than one. That second son has been linked with Hereward the Wake. The *De Gestis Herewardi* from 1150 states that Hereward was the son of Leofric of Bourne (near Croyland) and Ediva. Ingnulphus gives the same parentage and also connects Leofric with Croyland Abbey, which we know was connected to the family.

Two sources tell us that the Abbot of Peterborough was Leofric's nephew and Hereward's uncle.[42] Hereward and his rebels certainly sacked the abbey after William the Conqueror had placed a Norman bishop in the building. Among the rebels was Earl Morcar, Leofric's grandson and Hereward's nephew. After

9 *Victorian painting of Godiva and Leofric.*

the rebellion Hereward is said to have been reconciled to William and settled down with a gift of land. Domesday Book records that a Hereward held land in Warwickshire, Worcestershire and Lincolnshire, all part of the old kingdom of Mercia. Later sources such as the *Dictionary of National Biography* dismiss the connection between Leofric and Hereward, but the most recent book on Hereward, published in 1995,[43] goes into this issue in depth and in the end cannot dismiss its possibility.

There is also some debate about whether Godiva was even the sister of Thorold, again because of the dubious nature of many early charters. According to Burbidge, the relationship is confirmed by the *Chronicon Petroburgense*, where Thorold is described in Latin under the date 1050 as being vice count and brother of Godiva, countess. It is believed that Leofric was Godiva's second husband, and that she split the land of her unnamed late husband (an earl) amongst the churches in the Ely area in the reign of Cnut. Possibly it was this same Godiva who is recorded in the *Liber Eliensis* (chronicle of Ely Monastery) under the year 1022 as being in fear of death and giving more land (that of her late parents) to the monastery. It is not impossible that Godiva's first husband was the incumbent of Mercia, the Danish Earl Eglaf, who died around this time during a visit to Constantinople.

Apart from references usually concerning occasional bestowal of land or gifts, Godiva is not mentioned in any chronicles of her time. She does, however, appear in chronicles written many years after her death. The 14th-century Croyland Chronicles of Ingnulphus refer to her as 'the most beauteous of all women of her time'. Godiva's love of the church is often mentioned, and especially her devotion to the Virgin Mary. The fact that she had once been near to death may have had a direct effect on her devotion. As well as building new churches and chapels, she made gifts of land and of other items such as jewels melted down and recast for holy relics. After Leofric's death these became more modest. Her jewelled necklace was given to Coventry Abbey, and three cloaks, two curtains, two coverings for benches, two candlesticks and a book to Worcester Abbey. Godiva visited the abbey personally to make the gifts, 'for the health of his [Leofric's] and her soul',[44] and also because Leofric had taken lands off the abbey, promising their return after his death, and Godiva now wanted this extended until after her death.

Godiva was probably around 57 when Leofric died. Their son Aelfgar inherited the Mercian earldom and Godiva appears to have gone into retirement, supported by what remained of her lands. Some years later she may have gone into a religious house. She appears to have spent much time at the ancient Evesham Abbey, where she and Leofric built the church of Holy Trinity, and here she was buried. The Evesham Chroniclers claimed that Prior Aefic, her father confessor, had convinced Godiva to found a new Benedictine house for monks in Coventry.[45] *Evesham Notes & Queries* states that the last recorded visit of Godiva to Evesham

10   *The 'Godiva Window' of Holy Trinity Church.*

was to attend the funeral of Prior Aefic at Holy Trinity. In his excellent book *Old Coventry and Lady Godiva*, however, Dr Burbidge quotes this passage from the Evesham Chronicle: 'Then your worthy Prior Aefic departed from this daylight in the year of Our Lords Incarnation one thousand and thirty-eight, and his grave worthily exists in the same church of the Blessed Trinity near that of the same pious Countess Godiva, and of whom, so long as he lived, he was a friend.' According to the 'Douce Manuscript' at Oxford, her date of death was 10 September 1067.

So Godiva lived to see the death of her husband, the great Leofric of Mercia, and the death of her wayward son, Earl Aelfgar. She also witnessed her granddaughter Ealdgyth's becoming Queen of England by marriage to King Harold, and the destruction of Saxon England with the death of Harold on Senlac Hill. Her estates were redistributed amongst various Norman lords.

THE LEGENDARY RIDE

Whether or not Godiva's legendary naked ride through the market place of Coventry ever took place has been for centuries a source of debate. It was not written about in her lifetime, or the lifetimes of her children or grandchildren. In fact it wasn't mentioned by any of the chroniclers until over 150 years after her death, which is probably because it never happened. The original story, probably told to Roger of Wendover in 1190 by monks displaced from Coventry Priory, appears in Wendover's *Flores Historiarum*:

The Countess Godiva, who was a great lover of God's Mother, longing to free the town of Coventry from heavy bondage from the oppression of a heavy toll, often with urgent prayers besought her husband, that from regard to Jesus Christ and his mother, he would free the town from that service, and all other heavy burdens.

The earl sharply rebuked her for foolishly asking what was so much to his damage, and always forbade her ever more to speak to him again on the subject. She, on the other hand, with a woman's pertinacity, never ceased to exasperate her husband.

He at last gave her his answer: Mount your horse and ride naked, before all the people, through the market of the town, from one end to the other, and on your return, you shall have your request.

Godiva replied: But will you give me permission, if I am willing to do it? I will, said he. Whereupon the countess beloved of God, loosed her hair and let down her tresses, which covered the whole of her body, like a veil, and then mounting her horse and attended by two knights, she rode through the market-place, without being seen, except her fair legs.

Having completed the journey, she returned with gladness to her astonished husband, and obtained of him what she had asked for. Earl Leofric freed the town of Coventry and its inhabitants from the aforesaid service, and confirmed what he had done by charter.[46]

Wendover's *Historiarum* survives only as a 14th-century manuscript, so the above tale may not be the original. There are at least two other versions by Wendover, either written or revised by him or copied by others at Wendover's scriptorium at St Albans, where he was a priest and later prior. In another account attributed to Wendover, Leofric isn't 'astonished', but filled with admiration. A third account, most likely Wendover's original, states that Godiva rode through the market seen by none and Leofric considered that a miracle had taken place. This miracle is repeated, and dated to the year 1057, in an account written by Matthew of Westminster (this may be Matthew Paris) which must have been copied from Wendover. It states that Godiva completed the ride and returned rejoicing to her husband, who considered it a miracle. In his own *Chronica Majora*, written in the early 13th century, Matthew Paris repeats the miracle: 'hoc pro miraculo'.[47]

As these sources pre-date the 14th-century version above we can safely assume that we are dealing with a miracle. Godiva rode through the market place accompanied by two knights when it was full of people, and nobody saw her. It was a time of 'miracles', when the miraculous tales of the early chroniclers were known as 'monkish tales'. This is the basis of the Godiva legend wherein the countess, benefactor of the people, is forced to take drastic steps to save 'her' people from a 'burdensome servitude'.

The origins of the ride itself, regardless of Godiva's participation or otherwise, may lie in ancient fertility rituals dating back to Romano-Celtic Britain. In the south of Warwickshire, about twenty miles from Coventry at Southam, which once belonged to Godiva, a 'Godiva Procession' survived until about 1845, which bore some aspects of a pagan rite. Two women on horseback, one white, one black, called 'the Black and White Lady', were completely covered with drapes

11   *The Lady Godiva by Jules Lefebvre, 1907.*

of lace which made them virtually invisible to those looking upon them. It wasn't always a case of blacking up, either, for in 1794 it was recorded that, 'The inhabitants of that place have engaged a [real] Black Lady to accompany the celebrated Lady Godiva.'[48] Leading the two women was another important character, a man wearing a bull mask called 'brazen face'.

The white woman represented one aspect of the fertility goddess, the black woman the darker side. The fact that the two were referred to as a single 'lady' suggests they were regarded as one. An illuminated document of the Smiths' Company of Coventry shows Godiva followed by a black woman riding an elephant, and in one version of the 'Banbury Cross' rhyme we find, 'Ride a cock horse to Banbury Cross, to see a black lady ride on a white horse.'[49]

The man dressed as a bull was outlawed by the Church as late as the 7th century. The bull mask was symbolic of fertility, the 'brazen face' a symbol of the sun, the giver of life. Despite being outlawed, the 'Ooser' (as he was known) survived in rural England into the 20th century. This pre-Christian deity could be found in places such as Melbury Osmund in Dorset, where generations of the same family were guardians of the horned bull mask with bulging eyes. A bull mask was also used in Shillingston, Dorset in Christmas rituals with young girls.

It is known that fertility rites took place in the Romano-Celtic period wherein naked women blackened themselves with woad, one ancient ritual involving girls on horseback being led around the fields by a bull-masked man. In their original form they were believed to restore fertility to the land, and to give some assurance of good crops and healthy beasts. Such traditions can be traced back to the Neolithic period, when myths told of the earth-goddess being annually impregnated by her consort the sun-god, who then lost his power until the next fertility cycle.

The 'Godiva Window' which could once be seen in Holy Trinity Church depicted a woman, said to be Godiva, sitting side-saddle on a white horse in a yellow dress and holding in her hand a flowering hawthorn branch. The May tree was a fertility symbol associated with agricultural rites connected to the god Mars. A Romano-British bronze found in Wiltshire shows Epona, the goddess of horses who had connections with agricultural fertility, in similar style, with a horse and holding a branch probably of hawthorn. She also holds a dish and wheat, other symbols of agricultural fertility. It seems likely that an ancient ceremony was recalled by the monks, or by a monk, from Coventry who turned it into a miraculous tale of self-sacrifice, and thus the Godiva legend was born.

THE HOUSE THAT LEOFRIC BUILT?

It had always been believed that Coventry's first cathedral and monastery was founded by Earl Leofric and Lady Godiva but it has recently been suggested that they did not found the monastery but only endowed it. The arm of St Augustine was presented to Coventry church in 1022 and those who have chosen not to believe in the existence of St Osburg's claim that the only church which could have been extant at this time was St Mary's Monastery, the later Priory. The foundation date of 1043 has had to be recalculated back to 1022 or earlier. The confirmation charter of Edward the Confessor, the original source for the later date, already known to be a forgery, is now considered totally spurious.

For the foundation and endowment of St Mary's we rely mainly on charters which are known to be forgeries or, more properly, copies, with additions made later to help the prior with claims upon lands and liberties that were not strictly his. The earliest known charter relating to Leofric's foundation of the monastery exists as a copy made on 7 February 1267. It reads:

> In the Year of the Incarnation of our Lord one thousand and forty-three, I, Earl Leofric, by the counsel and advice of King Edward and Pope Alexander, who sent to me his letter written below, with a seal, and by the testimony of other devout men, laymen as well as churchmen, have caused the Church of Coventry to be dedicated in honour of God and Saint Mary His Mother, of Saint Peter the Apostle, of Saint Osburga the Virgin, and of All Saints.
>
> Therefore I have given these twenty-four towns together with a moiety of the town in which the Church, for the service of God, and for the food and clothing of the Abbot and monks serving God in the same place ...

The charter then goes on to name the following places: Honington, Newnham, Chadshunt, Bishop's Itchington, Ufton, Southam, Grandborough, Birdingbury, Marston, Hardwick, Wasperton, Chesterton, Southam in Gloucestershire, Ryton, half of Walsgrave upon Sowe, Marston in Gloucestershire, Salwarp in

Worcestershire, Eaton in the shire of Chester, Kilsby and Winwick in Northamptonshire, Burbage, Barwell, Scrapetoft, Packington and Potters Marston in Leicestershire. It adds that these lands are given with 'sac' and 'soc' (sake and soke), and toll and team and other liberties. The Domesday description of St Mary's lands fits quite closely with the charter.

The charters from this period, including the one by Edward the Confessor, contain two new privileges, the rights to have a coroner and a guild merchant.[50] This would give the prior the right, amongst other things, to form a guild, and thereby control the merchant class of Coventry. Charters and confirmation letters forged around 1148 to 1153 appear to have been produced to protect the rights of the church against episcopal control, to make sure the monks could choose their own prior and to protect the lands given for the upkeep of the house so that no lord could take them, as Ranulf II does with St Michael's chapels and tithes before he restores them on his deathbed.

Evidence that Leofric's charter may not have been a total fabrication is a papal bull of Alexander III which states, 'I, Alexander … do give licence to you my beloved son Leofric, to erect and endow the monastery …'[51] The bull goes on to state that no bishop or other powerful man 'shall presume to have it'. Alexander warns that if any man does so he will suffer excommunication. This is the forger's hand at work, protecting the church from outside espiscopal and baronial interference.

The confirmation charter of Edward the Confessor, if we are to believe it, was originally written shortly after Leofric's death in 1057. After a lengthy introduction it states that:

> The venerable Earl Leofric inspired by Divine Grace, and in imitation of the glorious hill, and the beloved of God, Alexander Chief Pontiff, hath builded the monastery of St. Mary, Mother of God, and of St. Peter, and of all Saints, in the town which is called Coventry (Couentre), and has adorned it with magnificent gifts … [there follows list of manors]. Therefore … I give and grant to Abbot Leofwine, and all that come who shall minister the place, the complete possession of the monastery …[52]

Another charter of Edward the Confessor, this time said by Dr Burbidge to be 'undisputed', is in the British Museum and is in Old English, not Latin.[53] It is addressed to Archbishop Edsie, who was bishop between 1038 and 1047, and bears out the contention that Leofric and Godiva endowed rather than founded the church.

The later confirmation charters of William I are also forgeries and are the first to mention the fact that Leofric had given the northern half of Coventry to the monastery. When it appeared, this charter caused many problems, as the earlier ones had made no mention of the north of Coventry belonging to the Priory, but we can no longer believe in these old charters and the foundation date of 4 October 1043 as our forebears did, and unless an unknown and totally genuine charter comes to light we can only speculate.

12 *Drawing by Thomas de Elmham of the 13th-century high altar of Canterbury, with relic beam and the other arm of Saint Augustine (19th-century engraving).*

We learn, again from forged charters, that the monastery and church of St Mary was dedicated by Edsie, Archbishop of Canterbury, and the monastery was to house 24 monks overlooked by Abbot Leofwine. Leofwine was the first known abbot, suggesting this was the beginning of the house of monks. He was quickly followed by Leofric, Earl Leofric's nephew. This Abbot Leofric rode with Harold to Hastings, of which journey the Anglo-Saxon Chronicle notes that, 'there, he was sickened, and came home and was dead soon thereafter'. It also lists amongst his churches that of Coventry, which Leofric the Earl, who was his uncle, 'before had made'. Nothing is known of this establishment apart from the fact that it housed the arm of St Augustine and the remains of the 'founding' mother, Saint Osburga. It would have been fairly small compared with the later medieval establishment, probably with an enlarged church measuring no more than about 100 feet. Around it would be a scattering of buildings, including the cells of the monks. William of Malmesbury says of the church, 'It was enriched and beautified with so much gold and silver that the walls seemed too narrow to contain it: and in the reign of William Rufus, Robert De Limesei [Limesey, the bishop of the church] scraped from one beam that supported the shrines, five hundred marks of silver.' This is probably the only description we have of the general interior of Leofric and Godiva's church before its replacement by a Norman building. On her deathbed Godiva gave a jewelled necklace to be placed around the neck of the church's main statue of the virgin and is supposed to have stipulated that those who prayed before it should say a prayer for each stone in the necklace.

One thing Malmesbury does make clear is that in Leofric's church the shrines of Augustine and Osburga were supported by oak beams smothered in silver leaf. There are a couple of floor tiles surviving from this building and a stone carved with a crude cross which was probably a door mantel. Experts have dated the Norman church to the beginning of the 12th century, just after the bishop's see was moved to Coventry. During recent excavations it was noted that a ditch running through the building was in-filled in the mid-12th century, so a new church could not have been started before this date, but the dating of the ditch may not be accurate, based as it is on what happened to fall into the excavated section of it and when. Stonework of around 1100 was found in the crossing piers, and parts of the south and north walls and outer aisles of the main building were Romanesque, which would suggest the work was begun by Robert de Limesey (in Coventry 1102-17), a noted pillager of the church who is recorded as having failed to repair it. He did, however, use stolen material from Coventry to build Lichfield and his palace in Coventry, so it is possible that at some time in his notorious Coventry career he may have begun the rebuilding.

The powerful Prior Laurence (1149-79), who built the Hospital of St John in Bishop Street, was also a notable builder and may have added later work. Building appears to have been ongoing during the bishopric of Hugh de Nonant (1185-98), for Richard of Devizes writing in about 1190 informs us that Nonant demolished the monks' workshops and diverted the materials to building the church which at this time was unfinished. He also sold goods belonging to the Priory to pay for stonemasons and plasterers. During this work a block of stone fell from a tower, just missing Nonant and killing a young monk next to him.

Burbidge records that the completion of this work was likely to have been in about 1220. Land was granted to the bishop to build a residence, probably the Bishops Palace, on a site which had housed the 'late mason' of the cathedral. This area includes land up to the 'garden' of the Earl of Chester, the ground surrounding the earl's house or the de-fortified bailey of the earl's defunct castle. In the Calendar of Close Rolls (1247-51) a royal grant records timber for building work, which could have been for some minor additions. In the following century, the Register of Bishop Robert de Norbury (1322-58) offered indulgences for forty days to anyone who would contribute to the fabric of the building, and recent excavation (1999-2001) has shown rebuilding work was done on the main church in the 13th and 14th centuries, and much of the outer building, i.e. frater, cloisters, and great Chapter House, site of two parliaments, all belongs to this period. Most of the north aisle belongs to the original Norman building, however, having been built upon a floater. A cut in the bedrock here probably formed the edge of the previous Saxon church. The south-west side of the south aisle, forming the chantry wall, appears to date from the 14th century, the mason's

13 *Seal of Roger Longespee de Meulan, 1258, showing stylised churches of Coventry and Lichfield, which gave rise to the belief that Coventry had three spires. The only known seal of Coventry Cathedral with church shows a building with short cupolas and pinnacles. It is now lost.*

'arrow' marks being the same as those in the undercroft of St Mary's Guildhall, but beyond about three columns the stonework is purely late Norman.

There appears to have been much work done in the 14th and 15th centuries. Floor tiles dating mainly from this time bear many different designs. The design featuring an SS collar of the Lancastrians and swan of the Bohuns is thought to have been first produced in 1381 to commemorate the marriage of Henry Bolingbroke (Henry IV) to Mary de Bohun. Many of the tiles were made locally at Stoke, where 14th-century tilers set up their kilns. The inside of the church was whitewashed and gilded, with carvings, such as a statue of St Paul, and face corbels, containing original colours such as red or pink.

This later church, which is estimated to have been 400-425 feet long, was entered by a stone gatehouse, originally overlooking a large market square. Over a central doorway was a stained-glass window whose colours were predominantly red designs painted on very dark green glass. Entrance was gained down a semi-circular stair of about four steps. Beyond the second pier on the right stood a chantry chapel, one of many side chapels in the building, inside which stood a large tomb, decorated with weepers and pinnacles. Near the crossing of the central tower was said to be a processional entrance and then a huge oak or stone rood screen. The side aisles beyond contained more chapels. The high altar and three chevet chapels marked the easternmost point of the building, one of the largest cathedrals in England.

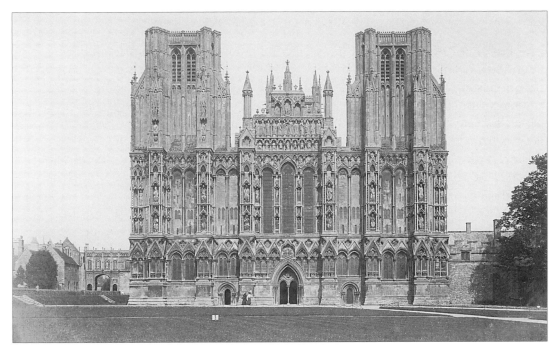

14   *The lower half of Wells Cathedral is of very much the same design as Coventry.*

In 1718 Willis Browne suggested in his book on mitred abbeys that St Mary's had three spires,[54] and since then it has generally been accepted that Coventry looked like Lichfield. Possibly the only evidence is a seal which shows the Bishop of Coventry and Lichfield standing before two three-spired buildings.

It was noted during excavations on the site of the crossing for the *Time Team* programme that the size of the crossing piers could not support the weight of a spire like Lichfield's. It could possibly support a smaller wooden structure, however, such as a wooden-tiled cupola with pinnacles. It was also noted during recent excavations that the crossing piers were Norman and that when the tower had been heightened some of the piers had to be strengthened. With this in mind it is unlikely that the massive stress of a spire would have been added. Also, during the excavation by the Northampton Archaeological Unit (1999-2001), the archaeologist in charge, Iain Soden, noted the absence of any remains pointing to the demolition of spires over the western towers. Coventry Priory was probably a building with towers and small wooden-slatted or lead-covered cupolas in the style of Selby in Northamptonshire,[55] or Wells Cathedral in Somerset, much of which was built in the same period as Coventry. The west front of Wells follows almost exactly the shape of Coventry, and what detail did survive of the west towers can also be found at Wells, including mouldings and blocked-in lancet windows.

THE EARLY BISHOPS OF COVENTRY

The last abbot of St Mary's Monastery was Leofwinus, who is noted as having attended a synod held in London in 1075. Shortly before his death around 1095 the monastery, despite the earlier charters, came into the hands of Robert de Limoges (usually called Limesey), Bishop of Chester. Limesey's former diocese, which he had recently acquired after leaving Lichfield, had suffered years of attacks from the Welsh and by 1086 much of east Cheshire was referred to as waste. It was required that all sees be moved into towns, and Limesey secured the sanction of Pope Paschal I and removed his see to Coventry on 18 April 1102, thereby becoming the first Bishop of Coventry and Lichfield, although the first six bishops styled themselves Bishop of Coventry. The role of abbot disappeared and the monastery became a priory. The bishop ruled over all, basing his stool in the city and his chair in the choir of the cathedral.

William of Malmesbury, in his *De Gesti Regnum*, states that Limesey 'eagerly took possession of it in a totally un-episcopal fashion, stealing the treasures … he gave no sign of worth whatever, for instead of repairing the sagging roofs, he wasted the sacred treasure … and might have been convicted of improper exactions had an accuser been forthcoming'. Limesey's behaviour soon caught the attention of Archbishop Lanfranc, who urged him to 'relieve that monastery of Coventry from all burdens, that thou restorest what thou hast taken, and that thou givest back whatsoever lands of the monastery to that same monastery which thou hast seized without delay'. Lanfranc also accused Limesey and his followers of eating all the monks' food. He suppressed their 'love of God' and learning, maintaining them at a level he believed he could control. It is no wonder the monastery had forged charters to protect them from such despotic espiscopal control. Before Limesey died in 1117 he dismissed the tradition of a bishop's being buried in his cathedral, insisting his body was laid to rest at Chester.

The see of Coventry and Lichfield remained vacant for four years until filled by one Robert Peche, who was laid to rest in the Chapter House of Coventry Cathedral. He was followed by Roger de Clinton, a crusading bishop who died while on crusade in Antioch.

It was in 1142, during Clinton's bishopric, that Earl Marmion of Tamworth desecrated the Priory by driving the monks out, and possibly killing some, when placing Coventry Castle under siege. After Clinton's death the monks of Coventry were summoned to Leicester for the purpose of electing a new bishop, the Prior of Canterbury, one Walter Durdent (1149-59). The clerks of both Lichfield and Chester objected and appealed to the Pope. The newly installed Prior of Coventry, Laurence, travelled to Rome and got the appeal overturned. Bishop Durdent was enthroned at Coventry and it is recorded that the first time he travelled to Lichfield he found the doors closed against him. Later Durdent and Prior

Laurence had an audience with the Pope, who decreed that the espiscopal chair should always remain at Coventry and the prior be the first to elect a bishop. Durdent excommunicated those who had repelled him from Lichfield and also the Earl of Chester, Ranulf Gernon. This was dropped after his death, when land at Styvechale was given in exchange for absolution. Durdent was buried in Coventry's Chapter House.

The last two bishops to style themselves 'of Coventry' were Richard Peche (1161), who resigned the bishopric and died soon after in 1182, and Gerard le Pucelle. The sixth bishop of Coventry was consecrated in 1183 and is considered the most scholarly of all. During his bishopric the scriptorium and library grew, but his life ended suddenly in 1185, it is believed by poisoning. He was also laid to rest in the great conference chamber, the Chapter House.

The bishops resided in a large 'palace' close to the south-east of the Priory in what was a much longer Priory Row (now under the new cathedral). It is thought to have been begun by Bishop Limesey, who robbed the monastic property to build it. It was added to by later bishops and was a huge three-bayed building with a tower, as can be seen on Speed's map of Coventry published in 1610. This was not the bishops' only residence, and a papal *bulla* issued on 4 September 1450 states that the palaces in Coventry and Lichfield and the bishop's castle and manor in Eccleshall and in Heywood are enough and that the bishops should not build or sustain any others. The palace was sold in 1547 to Nathaniel Lacey, Samuel Palmer and Obadiah Chambers for £105, with a reserve rent of one mark (13s. 4d.).

The next bishop was Hugh de Nonant, a noble holding the title of Sheriff of Staffordshire and one of King Richard the Lionheart's close advisers. He was also a monk-hater, and was once reported as saying, 'If I had my way there would not be a monk left in England. To the devil with all monks'.[56] He acquired the Priory of Coventry without election in 1189 by paying 300 marks to Richard I to fund his crusade. Nonant ignored the earlier papal decree and moved his espiscopal chair to Lichfield, home of secular canons but no monks, and then began to call himself Bishop of Coventry and Lichfield. It remained thus until 1837, when the diocese was merged with Worcester.

Nonant obtained licence to incorporate the prior's power with his own, thereby taking complete control of secular and religious affairs. Soon after, he held a synod and an argument broke out between himself and the monks, and they attacked him in front of the high altar, breaking his head open with the crucifix. Nonant petitioned William Longchamps, Bishop of Ely, King Richard's regent while he was crusading, for the monks to be expelled from their house. He accused them of deserting their rule and becoming 'contaminated by secular pollution' and, finally, of spilling his blood before the high altar. At a council it was decreed that the monks of Coventry should be expelled and replaced by more acceptable canons from Nonant's other seat of Lichfield.

15 *The seal of Richard Peche, Bishop of Coventry, 1161-1182 (19th-century engraving).*

16 *Seal of Roger Northburgh, 1322-60, with the arms of England.*

Moyses, the Prior of Coventry, went into exile in Rome, and died there in 1198, and the monks scattered. In Richard's absence Nonant became a great supporter of John and led attacks against Longchamps who, with Nonant's help, was deposed from office. Under John's regency Nonant held several offices, including Sheriff and Justice. When Richard returned to England he threw Nonant's brother into prison and deposed Nonant from his Coventry see. Nonant recovered his seat in 1194 after paying Richard 5,000 marks for his disloyalty.[57]

He died in the same year as Prior Moyses and repented his many sins on his deathbed. In his *Flores Historiarum* Roger of Wendover writes, 'he sent for all the religious men of Normandy, abbots and priors … and in the presence of all of them, purely and with contrite heart confessed all his sins … with many tears … So great was his show of penitence that all present wept with him.' Nonant then signed a document giving all his worldly goods to the church, his final act of atonement.

After the monks had been allowed back into the Priory a new prior was chosen, one Joybert. He set about the election of a new bishop and he and the monks chose a man known for his fairness, Geoffrey Muschamp. The prior worked to gain the house new privileges, including changes to their market, letters of protection and the return of the prior's barony, which was taken by King John but returned after Prior Joybert paid a 300-mark fine. In 1228 the Priory obtained the right to hold a yearly three-day fair from 2 October.

During the latter part of the priorship of Roger de Wooten (1236-48) the Priory fell on hard times and the monks approached their fellow brethren at Derley in Derbyshire for help. The Priory had become so impoverished it could not sustain the brothers within, who probably numbered just over twenty. Some left for Derley, where they remained until the Priory could afford to allow them back. Things improved greatly in 1249 when Roger de Montalt (or Mold) and Cecily, his wife, became benefactors, giving over their interests in Coventry and the advowson of St Michael and its chapels, retaining just the house on the estate of Cheylesmore. Other charters followed, including Henry III's confirmation of the forged charters of Leofric, and the letter of Pope Alexander confirming the rights to have a coroner and to found a merchant guild, rights which were unlikely ever to have been in the original charters.

One of the most notable bishops to appear during the 13th century was Walter Langton (1296-1322). Langton is first mentioned in 1291 as 'Walter, clerk of the Wardrobe',[58] in service to King Edward I. He became a major landowner, holding a large emparked estate in Ashley, Northamptonshire. After the Chancellor's death Walter held the Great Seal of England. In 1295 he became Lord High Treasurer and the following year the Bishop of Coventry and Lichfield. During his time as Treasurer Langton called in all the clipped coinage in the realm and, by new methods, restored the standard of silver and gold coinage. He was also a brilliant negotiator during the war with Scotland.

He continued in royal favour and took personal responsibility for arranging the funeral of his master and friend King Edward. On the accession of Edward II, Langton immediately found himself out of favour as he had often rebuked the prince's extravagant and unusual lifestyle to King Edward, and Edward II had Langton imprisoned. When he was eventually released he was allowed to retire to his diocese. He appears from then on to have spent much of his time at Lichfield. There he worked to restore the name of the English Church, which was falling into disrepute. He also built new additions to Lichfield and a new Bishop's Palace, its great hall extending 100 feet.[59] If he had time to add to Coventry Priory we do not know, but in 1321 he died and was laid to rest under an effigy in the Lady Chapel he had founded within Lichfield Cathedral. Langton left his bishopric very wealthy and the following Bishop of Coventry and Lichfield used some of Langton's fortune to add the three spires to Lichfield.

After the seat was relocated, many of the bishops looked upon Lichfield with more favour than Coventry. This may simply have been because Coventry, unlike Lichfield, was a house of Benedictine monks led by a powerful prior. The prior was quite capable of raising funds for rebuilding and funding, and the house had little need for a powerful figurehead, as it already had one. As the Earl of Chester was not resident in Coventry, the prior was the most powerful person; in Lichfield the bishop could build a court around himself with no one, prior or monks with charters, to question his divine power.

THE EARLS OF CHESTER AND COVENTRY CASTLE

It is not known exactly when Coventry came into the hands of the earls of Chester. It has been suggested that it may have been a gift during the reign of William Rufus for supporting the King during a revolt, but this is pure guesswork. The title dates to the reign of William the Conqueror. When he divided the shires of England among his feudal lords he needed someone strong to hold Cheshire against continuous attacks from the Welsh and possible combined attacks from united Welsh and Saxon forces. He chose his own nephew, Hugh Lupus (the 'Wolf'), to become the 1st Earl of Chester. Hugh was given land previously held by Leofric and Godiva's grandson, Earl Edwin, who had been imprisoned. It is said he married Matilda, the daughter of Earl Leofric's sister. This would not have brought him the estates, but later Lucy, daughter of Ivo de Taillebois, the niece of Earl Aelfgar, married the 3rd Earl, Ranulf de Meschines.

The 1st, 2nd and 3rd earls appear to have had nothing to do with Coventry. The 4th Earl, Ranulf Gernon (1129-53), was a different matter. He was described by Roger de Hovedon as 'a consummate warrior, glittering with arms'. Gernon was the stuff of ballads, with tales of his single-handed defeat of Lincoln Castle and his capture of King Stephen at the Battle of Lincoln sung in the streets. He supported the Empress Matilda and her son Henry against Stephen in the Barons' War. During this time Ranulf created a castle in Coventry which was besieged by Earl Marmion of Tamworth and King Stephen. For his part in this war Ranulf was later imprisoned and had to sign over his castles to the King.

He apparently made three charters relating to Coventry, the first of which was published by R.H.C. Davis and claims to date from 1145-6.[60] It gave Coventry 'unqualified' to his old adversary, Robert Marmion of Tamworth, who died while attacking the castle, but is believed to be suspect, and may have been fabricated by either Marmion II or III to claim rights to the town. If, of course, it were genuine it would imply that Marmion came to Coventry to take what he believed was his.

Ranulf's second charter confirms the Priory's rights, including the rights to tithes to St Michael's Church, within the castle, and to certain chapels around the area, namely Ansty, Shilton, Wyken, Binley, Whitley, Pinley, Stoke, Styvechale, Exhall, Foleshill, Keresley, Whoberley, Spon and Billesley. The charter goes on to say, 'These benefices aforesaid, with all their appurtenances, I have fully recognised as of and given to the Monastery of Coventry as to the mother church, freely, quietly and honourably, for ever, to be by them possessed for the salvation of my soul, and for the souls of my father and mother, my grandparents, and other ancestors.' There are some doubts about this charter, for when it was later confirmed by Earl Hugh II he made no mention of tithes ('decimis'), only appurtenances. After 1181 it is recorded that the clerks of St Michael received 69s. 6d. and were not in receipt of tithes. Therefore it seems that this charter, too, had been forged at a later date to claim non-existent rights.

His third charter, which may also be a forgery, gives the monks of Coventry the right twice daily, except for holidays, to take a cart to his wood under the supervision of foresters and gather what they need for fuel and building work.

Another charter, possibly dating to the 1120s (the original of which no longer exists), recognises the growth of Coventry, which could now be construed a city. It was confirmed in 1182 by King Henry II. The original charter grants Coventry liberties, including a portmanmoot and laws, and the same customs as the city of Lincoln.

Ranulf Gernon died in mysterious circumstances on 16 December 1153, only six months after he had regained Coventry. Roger of Wendover tells us that King Henry disinherited William Peverel for the murder by poison of Ranulf, 4th Earl of Chester. Ranulf's title was inherited by his six-year-old son Hugh Keviloc, named after Cyvelioc in Wales. Hugh (II) received his inheritance in 1162, when he was eighteen. During his minority a number of charters were issued and witnessed by his mother, the Countess Matilda. In 1173 he joined Robert of Leicester in a rebellion against Henry II. Henry sent a force into the Midlands led by Richard de Lucy, who besieged both Coventry and Leicester castles. Hugh was taken prisoner in 1173 and deprived of his lands in the following year. Coventry had to pay a fine of 200 marks to regain its liberties. In 1179 Hugh's lands were restored to him and the men of Coventry paid a reduced fine of 20 marks to rebuild what was destroyed during the attack on Coventry and its castle.

Hugh built a leper's hospital in Chapelfields for his friend, William de Auney, who contracted leprosy in the Holy Land. After his death Hugh had the house extended and built a chapel next to it dedicated to Mary Magdalen, to be used 'for the maintenance of such lepers who should happen to be in Coventry'. The chapel was attended by a priest and brothers and sisters who cared for the sick.

Hugh died in 1181 and the title was passed to his 11-year-old son Ranulf (III) Blundeville, 6th Earl of Chester. Blundeville was to hold the earldom for 50 years and became a national hero, along with Robin Hood. Ballads and rhymes commemorated him, and in *Piers Plowman* we find: 'I kan nought parfitly my Pater Noster As the priest it syngeth, But I kan rymes of Robin Hood, And Randolphe Erle of Chestre.' Blundeville gave the Grey Friars land in Coventry, and granted the city an eight-day fair. Charters of 1190-4 granted tithes of all his local lands for the upkeep of St Mary's, St Michael's, St Chad's and St Giles. A charter dated July 1192, confirming earlier grants made to St Mary's Priory,

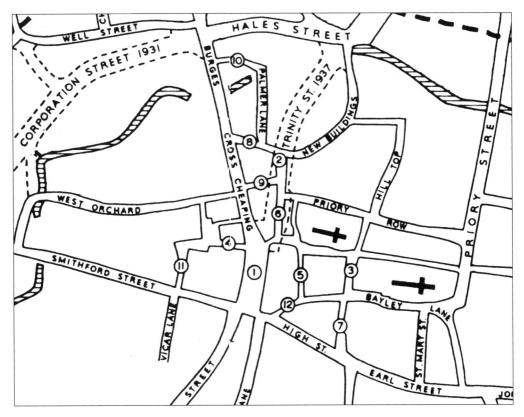

17 *Detail from 1923 Street Plan. 1. Broadgate, 2. Bull Ring, 3. Trinity Lane, 4. Market Place, 5. Derby Lane, 6. Great Butcher Row, 7. Hay Lane, 8. Ironmonger Row, 9. Little Butcher Row, 10. Lucas Lane, 11. Market Street, 12. Pepper Lane.*

Blundeville himself laid on the high altar, on top of which he placed his own gold ring as a gift.

Ranulf died on 28 October 1232, and as he had no heir Henry III made his own son Earl of Chester. Land was divided among his female relatives. His sister married the Earl of Arundel and acquired the old earl's half of the city. As the castle was ruinous the Earl built a moated manor house in Cheylesmore, which passed to the 7th Earl, then Roger de Mold, who had married the heiress Cecily. Through them it would eventually pass to Queen Isabella, wife of Edward II.

Coventry Castle has intrigued people for centuries and many antiquarians have linked it with Cheylesmore Manor House. Most likely it dates from the time of the Barons' Wars between Stephen and Matilda.[61] Between 1137 and around 1140 Gernon forced the local population into building him a motte-and-bailey castle. The motte would have stood at the highest point overlooking Broadgate, encircled by what is now High Street, Pepper Lane and Hay Lane; Bayley Lane and Earl Street marked the bailey area. Alternatively, the castle could have had no motte and been a 'ringwork' type. It was attacked by Robert Marmion of Tamworth, known as a man 'great at warre' who arrived in Coventry in late August 1143 as a supporter of Stephen, but was defeated and killed.[62]

In 1146 Stephen captured Ranulf and only released him on condition, the Chronicle states, 'that he gave hostages and swore on holy relics to yield up all his castles. Some he did yield up, but others he did not.'[63] One of the castles he yielded was Coventry. But Ranulf proved he could make oaths and break them, and quickly gathered a force to retake his castles and others belonging to the King. The *Gesta Stephani* ('Deeds of Stephen'), written shortly afterwards, tells us that Ranulf 'passed rapidly from one region to another with his unbridled army and by his ravages turned everything into desert and bare fields'. *Gesta Stephani* continues, 'Also in front of the Castle of Coventry ('ante castellum quoque Countrerii'), whither the kings men had withdrawn, the earl himself fortified a castle and valorously checked their sorties over the country, until the king arrived escorted by a fine and numerous body of knights, gave the garrison fresh supplies, of which they were in the greatest need and fought a number of engagements with the earl, who had laid ambushes for him at the most difficult points of his journey.' The first conflict resulted in heavy casualties and prisoners were taken. The King received a wound and yielded ground to Ranulf. Later he rejoined the fight and Ranulf himself was nearly killed and eventually put to flight. The 'Deeds' continue: 'He at length obtained the surrender of the earl's castle and demolished it'.[64] The reference is to the Earl's siege castle; Coventry Castle, held by King Stephen, is untouched.

After Ranulf's death the castle of Coventry must have remained in royal hands but it was later reacquired by Ranulf's son Hugh. In Hugh Keviloc's 'boundary charter' he refers to 'lata(m) porta(m) mei castelli', the broad gate of my castle. Hugh protects the rights of the Priory against his own people and forbids them to interfere with the monks' market. He also confirmed the boundary of the earl's land in relation to the Priory. The charter, however, is a forgery, probably used by the prior in his fight to retain lordship. It contains names of tenants both alive and many years dead!

When Keviloc rebelled, in 1173, Coventry was placed under siege by Richard de Lucy, which resulted in a victory for the king. No doubt the castle suffered considerable damage, and the last mention we have of it is in a charter of around 1199-1204, when Ranulf Blundeville forbade his constables to bring burghers into the castle to plead their causes ('Prohibeo et defendo constabularies meis ne eos aliqua causa castellum').

The motte (mound) of the first castle would have been between Hay Lane (from *haeg*, meaning enclosure) and Broadgate. The bailey ran down the hill and the course of its ditch appears to be mirrored by the present Bayley Lane. There is, however, a second ditch which suggests a square keep belonging to a later stage of the castle, now highly likely to be of stone. This ditch was referred to in a charter of 1293-7 as 'fossatum castelli', the castle ditch.[65] It was unearthed in 1894 and described as being 25 feet deep and full of black mud, running from Earl Street, across the High Street and under shops in Hay Lane, then curving sharply and cutting under the north-west corner of the tower of St Michael's. When it was noted in the 19th century that the tower had begun to lean slightly, and work took place to underpin it, workmen found it stood on a ditch cut into the bedrock. The ditch was deep and in it were unearthed remnants of a building and gravestones, all believed to be Norman. They may have been the remains of the original Norman chapel of St Michael, which stood in the bailey of the earl's castle. The ditch runs through the centre of the enlarged St Michael's and comes out under the central buttress of the east end. This buttress appeared to have been added because of poor foundations, and in the middle of the 19th century the castle ditch was found. Workmen dug through 26 feet of rubble without finding its bottom.

In the Langley Cartulary (no.275), 'in ballivo qui ducit ad ecclesiam sancti Michaelis',[66] refers to the church of St Michael's in the bailey. A charter (c.1220s) of William Crude gives to God, St Mary and the monks of Comb 12d. forever from rent to land in Coventry in the bailey ('in Balliva').[67] A few years after its destruction it appears that the earl had sold off all the land of Coventry Castle other than a small area referred to in 1307 as the 'earl's garden'. Another gift, this time to the church of St Michael, which may be connected to the castle, dates from about 1260. It refers to 'the entire stone house'[68] in Bayley Lane, formerly the property of Walter le buttere de Aula, or Walter of the Butter Hall. As the castle had a bakehouse (the 'castelbachous' mentioned in the Pittancer's Rental, 1410-11[69] and twice in the Corporation Deeds[70]), which was excavated in the present Castle Yard, a stone 'butter hall' could imply a dairy or, if the word is corrupted, a buttery, where the beer and wine butts were stored.

This second stage of the castle was of the later Norman type, with square keep and single hall (with no motte) and outbuildings. The defensive ditches were mainly squared, requiring the first ditch to be filled or re-cut. Entrance was gained over the ditched gate ('latam portam') at the top of Broadgate, near Pepper Lane, part of which was excavated in 1974 and found to be 24 feet wide and 21½ feet deep, dated to the mid-12th century by two sherds of Stamford Ware; then through a second V-shaped ditch, in Derby Lane, once called Tyrrel Lane[71] in reference to the defensive work; then across a third ditch, which lies under Hay Lane and completely encircles the keep; then through an entrance gate.

Caesar's Tower in St Mary's Hall has also been linked with Coventry Castle. The name is one normally attributed to castle towers, and in 1900 the base of the largely rebuilt tower was excavated and dated to the mid-12th century. The dating was based on the fact that the stones bore the marks of an adze, a tool normally used by Norman masons.

18 *A shorter and rebuilt Caesar's Tower at the rear of St Mary's Hall probably began life as part of Coventry Castle. (Joseph York)*

Until the late 19th century, remains of a massive wall were still attached to the kitchens of St Mary's Hall, behind Caesar's Tower. Of uncertain date, its size, at least six feet thick, suggests some connection to the castle site. During renovation work in 1914 to the south-east corner of the kitchen the foundations were exposed. Underneath was 're-vealed an enormous mass of masonry'[72] of which workmen tried to find the bottom but gave up at 12 feet. Finally, in the undercroft of the Hall are two wells which could have originally supplied the castle. T.W. Whitley stated in 1884 that somewhere around Bayley Lane was unearthed 'a large stone wall of great strength ... with much fallen stone around it'. He also noted that the wall followed the line of an intricate circular boundary stretching from Bayley Lane to Broadgate. This self-contained boundary, Whitley believed, may have been that of the castle and noted that it left the castle area heading down to the Sherbourne, as described on the boundary charter of Hugh Keviloc. The point at which the boundary passed into Broadgate was at number 18, where the castle entrance is believed to have been, and where Herman 'att the Castle Gate' once lived.

Coventry Castle was probably already in ruins when, in 1215, King John ordered the slighting of a number of castles. As he already held Kenilworth, Coventry would be expendable. The small area called the 'earl's garden' did not necessarily belong to the earl; it is a remnant of the bailey, or possibly a castle meadow. Coventry Castle's short and bloody history left its mark on the town. Present-day Broadgate is the 'latam portam' of the earl of Chester's castle.

Two

Medieval Coventry

The Earl's Half and the Prior's Half

Domesday Book of 1086 describes the settlement of Coventry thus: 'Land of Countess Godiva. 5 hides. Land for 20 ploughs. In lordship 3 ploughs; 7 slaves; 50 villagers and 12 smallholders with 20 ploughs. A mill at 3s; woodland 2 leagues long and as wide. Value before 1066 and later £12; now £11 by weight. Nicholas holds these lands of Countess Godiva for the Kings revenue.' The population has been estimated at about 350, but this does not include the northern half of the city belonging to Coventry monastery. It has been estimated that the real population of Coventry at the time of Domesday was around 1,000, a fairly large settlement by 11th-century standards.

By the year 1200 Coventry was prospering and much of its street pattern had been laid out. Two ancient roads, Bishop Street and Greyfriars Lane, and Earl Street and Smithford Street, went through the centre. There were well established suburbs on Barrs Hill, around the church of St Nicholas, in Gosford Street, Spon and around Hill Mill, at the top of Hill Street. It had grown large enough to support the bishopric and build a new cathedral. The new Priory was given the right by the earl of Chester to hold its own weekly timber and cattle markets, originally in Bishop and Cook Street then, in 1203, in the large open square before the Priory. The earl did not hold a market on the land in front of his castle, but still held some jurisdiction, as the market was administered by a joint court. After the death of Ranulf Blundeville in 1232 the prior appears to have obtained sole jurisdiction.

19 *Saxons ploughing (19th-century engraving).*

The earls of Chester had a major part to play in the growth of Coventry. In a charter confirmed in 1182 Ranulf II gave new merchants two years free from dues, and charters granted before and after 1200 gave the town the status of borough; burgesses held their land by free burgage, and not by paying rent or owing the lord service. The settlement was enclosed by a defensive ditch, the Red Ditch, which may have been an extension of the Earl's Ditch added to the castle defences, possibly during the Barons' War. By the 1260s this ditch, or an extension of it, passed around the settlement on Barrs Hill and enclosed all the town.

The area which became known as Little Park and Much Park Street was heavily settled, possibly because it lay by Earl Street and the south entrance to the castle. Deeds from the early 13th century show that Smithford Street was home to smiths and wheelwrights, and also housed dyers and weavers.[1] In Broadgate could be found goldsmiths and saddlers, and in Little and Much Park Street scabbard makers and cutlers. Also in this area were soap makers, Coventry soap being famous at the time. In the prior's half, there were large houses in the Well Street area around the Throstlewell and around West Orchard, such as the great stone house of Gerard de Alspath.

On 20 January 1345 Coventry was granted its Charter of Incorporation, which gave the place the yearly right to elect a mayor, bailiffs and have a commonalty (council). This charter is believed to be the first recorded example of municipal incorporation in the country and technically made Coventry a city. It was instigated by Queen Isabella, probably as part of her attempt to diminish the rights or ambitions of the prior.

References to the earl's and prior's halves have become a commonplace of Coventry history, giving the impression of a divided city, each side having its own courts and laws. This theory was first established by Mary Dormer Harris at the turn of the 20th century. In the 1960s a full version of the Tripartite Indenture of 1355 was discovered in the Lord Leigh Collection, held by the Shakespeare Birthplace Trust,[2] and close study revealed its purpose was not to unite the city, but to stop it splitting.

After the death of the last earl of Chester, his half of the city came into the hands of Roger de Mold who, to raise money for a crusade, sold it to the prior for a yearly rent of £100 and ten marks. He retained the rights to Cheylemore Manor and to hunt there when in residence. These residual rights were later inherited by Queen Isabella, who believed she had a bad deal and tried to regain through a lawsuit more of the former estate from the prior. The lawsuit failed, which angered Isabella, who proceeded to harass Coventry Priory in every way she could. She tried to cause a revolt at the portmanmoot (the town meeting on the moot hill in St Michael's churchyard) by inciting people to ignore the prior's overlordship, reject his coroner and boycott his market. A number of incidents included the breaking down of hedges and taking of wood from the prior's hunting park at Whitmore Park. Men had entered 'with force of arms', the prior's land at Sowe and Hawkesbury, and hay was stolen from the estate of Newland. One hundred cattle were stolen from the prior's estates and his corn was hijacked in front of the very gates of the Priory.

Isabella also accused the prior of ploughing up common land and she stopped her tenants from paying his rent. The prior hit back in various ways, by setting up his own separate portmanmoot and excluding the town's coroner from jurisdiction in his half. He began to sue various individuals for lost rights and encouraged rival craftsmen to set up in his part of the town. It was this state of affairs which forced all to agree to the Tripartite Indenture and stop the split.

From 1250, whenever business was done with the king, it was the burgesses of Coventry, not men from the earl's or prior's side, who were involved. Professor R.H.C Davis says Coventry was united as a whole town as early as the time of Ranulf Gernon, whose charter of 1145-6 gave 'Coventry' to Robert Marmion. He also points to an entry in the Pipe Rolls for 1183 which states that there was a mint in Coventry valued four times higher than that at Warwick, the expenses and profits of which were shared by prior and earl. Nor does the boundary charter of 1161-79 make mention of halves. Coventry did have a prior's and earl's half but they were divisions in name only. Coventry had two landlords but was run as a whole, as were other English towns at the time. Any division was based on loyalty to the lord, be he earl or prior. From 1250 Coventry's main landlord was the prior, and those in the old earl's half resented their new lord. Many of these people backed Queen Isabella when she attacked the prior's power.

CHURCHES AND MONASTERIES

As mentioned earlier, Osburga's and the Benedictine priory were the earliest monastic houses in Coventry. The Priory of St Mary had gained its wealth from endowments, as did the northern half of Coventry through the use of the forged charters. These charters, confirmed on 7 February 1267 by Henry III, claimed the right to a separate guild merchant and coroner. There were disturbances in the town when the Sheriff attempted to publish them and the prior's men were attacked. One John de Malecote, was killed. The prior chose not to pursue the merchant guild idea, but many were troubled by his evident ambitions, which would later lead to a group of 'gentlemen' trying to kill the prior through magic.

One of the most notable priors was Prior Laurence (1144-79), who founded the Hospital of St John, now the Old Grammar School, in Bishop Street. The hospital and chapel, which still remain, were set up in the reign of Henry II to care for the sick and infirm. Four years after his death, in 1183 Prior Laurence was succeeded by Prior Moyses. Moyses was chaplain to the Archbishop of Canterbury and came into the priory when it was under the bishopric of Gerard la Pucelle. Pucelle's reign was short and the following year Moyses had to deal with the monk-hating Bishop Nonant, who cast the monks from their house.

20 *The interior of the Hospital of St John. Here, before the altar, the beds of the sick would line the walls.*

21 *Monks chanting.*

Moyses' difficult priorship came to an end in 1198 when he died in Rome, and he did not live long enough to see himself and his monks back in Coventry Priory.

When the monks regained the Priory the Archbishop of Canterbury nominated Joybert as new prior, and after the death of Bishop Muschamp (1193-1208) the monks of Coventry nominated Joybert as their new bishop. The chapter at Lichfield disagreed as usual and nominated their own candidate. Both were rejected by papal legate and new elections were called, which resulted in the election of William de Cornhull.

In the reign of Edward II a dispute arose: the prior, Thomas de Pavy, sued one William Graump and others for infringing his market rights and selling goods at a 'fair' in Earl Street. Graump pleaded the charter of the earl of Chester, which gave them the same liberties as the burgesses of Lincoln. The court found for the prior and the Coventry men had to pay a fine of £60, a huge sum at that time. They were also ordered to sell only at the prior's Friday market.

A Coventry monk, William Irreys, was successfully elected prior in 1322, and it was during his reign that the problems with Isabella occurred. In 1349 the Black Death decimated the population, Prior Irreys himself fell victim and, because of the devastation, on 6 August an inquisition was taken of the Priory's current status, when it was discovered it had lost nearly all the land endowed on it by Leofric. This meant a substantial loss in yearly rental and tithe revenue, the Priory now depending almost solely upon its 'prior's half'. The rents from this had also dropped dramatically since many of the tenants had died. The Priory's two watermills and windmill in Radford, worth 40 shillings a year, lay idle as there was no one to work them. The total income of the Priory in 1349 appears to have been about £100 plus whatever was given in alms at its shrines.

In 1398 John Burghill, a Dominican friar and confessor to Richard II, became Bishop of Coventry and Lichfield. His time at Coventry was one of the most prosperous in its history. Burghill's 'obit' took place in Coventry Cathedral on 14 October 1409 and for the only time in the house's history a record survives of the names of the monks of the chapter:

> Richard Crosseby, prior, Rich. Luff, sub prior, Rog. Coton, Richard Warwyk, Jon. Napton, sacristan, Will Tuxford, Will Lyberd, Will Couentre, precentor, Thom. Fereby, treasurer, Adam Hoppusford, penitensiar, Will Maxtok, infirmarer, Nic. Caldecote, steward, Will Haloughton, pitancer, Gilb. Norton, succentor, Joh. Eaton, Tho. Clipston, primus scolaris, Jon. Burton, Tho. Pakyton, chaplain, Tho. Moreton, Jon. Woluey, refectorarius, Tho. Ascheby, secundus scolaris, Ric. Stoke, warden of the Lady Chapel, Will Bardon, Rich. Tholy, Tho. Derby, Ric. Abell.[3]

Richard Crosby (prior from 1399) held the post for 37 years. It was during his time that a parliament was first held there. Crosby had obviously noted the growing interest in pilgrimage in England and in 1410 held a synod at the Priory. It was decided to celebrate the church's founding mother St Osburga, and the synod called for her birthday to be celebrated henceforth as a double festival, 'every year forever', in memory of her saintly virtues and the miracles performed at her shrine. Usually regarded as the first festival associated with Osburga, this was actually an upgrading of her one-day festival recorded in the Warwickshire Eyres of 23 January 1302 as 'Sunday the feast of St. Osberg'. Probably in the course of new building work, the saint's relics were transferred to a new shrine in 1462. Coventry became an important place of pilgrimage because of the Priory and the shrine of Our Lady of the Tower, which appears to have consisted of a statue of the Virgin in a painted chamber in a tower near Whitefriars, in the city wall near New Gate, and was known throughout medieval England. A Lollard called John Bloomfield, tried for heresy in 1485, says of the shrine,

> That it was foolishness to go on a pilgrimage to the image of Our Lady of Doncaster, Walsingham, or of the Tower of Coventry, for a man might as well worship the Blessed Virgin by the fireside in the kitchen as in the aforesaid places, and as well might a man worship the Blessed Virgin when he seeth his mother or sister, as in visiting the images, because they are no more but dead stocks and stones.'[4]

This was, however, a minority view, and over the years Coventry Priory added to its store of relics; a list survives called 'The Inventorie of all manner of Reliques conteyned in the Cathedrall Church of Coventrie.' It includes the following:

First, a shrine of Saynt Oborne [St Osburga] of copper; Saynt Osborn's hedde, closed in copper and gylte; a parte of the Holye Crosse, in sylver and gylt; a relique of Thomas of Canterburie [Thomas à Becket] parte sylver and parte copper; a pece of oure Ladye's Tomb, closyd in copper; a relique of Saynt Ciscilie's foote, parte silver and parte copper; a Crosse with a relique of Saynte James, silver and gilt and sette with stones; an Image of Saynte George, with a bone of his, in shelde silver [later St George's shield was kept in St Mary's Hall]; an Armes of Saynte Justyne in sylver; an Arme of Saynte Jerome, in silver; an Arme of Saynte Augustine [Cnut's gift], in sylver; a relique of Saynte Andrewe, in copper and gylt; a Ribbe of Saynte Laurence, in sylver; an Arme of Saynte Sybvyne, in sylver; an Image of one of the Chylderne of Israelle, in sylver; a small Shryne of the Appostilles, of copper and gylt; a relique of Saynt Kateryn, in copper; a Barrell of Reliques of Confessors, of copper; four lytell Crosses, of copper; two Bagges of Reliques; Oure Ladyes Milk, in sylver and gylt.[5]

In Palmer Lane the Priory had a guesthouse for visiting pilgrims, among the best 'inns' in the land. It stood on the corner of Ironmonger Row and Palmer Lane (Marchels Lane before 1410), and throughout its various guises was known as the Pilgrim's Rest. The original inn may have been stone or stone and timber. The surviving drawings show a large timbered building, with jutting upper floors. The building was originally heavily decorated on the outside and inside with carved oak images of religious subjects, such as saints, and of the hunting world, such as deer and other animals.

22   *Pilgrims.*

The church of St Michael and All Saints stood within the bailey of Coventry Castle and in the 12th century was given over to Coventry Priory. Other chapels in this area included the Chapel on the Mount and the Chapel of the Cross. The Norman chapel of St Michael is thought to have stood on the south side of the building presently opposite Saint Mary's Guildhall, remnants of it unearthed in the 19th century having been dumped in the castle ditch under the north-east corner of the tower. Very little is known of the early history of the building except for the survival

23 *The Priory guesthouse in Palmer Lane.*

of the Early English south porch, which was added to the altered and extended Norman chapel around the year 1300. The western crypt, now known as the Chapel of the Cross, is also thought to date from this period. More is known of the later Perpendicular building, which belongs to the great re-building of the 14th century. The cost was largely defrayed by the Botoners, a family of wealthy merchants. There was once a brass plaque in the church which read:

> William and Adam built the tower, Ann and Mary built the spire;
> William and Adam built the church, Ann and Mary built the quire.

We know that William and Adam Botoner were both mayors of Coventry who gave £100 a year for 22 years to build the tower. The benefactions of their sisters cannot be confirmed, although there is no reason to doubt them. The lighting of such a building was expensive, and rents from properties were used solely for this purpose. The Drapers' Guild took responsibility for the lights on the rood loft and for the Lady Chapel, charging four pence to every master for every apprentice and four pence to every journeyman. Guy de Tyllebrooke, the 13th-century vicar of the church, gave all his property in Bayley Lane opposite so that its rent could be used to keep a light burning forever on the high altar.

The church stands some 240 feet long and 120 feet wide, its spires, once 303 feet, after restoration measuring about 295 feet. It was once considered the largest

24   *Pilgrim badges found in the Sherbourne in the 19th century.*

parish church in England, only St Nicholas's in Yarmouth challenging it in size. Its many side aisles were home to the craft guilds, which maintained priests there to pray for the souls of the guild brothers alive and dead. The guilds were the cappers, dyers, mercers, drapers, girdlers and smiths.

Holy Trinity stands close by and began life as the parish church attached to the Priory. Although we have no date for the establishment of this church we know it was on this site in 1139.[6] The earliest part of the existing church is the north porch with its blocked up 13th-century lancet windows. In 1391 the chancel, which was 'ruinated and decayed', was rebuilt, suggesting this was part of the original building. Like St Michael's, Holy Trinity had a number of guild chapels. It is recorded in 1392 that the Corpus Christi Guild endowed a priest to sing mass for the good estate of King Richard II and Queen Anne and also for the good of the whole of England. The chantry of the Holy Cross also employed a priest to sing a daily mass for the royal family and for members of the chantry.

One of the church's greatest treasures is the Doom Painting, one of the finest in the country. It depicts Christ on the throne of heaven surrounded by the 12 apostles. On his right kneels Mary, with the dead rising from their graves, and on the left is John the Baptist and, further away, the damned being driven into the jaws of hell by a demon. The painting has been dated to the period 1435 to 1460.

During Queen Isabella's enforced retirement at Castle Rising, in a letter dated 7 May 1344, she granted 'to the good people of the Guild of St. John the Baptist, in the town of Coventre, a piece of land called Babbelak in the said town, in order that they may there build a chapel in honour of God and St. John the Baptist.' At the same time a college of priests was founded in the

25 *New Street is said to have been constructed to house the builders of St Michael's in the 14th century.*

quadrangle opposite. As the land was part of the old lake bed, the church had to be built upon oak piles. It was completed and consecrated in 1350, and in 1357 William Walsheman, valet to the Queen and her sub-bailiff in Coventry, gave more land and added a new aisle. He also increased the number of priests at the college. In 1359 Edward of Woodstock, the Black Prince donated more land, now believed to be the area on which were built the tower and transept.[7]

William Woolfe, who was mayor in 1375, greatly helped the church and during his time the nave and aisle were built. The main building, therefore, dates from the 14th century, the clerestory and south nave dating to the 15th century. The Guild of St John joined the Guild of the Holy Trinity and St John's became their guild church. It is believed the guild paid a priest a wage of £6 13s. 6d. a year to act as schoolmaster and teach their children Latin. In 1362 Queen Isabella assisted in procuring a licence for Robert de Worthin, a priest, to become an anchorite and inhabit a cell attached to the north aisle.

26   *Interior of Holy Trinity in 1841.*

27 *An early 20th-century watercolour of Coventry in the 14th century, with Whitefriars and its church in the foreground. (Albert Peck)*

In 1230 Ranulf Blundeville gave land on the outskirts of the town to a new order called the Franciscans, founded by St Francis of Assisi and confirmed in 1215. These monks wore grey habits, were sworn to poverty, walked barefoot and preached the word of God outside their cloistered world. Many had grown tired of the insular ways of the Benedictine order, and the growth in its power and wealth, and saw the Franciscans as a return to true religious monasticism. The friars built a church and friary near the south entrance to the city around 1234. It is recorded in the Pipe Rolls of

28 *A Victorian idea of the Church of St John the Baptist in medieval times (19th-century engraving by Webster).*

29   *An 1820 engraving of Whitefriars Monastery.*

30   *Whitefriars Gate in Much Park Street.*

that year that Henry III allowed the friars to use timber from his woods at Kenilworth to shingle their oratory. Later, the Black Prince gave the friars stone from his quarry in Cheylesmore, the area later known as the Park Hollows, and the tower and spire of this second church, built around 1359, still survives. It stood at the crossing of a 250-foot-long building with cloisters to the south and burial ground on the site of the present Central Methodist Hall. Many skeletons were unearthed during the latter's construction and re-buried at the rear of the building. It may have also taken in the site of Ford's Hospital, for during the war J.B. Shelton unearthed encaustic tiles under the matron's room there following bomb damage.

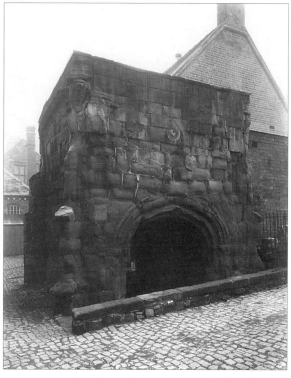

31 *Bachelor's Gate, where alms were distributed from White Friars, was destroyed in the Second World War.*

Others who contributed towards the construction of this building included such families as the Hastings, who built their own chapel within the church. Sir John de Hastings and his wife the Lady Isabella were both buried, dressed in friar's habit, in the Hastings Chapel. Other notables buried here were Roger de Mold and Cecily his wife, who were considered co-founders and lay in pride of place in the choir before the high altar, as well as Adam and William Botoner, builders of St Michael's, and John Ward, Coventry's first mayor. Many nobles were laid to rest in the robes of the Franciscan order, for it was believed that to wear the robes of St Francis was a certain passport into heaven.

The Grey Friars, or Friars Minor, appear to have suffered interference from Coventry Priory, and Queen Isabella, the Priory's natural enemy, wrote to the mayor and commonalty in their defence:

> Our beloved in God, the Friars Minor of Coventry, which are the foundation of our very honourable son, the King [Edward III] have certified to us that their customs, viz. processions and burials, are unreasonably impeded, to the consideration of which we will that you aid the said beloved in God, that they may enjoy all their customs, as they have formerly been accustomed to do, and that touching this matter they may not have further cause of complaint.[8]

32   *The Charterhouse.*

Another order, the White Friars or Carmelites, founded a house in Coventry around 1343 with the help of Sir John Poultney. All their houses were dedicated to the Virgin Mary and all the friars wore white in her honour. They lived austere lives and were popular with the people; Whitefriars was endowed with land and gifts of money, such as the huge sum of £300 left in 1354 by Lord Bassett of Drayton. The friary stood in over ten acres of grounds, all that survives being an inner postern gateway in Much Park Street and the main cloisters on the London Road. The church destroyed at the Dissolution was excavated in the 1960s and found to be 303 feet long, cruciform with a central tower. Records show that in 1579 the steeple was allowed to fall when the walls were being demolished.

It appears that the friars lived poorly, most of their income derived from offerings made by pilgrims to their famed shrine of Our Lady of the Tower. Dugdale states: 'This Chapell is in the tower of the Cittye Wall without New Gate, close by the roadway leading towards London. On the outside thereof was a picture of the blessed Virgin, richly painted, and within an image and her altar, whereat most travellers which passed by did offer more or lesse, out of confidence that their journey would be better blest.'[9] The shrine was considered lucky for travellers and many visited it to protect themselves on their journeys and pilgrimages. It was the practice of those who passed the shrine daily to salute it, and this gave a nearby inn the name 'Salutation'.

A short distance away stood the Charterhouse in Shortley, a corruption of the French 'Chartreuse'. This was home to the Carthusian order, which began, we are told, with a vision by its first prior, Robert Palmer, procurator of the London Charterhouse. The Coventry house, dedicated to St Anne, was the work of William, Lord Zouche of Harringworth. With the agreement of one Sir Baldwin Freville, Zouche gave land to the brothers for their foundation, but apparently the land didn't belong to either man to give away, and legal battles followed until finally it was acquired by John Langley in 1417. His family arms appear on a pennant held by a knight representing the Roman centurion Longinus on a wall painting in the building which still survives. Zouche died and his son, William, was entrusted to continue the foundation.

33 *A Carthusian monk (19th-century engraving).*

On 6 September 1385 Richard II, with Queen Anne in attendance, laid the foundation stone of St Anne's. Richard showed surprising favouritism towards this particular house, giving it more land than any other, and his connection brought many other benefactions. The notable Botoner family, who gave towards the construction of St Michael's and Greyfriars, gave money to St Anne's for new building work on the quire, church and cloisters, and for cells for the monks to live in. The order lived in separate cells and only gathered together for prayers. Coventry's order was considered one of the strictest in the country, and rebellious monks were sent here to learn their place.

THE CITY WALL

During the summer of 1639 John Taylor, the Water Poet, visited Coventry and wrote of it as 'a faire famous, sweet, and ancient city, so walled about with such strength and neatnesse as no city in England may compare with it'. The wall he was writing about eventually made Coventry the most powerful city in the centre of England. In 1329 Edward III gave the prior and the 'goodmen of Coventre' the right to duty on goods for sale in the market for a period of six years, in order to pay for a strong wall to enclose the city. The collection period for this murage tax was extended by another two years so the project could be completed by the holder of the Cheylesmore estate, John de Eltham.

Nothing happened, however, until 1356 when the City Annals record, 'Ric. Stoke, Mayor. He laid the first stone at Newgate, and there began the Town Wall, which was forty years a building. He got a good strike.' From New Gate (London Road entrance) the erection of the wall is believed to have commenced in a clockwise direction into the 'earl's half' of the city. Work was slow and on 20 November 1363 Edward III reaffirmed his charter giving rights to the 'Mayor, Bailiffs, and Goodmen of the city of Coventry to enclose with a wall of stone and lime'.[10] The work appears now to have finally got under way. In 1364 Edward licensed a tax on all traders in the city and on citizens, but initially the Priory was exempt. In 1366 more money was raised by taxes of a farthing for every sheep sold, four pence (a groat) for every hog and ox, a penny for every calf, two shillings for every cask of wine and four pence for every quarter of malt. The tax was particularly high on the victuallers who, in 1370, complained of their burden. The King revoked the tax and replaced it with another so that 'the Merchants and other rich men should be taxed with the meaner sort, according to their several abilities'.

By 1385 the wall had reached the south entrance to the city in Warwick/Greyfriars Lane. On 4 May Richard II gave the men of Coventry the right to continue with the wall on the condition that it enclosed Cheylesmore Manor House, actually running within 15 feet of the rear corner of the main hall. The stone for it he gave freely from the royal quarry at the Park Hollows. He also gave stone for the building of the great double-towered Greyfriars Gate, which stood next to the friary. He gave the mayor and bailiffs the right to seal woollen cloth with the city stamp, a privilege worth £24 a year, to further finance the wall. Richard gave stone for Spon Gate, by St John's Collegiate Church, and in 1399 he gave the commonalty of Coventry total ownership of the walls and gates and all the king's waste grounds around the city, any profits they could make from them to be used in the wall's construction and maintenance.

34 *John of Eltham inherited Cheylesmore manor.*

35 *Greyfriars Gate, south side (19th-century engraving).*

36 *Gosford Gate, east side (19th-century engraving).*

37 *Swanswell Gate.*

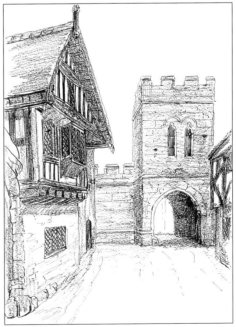

38 *Hill Street Gate by Florence Weston. (Coventry City Libraries, Local Studies)*

39 *Priory or Swanswell Gate showing rubble of wall.*

In a Letter Patent of Henry V, dated 11 May 1417, the wall appears to have neared completion, for the letter states that the city fathers had no land rents to pay for its completion and so had made collections from the poor. The King's charter gave the city the right under the Statute of Mortmain to acquire lands up to the yearly value of £40 to finish the work, and Henry VI licensed a messuage towards murage in 1423, the last mention in a royal document of the wall.[11]

Eileen Gooder's *Coventry Town Wall* contains a piece of information saved by the historian William Fretton from the Birmingham Reference Library fire which destroyed a huge amount of Coventry material in 1870. It refers to an agreement made in 1365 between Richard Stoke and the house of the Whitefriars to complete the wall from New Gate, down to Whitefriars Mill and Gosford Gate. The friars would supply two masons and two labourers and Stoke agreed to supply six masons over two years. The Whitefriars would have a postern gate and window, which could be walled up in times of danger. Despite this agreement, work on the wall from Whitefriars to the round tower by Whitefriars Mill wasn't finished until the year 1430. Yet Gosford Gate could have been constructed at the end of the 14th century and it was certainly in place in 1410, as the Pittancer's Rental of Coventry Priory proves.[12]

We know the wall had begun to creep across Priory land by 1404 because the prior later complained about loss of finance from the time when the wall was built. In 1423 it was ordered that all unfinished gates be completed. Permission was given to build up to (or from) one of these completed gates, the machicolated Bishops Gate in 1430.

By 1462 the wall between Swanswell Gate and Gosford Gate may have remained unfinished, and it was agreed with the prior to re-align it to encompass St Osburg's Pool and the prior's fish ponds. Following a disagreement, however, the prior refused to pay murage and the section was left unfinished until payments were resumed in 1499. Eileen Gooder informs us that, whether through lack of interest or money, just one mason, a man called John Smith, completed most of

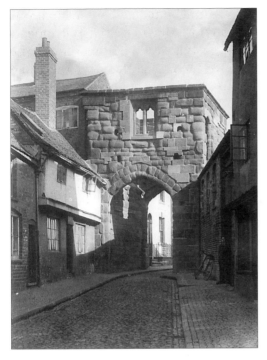

40   *Cook Street Gate from the city side.*

41   *Mill Lane Gate.*

this last section of Coventry's wall, building one or two perches (a local perch was about 24 feet) a year. He completed Bastille Gate in 1512-13 and finished his work in 1534.

This suggests that the work had taken 178 years, and John Leland appears to confirm the late completion date, noting on his tour between 1534 and 1543, it 'is but late sence the waulls of Coventry wer finished'. And yet in the 15th century two huge armies had set themselves outside an unwalled section of the city and been unable to get in. More likely is that a whole section of the wall, from the Swanswell Gate to Bastille Gate, was probably re-built on a different alignment, a tower base from the original section being unearthed near the old fire station some years ago. Poole notes that,

> It appears that a small portion of this wall as originally erected, was some years afterwards taken down and rebuilt on another site … [The prior] entreated that instead of it being built on the course of the river from the Priory Mill to the Bastil Mill … that it enclose his stews and St. Osburg's Pool.

This request was evidently complied with, as is proved by the surviving traces of the wall in a line forming the northern boundary of the Pool Meadow from Swanswell Gate. The first version of Bastille Gate may have existed earlier than the 1512-13 version mentioned in the Chamberlain's Accounts because the Leet Book in 1480 refers to the 'Derne yate, cald the Bastell'.

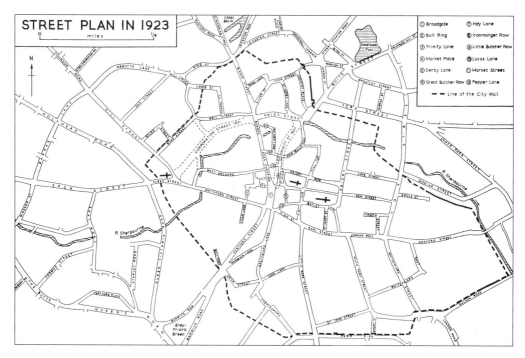

42   *Street Plan of 1923 showing line of city wall.*

In 1876 Fretton mentions traces of the first wall close to the Priory, which led people to think the Priory was fortified. John Leland's comment about the finished wall is probably a reference to the rebuilding of the section near to Gosford Gate and the circuit of Coventry's wall was probably completed well before 1462.

The wall itself is thought to have measured between 2 ⅛ and 2 ½ miles around and had 12 main gates. It consisted of two walls, the middle filled with rubble, and was between eight and nine feet thick. It made a complete circuit of the city at a height varying between 12 and 15 feet. Five gates straddled the main entrances to the city: Bishop's Gate (Bishop Street), Gosford Gate (Gosford Street), New Gate (London Road), Greyfriars Gate (Warwick Lane) and Spon Gate (Spon Street). The minor gates were Cook Street Gate (also known as Tower Gate), Swanswell (Hales Street, also known as Priory or Stour Gate), Bastille or Mill Lane Gate (Cox Street), Little Park Gate (Little Park Street), Cheylesmore Gate (Greyfriar Lane), Bablake or Hill Street Gate, and Well Street Gate (Well Street). Between 20 and 32 square and round towers could be used for cannon or munitions in times of trouble. Around the wall was a ditch, parts of which dated from the 12th century. The ditch was about 25 feet wide and could be flooded by opening 'splayers', which released water from the River Sherbourne or the Radford Brook.

In 1395 Sir William Bagot of Baginton Castle, with one hundred armed men, tried to breach two of the city gates and failed. This appears to have been an organised rising against the mayor and attempt to take control of the city.

ROYAL VISITS

One of the earliest mentions of royalty in Coventry dates to 1086, when William the Conqueror passed through on his way from Warwick to Nottingham.[13] King John is also recorded as visiting in 1192, when a deed relating to the church of Hoppe was witnessed by the whole chapter of the Priory. King Edward II is said to have been in Coventry on 28 February 1322,[14] when he appointed a levy to meet him here. He was back again in March 1332 with an army and marched north to fight at Tutbury Bridge. During one of his visits, Edward III held a joust in the city to which he wore a rare 'studded' suit of armour decorated with the heraldic arms of Sir Thomas Bradstone which he had borrowed for the occasion.[15] Edward's son, Edward of Woodstock, the Black Prince, was Lord of Cheylesmore and held court in the Manor House after the death of his grandmother, Queen Isabella. He is also traditionally associated with St Mary's Guildhall and is said to have given Coventry the right to use his three feathers on the city crest. Richard II visited on 6 September 1385 to lay the foundation stone of the house of the Carthusians, which bore the name of Anne, his beloved queen. It being the feast of Corpus Christi, the King and Queen were entertained by Coventry's famed Mystery Plays.

43   *A 14th-century joust (19th-century engraving).*

44 *Edward the Black Prince.*

When two of the King's favourites, Thomas Mowbray, Duke of Norfolk and Constable of Calais, and Henry Bolingbroke, Duke of Hereford, accused each other of treason, both men were arrested. Before an assembled Parliament Hereford then accused Norfolk of the murder of his 'dear uncle,' the Duke of Gloucester, something Norfolk had actually done on the King's behalf. Parliament diplomatically decided that the charges couldn't be proved and the matter was referred to trial by combat. At a select meeting at Windsor in April 1398 it was decided that Hereford and Norfolk should meet on St Lambert's Day, Monday 17 September, at Gosford Green in Coventry, and prove their words before God and the assembled people. The combat was heralded throughout the realm and thousands came from all over England and France to witness it. Norfolk spent the night at his castle at Caludon, Hereford stayed at Baginton Castle, home of Sir William Bagot, or at a tower outside the city.

Holinshed informs us that, 'the king came to Couentrie ... coming thither in great arraie, accompanied with the lords and gentlemen of their linages. The king caused a sumptuous scaffold or theatre, and roiall listes there to be erected and prepared.'[16] Both men's lances were taken to the Lord Marshall to be checked and returned. Then the Duke of Hereford closed his visor, threw his lance into the rest, and kicked his horse forward. The Duke of Norfolk had hardly moved when the King stood up and his heralds rushed into the list shouting 'Ho! Ho!' The dukes struggled to reign in their horses, were disarmed and told to return to their seats to await the King's word. Eventually the heralds called for silence and the King's secretary Sir John Bushy read aloud the results of their deliberations.

He praised the two knights, then stated that Henry, Duke of Hereford should leave the realm within 15 days, and not return for ten years unless the King ordered it. He was given a yearly income of £2,000, although all his lands were confiscated. Thomas Mowbray, Duke of Norfolk, because he had 'sown sedition in the realme by his words', was to leave the kingdom and never return, on pain of death. He was found guilty of embezzling money at Calais and his lands were confiscated to make up for the loss, though once it was made up he would receive £1,000 a year to support him in his exile. Both men were made to swear an oath that they would not continue with the argument while abroad. This they did and, with the stunned multitude, quietly left the field of combat.

The popular Henry Bolingbroke took his leave of the King at Eltham and, following pleas from John of Gaunt, was released from four years of his banishment. Then, Holinshed states, 'A wonder it was to see what number of people ran after him in euerie towne and street where he came, before he took the sea; lamenting and bewailing his departure, as who would saie, that when he departed, the onelie shield, defense, and comfort of the commonwealth was vaded and gone.'[17]

When Henry Bolingbroke's father, John of Gaunt, died, Richard seized his estate, and changed Henry's six-year banishment to life.[18] Bolingbroke was driven to claim the throne of England for himself by his descent through Henry III and Edward III. Richard II was captured and brought a prisoner to Coventry, then taken to London and forced to abdicate. Sir William Bagot of Baginton Castle, a member of the King's Council who stayed loyal to Richard and tried to save his life, was imprisoned in the Tower and his castle was confiscated. Henry later released him, however, in thanks for the kindness he had been shown when he stayed at Baginton before the combat. So began the reign of the House of Lancaster and its long and close association with Coventry.

On 6 October 1404 Henry summoned parliament to the Priory at Coventry. The Commons were made up of 71 knights and 12 burgesses. Because of its bias against the Church, the Parliament was later called the 'Parliamentum Indoctorum' or the 'Lack Learning' Parliament. No members from Coventry attended, but the prior and bishop were present. The Lords met in the Great Chamber and the Commons in the Chapter House.[19] Parliament argued against more taxes, the knights, nobles and burgesses suggesting that the king should get his extra money from the Church. It was noted that the Church held 'a third of the riches of the realm, and were not doing the King any personal service'.

The King supported their demand but Thomas of Arundel, Archbishop of Canterbury, argued against it, saying that the realm would be in spiritual danger if the Church were deprived, and as long as he was Archbishop he would fight such injustice.[20] He dropped to his knees and appealed to the King's conscience, saying that to deprive the Church was the most heinous crime a prince could commit.

45 *Sir William Bagot of Baginton Castle, the first man to attempt to take walled Coventry (19th-century engraving).*

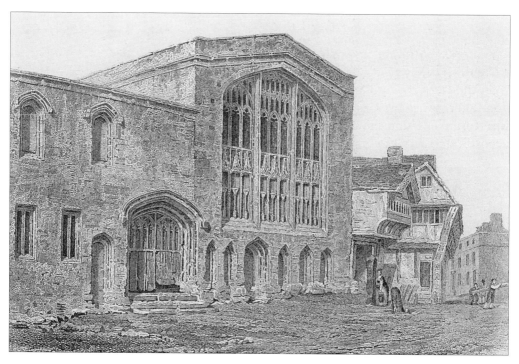

46 *St Mary's Hall in Bayley Lane (early 19th-century engraving).*

His plea worked. Henry informed him that he was firmly resolved to support the Church and hoped to leave it in a better state than he found it. The Commons adjourned to the Chapter House and continued with their petition, bringing in a bill calling for the seizure of clerical revenues. The petition was thrown out by the Lords, and extra taxes on wine, wool, skins and other merchandise were imposed to raise revenue.

Parliament ended after a month because Coventry could no longer support the hundreds flooding into the city, provisions were running short and there was a lack of lodgings.

In 1412 Henry was again in Coventry with his son when both were made members of the Trinity Guild. Three years later his son was crowned Henry V and soon after entered France to claim that throne from the mad King Charles VI. In 1418 he borrowed 200 marks from the mayor and commonalty, and gave in pledge for this a jewelled collar known as the 'Ikelton Collar'. Made of gold, it weighed 36 ounces and was decorated with four rubies, four sapphires, 32 large and 53 small pearls, and was valued at £500. It was kept in the great five-key chest in the Treasury in Saint Mary's Hall. On 21 March 1421 Henry came again to Coventry with his French Queen Catherine. The mayor presented him with 100 marks and what was to become the traditional Coventry gift, a highly ornate and tall golden cup.

THE GUILDS OF COVENTRY

The guilds, both merchant and trade, formed an important part of the fabric of Coventry society until after the Dissolution. The prior since 1267 had legally held the right to found a merchant guild but chose not to use it, and the right was taken away by a statute of 1335 permitting trade free from the guilds' interference. Guild members could sell in Coventry without toll, however, and, according to a 1333 charter, were also immune from tolls in any part of the land.

47   *The great medieval kitchen of St Mary's Hall (19th-century engraving).*

It was later agreed that 'quayage' at Bristol dock was half price for Coventry merchants. The guild also acted like an insurance company, helping members financially when ill or when unforeseen circumstances had impoverished them, and providing loans to extend business. The guild church looked after members' souls.

The first merchant guild was formed in 1340, on the pretext that Coventry merchants needed a brotherhood. Selling merchandise here was more difficult, as a 14th-century document said, 'pur loynteignitte de la mere', 'because of the distance from the sea'. It was to found chantries, bestow alms and carry out other charitable works. The Guild of St Mary acquired a site in Bayley Lane, part of the site of the old Coventry Castle, which had originally been granted to William Cole by the vicar of St Michael's, Guy de Tyllebrooke, on condition that a lamp was kept burning on the high altar of the church. Cole gave the land to the guild on condition that Tyllebrooke's wishes were observed.

Work quickly got under way to provide a meeting place for the guild. When completed it comprised a gatehouse, kitchen, undercroft and hall, the upper part of which was timbered. The hall was about 20 feet shorter than the present one and stood behind three shops fronting Bayley Lane. Meetings were instituted in the completed building on 21 September 1342, when an ordinance decreed that the guild's annual meeting was to be held 'en la salle nostre dame', in the hall of Our Lady, Saint Mary's Guildhall.[21] The guild maintained the church of St John the Baptist and chapels in St Michael's and the Priory.

In 1342 a second guild was established after Edward III gave John Holland, a priest, John Lemman, Thomas Porter, Richard (some sources say Walter) de Stoke, Peter de Stoke and William Welnesburgh leave to form a guild consisting of themselves and others who wished to join in honour of St John the Baptist. In 1344 the guild received land from Queen Isabella on which to build the church of St John the Baptist. It also built a meeting place called Bablake Hall. By 1393 there were nine priests serving the church, the Hospital of St John and the Lady Chapel of St Michael.

A third guild, formed in 1343, the Guild of St Catherine, appears to be closely associated with the Guild of St John for its priests held mass in St John's. The Guild of the Holy Trinity was created by licence on 23 March 1364. The creation of the first Trinity Guild appears to have been the catalyst which unified and empowered the separate guilds, and Letters Patent of King Richard II dated 1392 granted the guilds of St Mary, St John, St Catherine and Trinity the right to amalgamate. They then became the powerful United Guild of Saint Mary, Saint John the Baptist, the Holy Trinity and Saint Catherine, which was shortened for convenience to the Guild of the Holy Trinity or, more simply, the Trinity Guild.

Creation of the Trinity Guild made the merchants even more powerful. Between 1394 and 1414 they set about the enlargement of St Mary's Guildhall, which mainly involved the removal of shops, lengthening of the hall, replacement of timber with stonework, and windows and a new roof decorated with oak angels and beasts. The gatehouse was also enlarged or rebuilt.

The Guild of the Holy Trinity was made up of the most powerful men and women in the city. It was therefore natural that its hall should become the seat of corporate power. The City Leet was based there, using what is now called the Old Council Chamber for their meetings. New laws instigated by the Leet were proclaimed from a balcony which once faced Bayley Lane, and by the early 1400s the hall was regularly referred to as the Council House. All mayors of Coventry were and still are sworn into office in the Guildhall, and all ex-mayors of Coventry took the post of Master of the Guild. The Treasury in Caesar's Tower housed the charters and silver of both Guild and Council. Members of the Guild formed an oligarchy, and between 1420 and 1444 all the senior officers of the city, the mayor, recorder, coroner, justices, bailiffs, chamberlains and wardens, and nearly all members of the Leet were members of the Trinity Guild. The Trinity Guild became so powerful that notable figures such as Henry IV, Henry V (when Prince of Wales), Henry VI, John of Gaunt, Cardinal Henry Beaufort and the celebrated Dick Whittington joined its ranks.

The Guild of Corpus Christi was created by Robert Chandos and 18 others, 'in honour of the Body and Blood of our blessed Saviour', and licensed by Edward III on 26 May 1348. It maintained priests who sang mass at St Nicholas's Church in St Nicholas Street, although this may pre-date the guild by many centuries, possibly being the very church said to have been founded here by St Chad. Originally based in a building in Mill Lane, the guild later based itself in St Nicholas's Hall (sometimes called the Leather Hall) in West Orchard, after which move it was renamed the Guild of Corpus Christi and St Nicholas. In 1392 John Scardeburg of Coventry, amongst others, gave the guild 29 messuages, eight acres of land and 18 pence a year towards its maintenance, but very little survives of the early history of the guild, which was the most powerful of those based within the prior's 'estate'.

Other guilds in the city were trade based. The Shearmen and Tailors' Guild, which originally included the Fullers and Walkers, was in fact the earliest trade guild formed in the city and was named the Guild of St Anne. It was formed sometime in the reign of Richard II (Reader suggests 1393) and claimed to have been formed for purely religious reasons. It was the first of the 'City Companies', trade guilds made up of journeymen who would try to emulate the great guilds of their masters, and was considered troublesome by the merchant guilds. They used their influence to crush the journeymen's guild in 1407, but it was revived, then crushed again in 1414. It reformed once more in 1425, calling itself the Guild of St George, and returned to its meeting place, the Chapel of Saint George, which stood partially on Gosford Bridge in Gosford Street. The City Annals inform us that Laurence Cook founded St George's Chapel and was mayor in 1414 and

48   *St George's Chapel in Gosford Street (19th-century engraving).*

1429. In the year of its re-birth the guild was again suppressed with a writ issued by the mayor stopping 'unlawful' gatherings. The guild appears to have re-emerged in 1433, when Cook had the chapel re-consecrated. It was finally dissolved in 1439 and re-emerged as the Nativity Guild, the Guild of Our Lord Jesus Christ.

The Dyers were established sometime in the early 1400s. One of the earliest references to them is in 1448, when they supplied 37 armed men. The earliest reference to the Broadweavers and Clothiers is in 1435, when a parcel of land adjoining the pageant house of the Tailors was granted to them for eighty years to raise a pageant house on the site. Rules for the Pinners and Tylers Company were agreed upon in 1414, before the mayor Laurence Cook. The rules still exist and read:

> In the Name of God, Amen.
> These are the penalties and ordinances of the Tylers Craft of Coventry. First it is ordained, that every year they shall come to White Friars, on St. Stephen's Day, and there in worship of God and Our Lady ... to go honestly each together and eat and drink; and then to choose two good men to be Keepers for the next yere ensewing ... Also every man of the craft shall come together four times in a year at the master's assignment to pay their quarteridge and also for to speak of things that are needful and profitable for the craft ... every man to pay a penalty of 4d. for wax to make candle to burn in their chapel in St. Michael ... Those men who have been chosen masters for the year, to buy an honest livery, that the craft may be honestly clothed in against Corpus Christi Day.[22]

The rules also state that no man take on an apprentice for less than seven years and no apprentice be set to work before being brought before the craft masters. If any craftsman dared to 'rebel in word or deed' he should be fined 6s. 8d., half of which would go towards the repair of the town wall.

LIFE IN MEDIEVAL COVENTRY

By 1280 the population of Coventry was over 5,000,[23] and the city was growing ever more prosperous, mainly on the back of sheep. The town was a centre of the Midlands wool trade, producing cloth that was sold throughout England and Europe. In 1398 the wool of one merchant valued at £200 lay in the port of Stralsund on the Baltic coast. Special buildings were being created for the trade such as the Wool Hall, which sold wool, and the Drapery, which sold finished cloth. Both were in Bayley Lane. The trade drew 'foreigners' into Coventry, and by early 1349 it is estimated that 51 per cent of the population were immigrants from the surrounding counties and as far away as London, and the south and east coasts.[24] The area around Little and Much Park Streets was leased out by Queen Isabella in quarter-acre plots to 88 different individuals, and many of the medieval city's finest houses were constructed here.

In 1349, the year of the Black Death, the City Annals record, 'A great pestilence happened in this citty, and throughout the realme, the living scarcely sufficed to bury the dead.' A second version of the annals informs us that, 'When Churchyards were not sufficient and large enough to bury the Dead, then certain fields were purchased for that purpose.' After the plague English society changed for everyone, from craftsman to agricultural labourer. Suddenly workers were in a position to demand higher wages for their sought-after labour. Landowners resisted their demands and tried to keep wages down, which caused much discontent in the kingdom. Discontent turned to full rebellion when a poll tax of a shilling a head was imposed on the populace.

One of the leaders of this rebellion, who appears to have a Coventry connection, was a priest called John Ball. In 1381 he spoke to an audience of thousands on Blackheath in London, ending with a question:

> When Adam delved and Eve span,
> Who was then the gentleman?

His words stirred class hatred, and an army of over 100,000 marched on London, slaughtering officials as they went. The 14-year-old King Richard II managed to turn the tide by promises he could not fulfil, but the second leader of the rebellion, Wat Tyler, was killed by the Mayor of London. John Ball fled to Coventry and was hidden away by followers, or possibly relatives, until he was finally captured and executed in St Albans.

The Feast of Corpus Christi was of major importance to the city, involving many in the communities of church, council, guilds and general public. The Corpus Christi Procession was performed in the early morning, before the commencement of the Mystery Plays, also known as the Corpus Christi Plays. It was a major spectacle, members of the Trinity and Corpus Christi Guilds, dressed in their finest gowns, walking behind a priest, who carried the host in a golden cup beneath a richly decorated canopy borne by four burgesses in full regalia. They were followed by a man bearing a processional cross, then guildsmen bearing banners of their guilds and the city minstrels, the waits. Then followed all the clergy of the city, the council and magistrates and members of all the trade guilds bearing banners. The entire procession was on foot, except for the mayor and masters of the guilds. At the rear was a pageant showing the Annunciation, followed by saints, virgins and the apostles, and the Virgin wearing a beautiful crown. Accounts of the Corpus Christi Guild read, 'Payd for a Crown of sylver and gyld for the Mare [Mary] on Corpus xpi [Christi] day xiiiijs. ixd. [15s. 9d.].' The procession was so important it drew many visitors to the city to witness the spectacle. It also heralded the beginning of an eight-day fair and market, decreed in 1217 by a charter of Henry III.

Another important procession took place on St George's Day and was known as 'Riding the George'. St George was accompanied by the Princess Sabra and a dragon. Such rides were not uncommon in England, but Coventry has had a special connection with St George since the time of Edward III, when the saint's birthplace was named as Coventry. Coventry's 'riding' was bigger than most and drew many to the city, including kings and nobles. An English legend was created whereby St George was born at Caludon Castle, the son of Lord Albert. He was taken at birth and brought up to manhood by the enchantress Kalyb, then fought dragons, lions and the infidel, before returning to Coventry with the princess. One story of his return says that Coventry was being terrorised by a dragon and

George came back to kill it, then died of his wounds and was buried in Coventry in great state; another version claims he returned with his Egyptian princess, had three sons, one of whom was Sir Guy of Warwick, and lived out a quiet and peaceful life.

A shrine to George with his statue stood in the Priory, and a chapel and guild in Gosford Street were dedicated to him. A huge, highly ornate, silver-gilt cup engraved with the image of St George was stored in the Guildhall Treasury, and the Hall also held his shield, which may originally have been a silver shield reliquary housed in the Priory before the Dissolution.

The prosperity brought to Coventry by the cloth trade meant that by 1377, despite the Black Death, Coventry had a population of 9,000 and was thought to be the fourth largest city after London, Bristol and York. It was surrounded by common land known as Michaelmas Lands, upon which many of the commoners depended for their survival. It was enclosed for cultivation in strips every year from Candlemas Day (2 February) to Michaelmas Day (29 September), after which it was thrown open for the commoners to use again. Common land comprising meadow was known as Lammas Lands, and their enclosure lasted from Candlemas to Lammas Day (1 August). Rights to the Lammas Lands are thought to date back to the Saxon period. In the 12th century Walter of Coventry gave over hundreds of acres of Lammas lands to the commoners, his deed of gift reading, 'Know all that be, or shall be, that I, Walter of Coventrye, have given, and by this charter confirmed to all the Comburgisses of Coventrye, Common of all the pasture for all the cattle in all my landes, as well now of inclosed as [or] otherwise, as heretofore time they hade it: to have and to holde to them and to their Heires in Fee and Inheritence for ever.'[25]

Many a battle would be fought over rights to the hundreds of acres of common lands which encircled the city. In 1384 the mayor informed the commoners that the Poddycroft and other common land had been rented to the Trinity Guild, but the commoners refused to comply and constantly broke down the enclosure fences put up by the new owners. They continued to invade the land *en masse*, and in 1414 it was decreed by the Leet that anyone found trespassing on the former common land would be arrested and imprisoned until they made amends for their crime. In 1421, 134 citizens were summoned to the Guildhall and approved the giving over of the Poddycroft, the Mirefield and the Stivichall Hiron to the guildsmen. In retaliation the commoners destroyed the gardens, including that of Julius Giles (mayor in 1426), which had encroached on common land near Greyfriars Gate.

In 1285 the right to toll saleable goods to pay for the paving of the streets was granted. This appears not to have been successful and the right was sought again in 1305. In 1332 work began on improving the water supply and permission was given to erect a conduit, 20 feet by 10 feet, in Cross Cheaping. It utilised an already existing water supply.

Grammar schools were set up in the Priory and at Bablake, where children of guild members were educated. There are two references to these schools in the Coventry Leet Book, the first dated 1425 stating, 'John Barton to come to Coventry, if he will, and keep a grammer school, if he knows well how to teach children and keep school.' The second entry, at the Easter Leet of 1429, states that, 'Also they ordeyne that mayster John Pynchard, skolemayster of Grammer, shall have the place that he duelleth Inne for xis [11 shillings] ye yere, whyles that he duellithe In hit & holdythe gramer skole hym-self ther-Inne.'

CRIME AND PUNISHMENT

The treatment of criminals in Coventry does not become apparent until the 12th century. In 1154-6 it is recorded that the Earl of Chester, Ranulf Gernon, gave a special piece of land in Styvechale on which men could fight judicial combat to prove their innocence. The earliest recorded execution took place sometime in the reign of Henry III. An early chronicler informs us that in his reign the people were overtaxed and Henry wasted money and showed contempt for ancient English law. The people and barons of England were turning against the King and, in 1239,

> A counsel had been held until late one winter's eve at the Royal manor of Woodstock, to consider and remedy the growing troubles of the State, but as deepening shadows grew apace the King left the hall, tired and weary, for the rest of his chamber. But with his mind filled with anxious cares, sleep forsook him, and luckily it was so, for a grating noise, as if someone was endeavouring to undo the fastenings of the window aroused him from his reverie, so pulling the arras he beheld a tall figure busily unfastening the lattice. Noiselessly he called his attendants from the adjoining room, who, after a struggle, succeeded in effecting a capture, and when the prisoner was brought before the King, he said he was a priest named Ribbaud, and was connected with a northern monastery. He likewise confessed to being hired by conspirators to take the King's life.[26]

The priest was put on trial, found guilty of attempted regicide and sentenced to be 'sent to Coventry'. He was executed in Broadgate. His hands and feet were tied to four 'wilde horses', which were sent in different directions, dislocating all his bones. His feet were then cut free and he was dragged until dead, then hanged, drawn and quartered, his remains sent to be displayed in different cities, a lesson to all would-be regicides.

The first recorded murder in Coventry (and the first mention of a Shakespeare in Warwickshire) was in 1358, when Thomas Shakespeare, a mercer, killed a goldsmith in Coventry by striking him with a sword. An inquest was held and Shakespeare's goods, valued at two shillings, were confiscated. Thomas Shakespeare fled and was no doubt outlawed. A multiple murder took place in Coventry Priory in 1394 which is recorded in the Roll of John Houland, the coroner of Coventry. It reads,

Monday before the Feast of Epiphany in the 17th year of the reign of Richard the Second, John Cristleton, his son William and their servant, Ralph Giffard, were found dead, suffered by axe wounds. An inquest was held upon the bodies before twelve jurors. It was sworn that on Wednesday before the Feast of Our Lord's Circumcision, one Geoffrey Wytles at night entered the Priory and in a house called the Sextern where the victims dwelled. Here he did slay and traitorously murder them, robbing them of 40 marks and £10 worth of jewellery.

The murder weapon, an axe, was left near the bodies. Wytles escaped and was never brought to justice.

There are some interesting records in the Warwickshire Eyres. One dating from the mid-1200s informs us that a John de Corle struck William de Parker on the head with an axe, resulting two weeks later in his death. The Eyres record that after he had committed the deed Corle claimed sanctuary in the church of St Mary's Priory, and was visited by the coroner who took his confession. He no doubt saved himself from a grisly execution and then left the realm.

Sanctuary was often the only way the criminal could save himself from execution. Adam de Wattell and Margery of Coventry already had a hue and cry raised after them, so placed themselves in St Mary's in 1262 and acknowledged before the coroner that they were thieves. Even the captured criminal still had a chance if he or she could break out of prison and claim sanctuary. This appears to have been a common event in medieval Coventry, implying that the security of prisons left a little to be desired. In the early 1200s Walter of Dunhamlyde was caught in the city passing false coinage. He would certainly have faced the gallows had he not escaped and claimed sanctuary in St Michael's Church. There he admitted to the coroner that he was a thief and forger and swore to leave the realm.

In the 1230s William Grom and many others were taken and imprisoned in Roger de Montalt's prison. All escaped and fled except William, who went to St Michael's and confessed larceny before the coroner. This is possibly one of the earliest references to an actual prison in Coventry, owned by de Montalt and probably within a short distance of St Michael's. It is known that both the earl and prior had their own prisons, the prior's being to the north of the Priory. The earl's, later Montalt's prison, was in the ruins of Coventry Castle. Most castles held prisons or dungeons and it was not uncommon for redundant castles to be used as prisons. Montalt's prison may have been in a poor condition and even rebuilt, for in the Charter of Incorporation of 1345 it is stated that, 'We moreover will and grant for us and our heirs, that a certain prison shall be had and made in the same vill within the tenure of our said mother [in the earl's half] for the chastising of malefactors there apprehended.' As late as the 16th century the gaol is known to have been in Bayley Lane, and there are often references to the Gaol Hall there. The Gaol Hall had a close connection with the Guildhall and both are often mentioned together in late medieval documents. The 16th-century martyrdom of Lawrence Saunders contains a reference to the gaol keeper being visited in the Guildhall.

Executions in Coventry at the time were public spectacles held in the centre of the city, namely Broadgate/Cross Cheaping. Much of this area was originally a large triangular market place in front of the Priory, which was later infilled by Great and Little Butcher Rows, Bull Ring, the south of Palmer Lane and the west side of Cross Cheaping. This with other places around the city was home to a number of executions, not only of commoners but of lords, who were 'sent to Coventry' especially for execution, a one-way trip after which no one would ever speak to them again.

Minor crime was originally dealt with by the portmanmoot, a large assembly of the commonalty of the city, plus the city bailiff, justice and clerk, which met on set dates on the moot mound under the elm in St Michael's churchyard. More serious offences were dealt with by the County or the Sheriffs Court, or before a special Court Leet convened by the earl or prior. This was superceded by the City Leet, which appears to have first met on 14 October 1414. It consisted of 24 'honest and lawful' men, mainly senior members of the Trinity Guild. Most of the laws were passed by an inner group of 12, led by the mayor, in the 'Old Council Chamber' of the Guildhall.

Three

LANCASTRIAN COVENTRY AND HENRY VI

A ROYAL CITY

During the reign of King Henry VI and his Queen, Margaret of Anjou, Coventry's history was linked with national history, in peace but mainly in war. The city even became known as Margaret's 'secret harbour', and in 1459 the King and Queen were in the city every month except for April. After the premature death in 1422 of the illustrious Henry V, his Queen, Catherine of Valois, found herself a widow with a nine-month-old son. The widow Catherine married Owen Tudor, and in 1428 Henry was made ward of local lord Richard Beauchamp, Earl of Warwick. The eight-year-old boy was crowned Henry VI of England at Westminster in 1429 and two years later was taken to Paris and crowned Henry, King of France. Warwick wrote in 1432 that as Henry had

49 *Henry VI and Margaret of Anjou being presented with a book by a young John Talbot (19th-century engraving).*

50 *Cardinal Beaufort, member of the Trinity Guild, in the Coventry Tapestry, St Mary's Hall. (Craig Taylor)*

grown in stature and knowledge of his authority as king he had come to resent the earl's chastisements, and the earl requested that the council assist him in controlling the 'king's person'.

Coventry's first connection with Henry, who at the time had no power and was led by a council, was in 1424 when the city loaned the sum of £101 2s. 11¾d. for the French war. In 1429 more money was requested for the ransom of England's most famed warrior, John Talbot, Earl of Shrewsbury, who had been taken prisoner at Patay. The sum of 23 marks (£15 6s. 8d.) was raised, and with other monies from elsewhere Lord Talbot, a regular visitor to Coventry, was released. More money was sought in March 1430 when Henry requested and received £100. The Leet Book records that Henry came to Coventry for the first time on 12 June 1434, no doubt as a small boy in the company of the Earl of Warwick. He received a silver-gilt cup worth ten marks. Prompted by this visit, the following year the city gave £100 7s. 4d. to the King.

Much of this money was for England's war against France. Despite the fact that Henry was officially King of France, the French, led by Joan of Arc, had begun to retake the country. The 'Maid's Rebellion' was crushed, however, and the King's uncle Cardinal Beaufort, who can be seen on the Coventry Tapestry in St Mary's Hall, a member of the Trinity Guild and regular visitor to Coventry, was one of the judges at her trial.

51 *Henry VI at mass in St Michael's Church (19th-century engraving).*

It wasn't until he was 18, in 1439, that Henry had any control over his government. The City Annals record how, in 1437, 'King Henry came to Coventry, and kept Christmas at Kenilworth.' In 1445 he married the beautiful Margaret of Anjou, daughter of Rene, Duke of Anjou and titular King of Sicily. The marriage was brokered by favourite, William de la Pole, later Duke of Suffolk, who married the dowerless Queen in proxy for the King before bringing her to England. He also handed Maine and Anjou over to her father, something which would later bring about his downfall and assist with the loss of France.

In 1448 Coventry Companies supplied 600 armed men to fight in the Scottish and ongoing French wars under the banner of the Black Ram, symbol of

Coventry's wool trade. After a disturbance in Kent the city was put on general alert, and the Leet ordained that certain wealthy citizens of the city should provide themselves and others with weapons and armour. In June 1450 the men of Kent rebelled again, this time led by Jack Cade and John Mortimer. A force of 50,000 armed men marched on London and the royal household was forced to flee north, some sources say to Coventry, others to Kenilworth, although it is most likely to have been Coventry for it is recorded that the Earl of Wiltshire was summoned to Coventry to Henry's presence.[1] The King then led a force to crush the rebellion. But things were to get worse.

With the losses in France and the recent unrest, England was becoming unstable. Civil war seemed inevitable and towns and cities began to equip themselves for such an event. In March 1451 it was ordained that all Coventry's ditches should be be cleaned, and dams made ready for flooding. All the city gates were to have a portcullis, and a postern was made over Spon Gate. Chains were hung across the main thoroughfares to stop large groups of horsemen riding through the city. Every household was to supply someone for the city watch. In June the Leet ordained that, 'ther shulde be made iiij gonnes of brasse, ij greter and ij smaller; the greater arn called serpentynes.'[2] The guns were made and brought in from Bristol, bound in the city with iron bands and placed with gunpowder and ammunition in Bablake Gate.

On 21 September 1451 Henry came to Coventry, no doubt to reassure himself that the best defended city in the heart of England was truly Lancastrian. The whole event is recorded in the Coventry Leet Book, which, translated into modern English, reads:

> The King our Sovereign Lord came from Leicester toward Coventry, the mayor being then Richard Boys, and his worthy brethren, arrayed in scarlet, and all the commonalty clad in green gowns and red hoods, in Hazelwood beyond the Broad Oak, on horseback attended the coming of our sovereign lord. And also some of them had sight of our sovereign lord present and the mayor and his peers lighted on foot and meekly kneeling on their knees and did unto our sovereign lord their due observance.

During the visit Henry conferred a rare honour on the city by making it a county, the City and County of Coventry. This honour was confirmed by charter, on 26 November, which begins:

> The City or Town of Coventry, aforesaid, with Radford, Keresley, Folkeshull, Eccleshall, Anstey, Shulton, Calwedon, Wikely [Wyken], Henley, Wood-end, Stoke, Bigginge, Whitley, Pinley, Asthull, Hernehall, Horwell and Whabberley, Hamlets of the City or Town aforesaid and that part of Sowne [Walsgrave-on-Sow] … and Stivichall, which are within … and part of the County of Warwick, shall from the feast of St. Nicholas [6th December 1451] next coming, be one entire County of itself, corporated in deed and in name, and distinct and wholly separated from the said County of Warwick, for ever, [and] shall be forever distinctly and separately named, called, and entitled the County of the City of Coventry.[3]

52 *John Talbot, Earl of Shrewsbury, a regular Coventry visitor, from the Coventry Tapestry. (Craig Taylor)*

The new county was some thirty square miles in area and Coventry was now an assize town, distinct from the county town of Warwick. It was to remain the case until 1842. The charter also confirmed Henry's promise to promote Coventry's bailiffs to sheriffs who took their oath before the mayor in the Guildhall. The sheriffs were ordered to hold a court on one Tuesday every month and the coroner was to be coroner of the county. Finally, the charter granted that the mayor, sheriffs and commonalty would be free from 'Toll, Passage, Pantage, Murage, and Pavage' for goods and merchandise throughout the realm.

In 1453 that campaigner of forty battles, John Talbot, Earl of Shrewsbury, after making headway in France, fell with his first son at the Battle of Castillon, and in July or August Henry suffered his first bout of mental illness (possibly catatonic schizophrenia). He went into a stupor and was unable to speak or recognise those about him, including his son Edward, who was born in October. The Duke of York was made Protector, much to the annoyance of Queen Margaret. Henry did not make a recovery until the end of 1454, and in the following year, according to Polydore Vergil, the Dukes of Somerset and Buckingham warned the Queen that the Duke of York was plotting to kill the King: 'The queen, much moved by this warning, and afraid both for herself and her husband, took occasion [to] persuade him [to] withdraw to Coventry. [The] King, seeing himself in danger, rode there and calling an assembly of friends discharged Richard Duke of York of the protectorship.'[4]

Coventry sent one hundred men wearing jacks and salettes and armed with bows and arrows to the first battle of the Wars of the Roses in the streets of St Albans. It was during this skirmish that York's enemy, the Duke of Somerset, the royal favourite, was targeted and killed along with other lords who supported him. Henry sustained an arrow wound to the neck and fell into the hands of the Yorkists. Their lords swore allegiance to the King and Henry, no doubt under pressure, made York Constable of England and the Earl of Warwick, another Yorkist, Captain of Calais.

Within months Henry appears to have had a relapse and the Duke of York was again made Protector. His illness lasted until February 1456.

THE ROYAL COURT MOVES TO COVENTRY

By 1456 Margaret was a sworn enemy of the Duke of York for he was a threat to her son's inheriting the throne. London was increasingly acquiring Yorkist sympathies so the Queen looked north to Coventry and decided she would move the whole of the royal court there. The Coventry Leet Book records that

on 28 August 1456 the mayor, together with 91 councillors, met at St Mary's Guildhall and agreed to the collection of £100, £50 for the Queen and the same for Edward, Prince of Wales, and two silver-gilt cups valued at £10 10s. John Wedurby of Leicester was hired to organise the Queen's welcome, which took place on 14 September.

In *Lancaster and York, The Wars of the Roses*, Alison Weir says that, 'Coventry became the seat of government ... the premier residence of the sovereign. Here Margaret would create a centre of patronage, surrounding herself with artists, musicians and scholars in an attempt to re-create the splendours of the former courts based in the palaces of the Thames Valley.'[5]

53 *Margaret of Anjou taking mass in St Michael's Church.*

54 *Richard Neville, the Earl of Warwick (right) and the Duke of Gloucester from a 15th-century drawing (19th-century engraving).*

At a council held in the city on 7 October York's supporters, the Bourchiers, who wielded great power during the King's illness, were dismissed. They were replaced by the Bishop of Winchester, who was made Chancellor, and John Talbot, Earl of Shrewsbury, second son of the great warrior Talbot, who was made Lord High Treasurer. York and the Earl of Warwick swore to keep the peace. Other Yorkists were replaced by men loyal to the Queen, and the Duke of York and Earl of Warwick were effectively isolated.

It was probably during this period that Henry was again enrolled as a member of the Trinity Guild (he had been made a member when Prince of Wales).[6] On 7 December 1456 his jewels were removed from London and brought to Coventry.[7] The court also began to bring revenue into the city and fines were made on inheritance, those in the first year amounting to £1,089. It is recorded that they were to be paid into the 'chamber or jewel house, Coventry'.[8]

Henry left Coventry for Kenilworth, his other Midland home, on 14 March, and was accompanied by the mayor and city worthies to the 'newe Crosse upon the heth at the utter syde of the franchice [city boundary] and there took their leave'.[9] Two days later the Queen left for Coleshill accompanied by the mayor with his mace and the sheriffs with their wands, a reflection of Margaret's power at this time, such treatment usually only being afforded to the King himself. Margaret had become the power behind the throne and it was she who now effectively led the Lancastrians.

At the beginning of 1458 York's support still included that of the Earl of Warwick, who was successfully holding the post of Lord Admiral of England. A last attempt was made to remove the threat he posed by appointing him Lieutenant of Ireland, but he took the post and stayed where he was, sending a deputy instead. Henry sought to reconcile the two sides at a great council held in London. Later that year the Earl of Warwick's popularity rose after he defeated 28 Spanish ships with just 16 of his own. Soon afterwards he destroyed three Genoese ships which were protected by treaty and Margaret had him recalled to court to explain himself. She tried to get Warwick dismissed from the post and replaced by the Duke of Somerset. Warwick refused to resign until his term was up, however, unless ordered to do so by Parliament.

At a council in Coventry on 9 November a brawl began between one of the Queen's men and one of the Earl's. Warwick's man injured the other and fled, whereupon it is said a cry was raised for Warwick, who came to see what the problem was and was pursued by men 'entendynge to slayen hym'.[10] The Yorkists believed the attempt on Warwick's life was the work of the Queen and the Queen blamed Warwick and tried to have him arrested for creating a disturbance. Meanwhile Warwick returned to the safety of Warwick Castle.

WAR

By 1459 Margaret was becoming unpopular. An entry from the pro-Yorkist *English Chronicle* sums it up:

> The queene, with such as were of her affinyty, ruled the realme as she lyked, gathering riches innumerable. The office[r]s of the rea[l]m, and specially the erle of Wylshyre, tresorere of Engelond, for to enryche hymself, peled [stripped] the por peple and disheryted ryghtefulle eyres and dede meny wronges. The quene was defamyd and denonyced, that he who was called prynce was not her sonne, but a bastard conceved in adulterie.[11]

Those of the Yorkist alliance considered the King a simpleton, and the Queen tried to persuade Henry to renounce the throne in favour of his son. He refused so Margaret decided to take the situation in hand and began to raise support amongst her levies in Cheshire, where she made the Prince bestow enamelled white swan badges of the House of Lancaster on those who would help 'through their strength to make her son king'.[12]

Margaret returned to Coventry in February 1459, this time with an army consisting of her Cheshire levies. She stayed for two months, with her army encamped outside, and was urged by Sir William Herbert to strike at the Yorkists before they too had time to muster. In April she persuaded Henry to support her by summoning his magnates to meet him armed at Leicester on 10 May. She also issued a Bill for conscription, something never before employed in England. York used this for propaganda purposes, condemning the Bill. The Duke of

Somerset and his followers responded to her call, as did Coventry which sent 40 armed men. In the north and south the Yorkists began to arm and the Queen accused them of treason.

At a Great Council convened in Coventry Priory on 7 June, the Queen summoned the Yorkist leaders, the Duke of York, the Earls of Warwick, Salisbury, and Arundel, the Archbishop of Canterbury, the Bishop of Exeter and Viscount Bourchier, but they failed to attend for fear of the Queen, who then pronounced them traitors. York and Salisbury wrote to Warwick pleading for help, as the Queen intended their ruin, and Warwick responded by raising 200 men-at-arms and 400 archers and bringing them from Calais, with the intention, it is said, of marching to the King to plead their case. Warwick headed for his castle, only to find it had been taken by the Queen's men, so he was forced to march for Ludlow as the larger royal army of 8,000 men-at-arms blocked his way to Coventry.

The royal family arrived again in Coventry on 19 September, four days before parts of the Yorkist and Lancastrian armies clashed at Blore Heath. The war had restarted and the Yorkists had the first victory. Benet's Chronicle states that shortly after this, 'the Duke of York, and the earls of Warwick and Salisbury, assembled an army of 25,000 near Worcester. The King and his lords with 40,000 men arrayed for war and banner unfurled advanced towards them.'[13] York, out-numbered, fled to Wales, then Ireland, and Warwick retreated to Calais. York left his wife and two sons at his castle at Ludlow and the royal army marched on the town and ransacked it. The Yorkists fled. A parliament was summoned to assemble in Coventry on 20 November, but there was no place for Yorkists. The Rolls of Parliament later refer to the matter, noting that there 'were named, returned, and accepted, som of theym withoute any dieu and free election, and some of theym withoute any election, ayenst the cours of youre lawes and the liberties of the Commons of this youre Realme.'[14] Parliament discussed whether to pardon or punish the Yorkist lords, but Margaret had already made up her mind and even brought along as prisoner the wife of York, the Duchess Cecily, and his sons Richard (later Richard III) and George (later Duke of Clarence) to witness what she hoped would be his defeat. The Rolls for 1459 record some of what was said at a session later called by the Yorkists the Parliamentum Diabolicum, or the 'Parliament of Devils'. The following was addressed to King Henry, who despite everything was still considering a pardon:

> Let it please your highness, by the advice and consent of your lords, spiritual and temporal, and your Commons assembled in this Parliament [that they] ordain, establish and enact [that] Richard, Duke of York, Edward Earl of March, Richard Earl of Salisbury, Edmund Earl of Rutland, Richard Earl of Warwick for their treacherous levying of war against your most noble person at Ludford, be declared attainted of high treason, as false traitors and enemies against your most noble person ...[15]

This was said to be the first Bill of Attainder in an English Parliament. It denied a total of 23 Yorkist lords their rights as nobles, and their property and lives were forfeit to the Crown. Henry got a clause added, stating that the men were not necessarily banished for life since he held the prerogative to pardon. The sentence of the lords was announced before the Priory gate, 'cryed opynly and proclaimed as for rebellis and traytoures; and theyre tenauntes and there men spoyled of theyre goodes, maimed, bete and slayne without eny pyte'.[16] Parliament was brought to an end on 20 December, much to the relief of the city, which was running short of supplies.

The young Duke of Somerset was made Captain of Calais, but on his herald's arrival he found the city under the control of the Earl of Warwick. Somerset was informed and sailed for France but lost most of his baggage and arms to the waiting Earl. It is recorded that Warwick built up his forces at Calais and that he and Somerset occasionally 'bickered'. The Duke of York was doing much the same in Ireland, waiting and growing in strength.

On 7 January 1460 Warwick raided Sandwich, taking Lord Rivers and his son prisoner. He later had them executed on Gosford Green. Henry returned to London and sent out commissions of array, including one to Coventry dated 2 February, but the summons arrived between mayors and was not dealt with for two weeks.[17] The Leet Book records that, on the same day, the mayor and his council visited the Duke of Buckingham, who came to stay in the city at the *Angel Inn*, possibly to see why the King's command appeared to have gone unheeded.[18] The Duke was killed at Northampton six months after this event.

Following the royal army's violation of Ludlow and Newbury, the Coventry Act of Attainder, and Margaret's unpatriotic dealings with the French and Irish, there appears to have been a resurgence in Yorkist sympathies in England, and it may be that Coventry's retiring mayor shared them. On 20 February the council gathered at St Mary's Hall and ordered that 40 men should be armed and sent to the King, to prevent Richard, the late Duke of York, from re-entering the kingdom.

The Yorkists took control of Sandwich while Henry was in Coventry, and on 25 June executed the King's man with 12 others on the beach at Calais. They demanded that the Act of Attainder be reversed, or they would use force of arms in their fight for justice. On 26 June Warwick, Salisbury, March (later King Edward IV) and Fauconberg left for England with 2,000 men. By the time they reached Blackheath their force had swelled to 20,000. While the Yorkists flocked to Warwick's standard in London, the King made a call to arms at Coventry.

On 5 July Warwick set out to meet Henry at Northampton where the royal army lay in wait. Henry had left Margaret and Edward within the safety of the walls of Coventry.[19] This was the last time Henry would see the city. Warwick sought an audience with the King, assuming things could still be amicably restored, but his pleas were rejected and his army marched to the attack. The battle, which took place in heavy rain, was over in half an hour, after Lord Grey turned coat and helped the Earl of March into the heart of the Lancastrian camp. About three hundred Lancastrians died, many drowning in the Nene. Those who died surrounding the King's tent included Treasurer Lord Shrewsbury and the Duke of Buckingham. Henry was taken and escorted back to London, and on hearing the news Margaret and the Prince fled to Harlech Castle in Wales.

The Duke of York landed in England in early September and at a Parliament held in London on 7 October the Act of Attainder was reversed.[20] On the 10th York entered London with 500 men, preceded by heralds and trumpets and his bare sword carried before him like a king. On 16 October York put to the House of Lords a formal claim to the throne of England based on his descent from Henry III. Henry agreed to name him his successor, by-passing his own son in York's favour, and also gave him the title of Prince of Wales. A week later York proclaimed himself Protector. From Wales, Margaret sent forth summons calling her men to arms, then headed to Scotland. The Lancastrians gathered in the north of England, while Exeter and Somerset raised the West Country and then marched through Coventry on their way to meet them.

On 9 December York headed north with an army of 6,000, but it was defeated at Wakefield and 2,500 were slaughtered. York himself was beheaded, but Margaret allowed her northern army to run riot in the south-eastern shires and any Lancastrian affiliation in those areas quickly disappeared. Early in 1461 Warwick raised an army in London to take on the northern 'rebels', which marched, taking King Henry with them, to St Albans, where battle was given and won by Margaret's army.[21] London was now open to the northern army and the city was assured by the King and Queen that it wouldn't be pillaged. But the army was beaten to its prize by Warwick and the young Earl of March and so turned again northwards. Warwick had to decide whether to follow Henry or support the Earl of March in his claim to the throne. He chose Edward, Earl of March and was to become known as Warwick the King Maker.

COVENTRY CHANGES SIDES

Henry VI was deposed and Edward, Earl of March, eldest son of the late Duke of York, was declared Edward IV of England at Westminster Abbey. The Earl of Warwick headed north to raise troops for the final destruction of the Lancastrian cause. A letter was sent ahead of him to Coventry ordering the city to supply 'defensible men' to the King's cause. Money was levied from each ward to pay for 100 armed men, who joined Warwick on his march to Towton. They went into battle under the flag of the Black Ram, which is remembered in an ancient rhyme:

> The White Ship of Brystow, he feryed not that fray,
> The Black Ram of Coventre, he said not one nay;
> The Wolf cam fro Worcetre, ful sore he thought to byte,
> The Dragon cam fro Glowcestre, he bent his tayle to smyte.

Lancastrian and Yorkist armies fought in a snow storm for over ten hours in one of the bloodiest battles ever fought on English soil, which ended with a Yorkist victory. An estimated 40,000[22] were killed, and nine days after the battle the Chancellor of England described how the bodies were spread over an area six miles by three.[23]

Henry, Margaret and the Prince fled north and the Earl of Warwick was sent to pursue them. A memorandum of this event, recorded in the Coventry Leet Book dated 14 June, states 'that alle these persones following payde as here foloweth to the xi ii [£11 2s.] which was yeven to my lord of Warrewyk for the wages of the xl men that went with hym out of the Cite at his Jorney ynto the north for to resist Kyng Herry and queen Marget.' The pursuit failed as the royal family reached the safety of Scotland.

In late June, shortly before his coronation, Edward IV made his first official visit to Coventry and was presented with a silver cup filled with £100 in gold. Pageants were set up depicting scenes such as Samson, the 'strongman', defeating his enemies. This first meeting of the Yorkist king and the Lancastrian stronghold proved most amicable. With a Yorkist monarch on the throne and the local lord, Warwick, also on the Yorkist side, Coventry had little choice but to play the Vicar of Bray, serving whichever side was in power. But the town was still Lancastrian at heart and would later show its true colours.

By the beginning of 1462 Lancastrian sentiments appear to have been re-emerging. In the city unspecified problems regarding the old allegiance had emerged and Edward feared that civil unrest would ensue. On 7 July he wrote to the mayor ordering him to make a proclamation in Coventry against breaches of the peace, wearing livery without warrant, and people taking the law into their own hands. Any offenders should be imprisoned or sent to him. But after a defeat at Holybank Ford the royal family fled to Bamborough Castle, and it was from here that Margaret fled to France with Prince Edward; they were never to see Henry again.

At the beginning of 1464 Edward presided over an argument as to whether Cheylesmore Park was owned by the king or the city. The case was heard in the Chapter House of the Priory before Edward and the Constable and chief judges of England. No verdict was returned so it was recalled in London and the city

55 *Monks and lawyers meeting in a Chapter House.*

56 *The* Golden Cross *in Hay Lane, said to stand on the site of the mint in Edward IV's reign.*

won. Following the battles of Hedgely Moor and Hexham, Lancastrian resistance came to an end for now. Henry was betrayed and captured on 29 June 1465 and taken prisoner to London, led through the streets, with his feet tied to his stirrups, by the Earl of Warwick. He would remain a prisoner in the Tower until his restoration in October 1470.

Richard Neville, Earl of Warwick, was now the second most powerful man in England. He sought an alliance with France and began earnest negotiations to set up a marriage between Edward and the sister-in-law of Louis XI, but five months later Edward admitted 'in merry guise' that he was already secretly married to a commoner, Elizabeth Woodville, a Lancastrian widow with two children, related to the Greys of Astley Castle, just north of Coventry. Warwick was humiliated.

Elizabeth was enthroned in May 1465 and the royal couple spent Christmas of that year at Coventry Priory. It was probably during this time that Edward gave Coventry the right to mint his new 'light coinage'. These gold and silver coins bore a 'C' for Coventry under the king's head and CIVITAS COVENTRE on the reverse, and consisted of gold ryals, half ryals, silver groats and half-groats. They were struck at a mint which is traditionally said to have stood on the site of the *Golden Cross* public house on the corner of Hay Lane.[24]

57 *A Coventry silver groat of Edward IV (19th-century engraving).*

By the end of 1467 rumours were circulating that the Earl of Warwick had been plotting with Margaret of Anjou. That Christmas at Coventry Edward summoned Warwick to his side in order to 'keep an eye on him'.[25] A messenger from Margaret was intercepted and Edward summoned Warwick to explain himself but the Earl refused to attend. Warwick was summoned again on 7 February 1468 and again refused. Following mediation by his brother, the Archbishop, Warwick agreed to attend a council with the King in Coventry, but he could not be reconciled with the Woodvilles. He also refused to raise archers for Brittany and warned Edward of the dangers of making foreign alliances.[26] For Edward had decided to renew his claim to the French throne and the response of Louis XI was to restore to favour the exiled Margaret and Edward. Lancastrian forces began to rise again. The Earl of Warwick meanwhile forged an alliance with Edward's younger brother, the Duke of Clarence, who wished to marry Warwick's daughter, Isabel.[27]

Following the Lancastrian defeat at Losecoat Field, Warwick and Clarence marched south-west to Coventry where they received a summons to appear before the King and disband their men. The men declined the invitation. It is likely that the Duke of Clarence borrowed 300 marks from Coventry at this time, leaving a coronal encrusted with rubies, diamonds and sapphires for his pledge. It was kept for some time in the great chest in the Treasury of St Mary's Hall. The Coventry Leet Book of July 1470 tells us that then '[the] duke of Clarans & the yrle of Warwic went out of Þe londe & went to Þe kyng of France, & Þere were gretly cheryshed; & Þer was a marriage made by-twyx prinse Edward & a dohgter off Þe sayd yrle of Warwic.'[28] Edward marched south in pursuit of them and entered Coventry with his army on 3 April. The army camped outside the city walls for three days before the King continued his journey, taking 40 Coventry men with him.

The marriage between the exiled Edward, Prince of Wales, and Anne Neville, daughter of the Earl of Warwick, was contracted after Warwick had decided to join the Lancastrian cause. Louis XI, Warwick's friend, convinced the exiled Queen Margaret that her hated enemy could be a route back to the throne of

58 *Cheylesmore Manor gatehouse. (John Ashby)*

England. Clarence now saw his only possibility of acquiring the throne slipping away, a fact which would later have major consequences for Coventry.

A rising in the north distracted Edward, who took with him the 40 men from Coventry. Within a few days Warwick and Clarence, with the Bastard of Fauconberg, Jasper Tudor, the Earl of Oxford and other Lancastrians, landed in Devon and passed through the West Country proclaiming Henry VI. Eventually their army marched unopposed into London. It continued north and the Leet Book records the growing numbers: 'So there they drew to them much people and they came to Coventry, they were 30,000.' Edward's armies deserted or joined Henry, and Edward was forced to flee to Burgundy. On 3 October 1470 Henry was released from his five-year imprisonment in the Tower and three days later Warwick and Clarence returned to London in triumph. Henry 'was restorede to the crowne ageyne ... Whereof alle his goode lovers were fulle gladde.'[29]

By March 1471 Edward was threatening to invade, and the Leet Book records that Coventry was again on alert, Cheylesmore Gate being armed with a breech-loading cannon with two chambers, and a handgun and 32 shot. Robert Onley, later to become Sir Robert, took delivery of a serpentine cannon, and a staff gun with chamber and 16 shot; John Wilgriss of a 'grett gunne', a chamber and a staff gun. On 15 March Edward landed at Ravenspur with just 500 men, saying he had returned simply to claim the Duchy of York. At York he swore an oath on the truth of his claim and swore that he was Henry's man. By the time he reached Leicester he had 3,000 men. Despite having a larger force than Edward's, Warwick decided to withdraw his army of 6-7,000 within the walls of Coventry, where he waited for reinforcements from other lords, including Clarence, who had probably already decided to turn coat and support his brother.

On 29 March 1471 Edward arrived at Coventry after spending the night at Coombe Abbey, and his army spread out over the Gosford Green area. It is said that he 'stood before the walls and shouted out his defiance of Warwick',[30] but Warwick gave no answer. For three days heralds came to Gosford Gate and demanded entrance, but the only reply the Earl gave was, 'that he had rather be like himselfe than like a false and perjured duke; and that he was fullie determined never to leave warre till he had either lost his owne life or uterllie subdued his enemies.'[31] Edward then decided he would lose the initiative by sitting outside Coventry so he headed for London.

He met Clarence's army of about 4,000 men heading up the same Banbury Road. The two men were reconciled and then marched on Warwick and took possession of the castle. On 5 April the greatly enlarged army marched back on Coventry, and outside the city walls Edward declared himself king and demanded entrance. Warwick still refused to deal with him so Edward headed back to London, in the words of the 'Arrival', 'not thinking it behoveful to assail nor to tarry for the asseiging thereof, as well for the avoidance of great slaughter that should thereby ensue, and for that it was thought more expedient to them to draw towards London'.[32] Edward entered in triumph and is said to have shaken hands with King Henry, who said, 'I know in your hands my life will not be in danger.'

Within days Warwick left the safety of Coventry's walls, marching south with an army now numbering up to thirty thousand. Amongst them the Leet Book records Coventry men numbering 20 horsemen and 20 foot soldiers. Edward marched north and the two armies clashed at Barnet. The battle was fought in the fog, and despite being outnumbered the Yorkists won the day. Richard Neville, Earl of Warwick, was cut down by troops and his bloodied body left naked on the battlefield. His remains were afterwards put on public display in St Paul's so all would know that the great King Maker was dead. Henry, who had been part of Edward's baggage train, was returned to London and his cell in the Tower. He would never be seen alive again.

His son was slain at Tewkesbury on 4 May. Edward arrived in Coventry fresh from his victory and ordered a muster of troops, then punished the city for supporting Warwick and the Lancastrian cause by confiscating the civic sword and removing the city's liberties. This probably included the right to strike coinage, for no Coventry coins are found after this date.[33] On 11 May Margaret of Anjou and the Prince's widow, Anne Neville, were brought as prisoners to Coventry and delivered to Edward, and on the 14th Edward left with Margaret for London; Anne was consigned to the care of his brother, Clarence. Margaret was imprisoned in the Tower, and on the day of Edward's triumphant entry into London Henry VI was murdered in his cell. His body was put on public view in St Paul's and Blackfriars, and on both occasions it is said to have bled, proving that Henry was murdered. It was then interred at Chertsey Abbey and thus began one of the greatest cults in England, that of Saint Henry of Windsor.

On 20 June 1472 the Leet Book records that Edward sent a pardon to Coventry, 'for the tyme Þat Ric. late Erle of Warwyke with oder to hym them accompanied kept the Citee in defence agenst his Royall highness in the Lenton next afore Barnett ffeld'.[34] The pardon came at a price, 500 marks, but most of the confiscated liberties were restored. Nine days later, it is recorded that 'alle the Plate and Jewels, except a Coronalle, that laie in plegge in seynt Marie hall for CCC markes lent upon hem to the Duk of Clarence, returned'. Edward put pressure on the city for the return of the Duke's coronal and half of the money he still owed the city was dropped.

On 28 April 1474 Edward's son, Edward, Prince of Wales, came to Coventry and the mayor and his brethren and 'divers of the Cominalte', dressed in green and blue, met him on horseback at New Cross in Radford. The Prince, being at that time only four years of age, sat in a chair fitted to the side of a horse. The mayor presented him with the usual Coventry Cup, a tall decorated chalice, inside which were 100 marks in silver, covered by a 'kerchyff of Pleasaunce'.[35] The Prince was welcomed at Spon Gate with a verse of greeting which acknowledged his true royal blood. Upon the Conduit stood Coventry's own St George, armed with 'a kyng's daughter knelyng a fore hym with a lambe, and the father & moder beying in a toure a boven, beholding Seint George saving their daughter from the dragon'.[36]

During Edward's visit the commons of the city were asked to swear allegiance to the Prince, which they did. The mayor was also given the honour of having the Prince as godfather to his own son. After the visit Queen Elizabeth sent the mayor and brethren 12 fat bucks for the enjoyment of themselves and their wives. Edward came again in 1478 and stayed at Cheylesmore Manor House for some time. During this visit he was enrolled as a member of both the Holy Trinity and Corpus Christi Guilds.[37] It seems the Prince was a regular visitor to his manor at Cheylesmore and on 21 December he officially requested the city's aid to raise money to fund a war against France. On 24 December he requested that all men of a certain income should attend him to hear his 'pleasure'.

King Edward could never be sure of Coventry's allegiance and in 1477 he sent Sir Thomas Vaughan to the city to seek out seditious persons 'which myght sow eny sysme betwixt the kynges goode grace and eny his lordez or Þe cominalte of Þis roialme, that then euery suche persone haue open punysshement'.[38] He also suspected that pledges or jewels belonging to the late Earl of Warwick and the imprisoned Duke of Clarence were still in the city, and ordered a search, but none were found.

Religion

During the late 14th century a religious cult supported by John of Gaunt formed around the leadership of John Wycliff, who defied the power of the Pope, questioned many aspects of the Catholic faith and published religious tracts and an English version of the Bible. Such things were considered heresy but this didn't stop the followers of Wycliff, called Lollards, from spreading the word. During the later years of his life Wycliff was rector at Lutterworth, some fifteen miles from Coventry, and it was from here that he sent out his preachers, so the Lollard belief was well established in Coventry.

The first recorded Lollard preacher in the city was William Swynderby, who came in 1382 but was quickly driven away by the established church. Another known Lollard connected with Coventry was Nicholas Hereford, who helped Wycliff with his English translation of the Bible. For his work he was imprisoned, but he later recanted and, thereafter, scaled the heights of the established church. He finally retired to Coventry's St Anne's Friary (Charterhouse), where he died in 1417.[39]

The Coventry Leet Book of 1424 informs us that:

> John Grace was at that time a famous man among the people, whereas he had preached saying that he was a gracious man in saying, and a holy liver, and many marvels made and showed, for which saying many men trusted that it was so … it was said he was not licentiate, nor no licence had to preach. And at the same day, at afternoon, when evensong was done, Richard Crosby, Prior of St. Mary Church in Coventry, was purposed to have gone into the pulpit in Trinity Church … and then to have denounced accursed all those that heard the sermon of the said John Grace.

John Bredon, head of the Grey Friars, also joined in the condemnation of the vast number of Coventrians who chose to listen to Grace. The two most powerful clergy in the city only riled the people, however, and both men found themselves trapped in Holy Trinity fearful of what would happen if they left the safety of the building.

The mayor was summoned to appease the people, who by now may have gathered outside the church. Rumours were circulating in the county that 'the comens of Coventre wer risen, and wold have distroyd the priour and the seid frer'.[40] The incident came to nothing, but the following year the King sent the Earl of Warwick to Coventry to investigate the event and the spread of Lollardism.

The city franchises were in danger of being confiscated, until £80 was paid and all was well. Grace was arrested and brought back to Coventry and lodged in the gaol, where he faced an inquisition and, we are told, was 'dealt with', but in what manner we do not know. In 1431 there was an unsuccessful Lollard rising under a certain Jack Sharpe. Coventry men were implicated and arrests were made in the area.[41] Those arrested were executed for treason. The end of Grace and Sharpe was not the last the city fathers would hear of this problem, however.

59 *A friar preaching in the 14th century.*

In 1438 Friar Bredon of Greyfriars preached against the Priory of St Mary. He nailed notices to the door of the Priory which stated he would deliver the people of Coventry from the Pharaoh, meaning the prior.[42] For saying these things Bredon was ordered by King Henry to be removed to a friary, forty or fifty miles away, and forbidden to visit Coventry or to speak out again. Later the King sent a letter to the mayor saying that Bredon was to recant in all the parish churches of the city and if he refused he was to be arrested and imprisoned. Friar Bredon paid his penance by public acts of recantation, renouncing his previous words and adding that the taking of funeral candles by the monks of St Mary's was both laudable and commendable. Despite his public humiliation, Bredon could not keep his opinions to himself and only months after this event he was in trouble again, this time with the city fathers.

Education at this time was mainly in the hands of priests, and the interest in Lollard beliefs was thought to have been partly instilled in the young by the new private grammar school teachers who began to appear in the city. In 1439 the Church began to show concern at this corruption of young minds against the true faith, and the Coventry Leet Book of that year records a deputation led by the mayor and six of the council to meet the prior to discuss the problem. They were willing for the prior to run a 'skole of Gramer' for his brethren and the 'children of the aumbry', who may be the choirboys, but insisted that 'every man of this city be at his free choice to send his child to school to what teacher of grammar he liketh'. No doubt the prior would have liked to see the end of the private grammar teacher and to have education based solely on the established religion, but the grip of the established church in Coventry, as in other parts of England, was beginning to loosen.

60   *The parish church of St Michael.*

The church of St Michael, with its chapels and 11 altars, was the largest parish church in the land. It is thought to have been completed by the mid-15th century, and some historians believe the visit by Henry VI to hold mass was to commemorate its completion. A tradition states that the west entrance to the church was made for this visit. The octagon and spire, which measures 125 feet 9 inches, was erected in the 1430s. Christopher Wren thought St Michael's one of the finest churches in the land, though other writers have considered its exterior 'big and bare'.[43] In the medieval period, of course, churches were painted with bright colours, and the tower contained numerous statues of saints such as George and Michael, all of which were painted. In the 1880s, during the restoration of the tower by the clerk of works, G.R. Webster, it was noted that paint still remained in the protected areas when the statues were removed.

The Doom Painting at nearby Holy Trinity church was rediscovered when whitewash was being removed in 1831. And another church painting, this time of the 14th century, was discovered in December 2000 during the dig at Coventry Priory. It shows the heads of four kings, and is said to date from 1360 to 1380. It represents the Vision of St John the Divine and was possibly painted on the Chapter House wall during the building's upgrading. The fragment is of international interest and a report from art historian Miriam Gill states that, 'Comparisons of the Coventry fragment with the closely related subject of Elders adoring Christ in Majesty at Westminster quickly reveals the superior quality of the Coventry painting.'[44] Another piece of the painting was discovered in 2002.

Stained glass was produced at a Coventry workshop by John Thornton, one of the 15th century's finest stained glass artists, and his work adorned St Michael's and St Mary's Guildhall (where some still remains in the oriel window). His most famous commission was the great east window of York Minster, which dates to between 1405 and 1407. It is recorded he was paid four shillings a week for this commission, because of his masterly work. Remains of larger panels from St Michael's are still to be seen in the new Cathedral.

In 1464 a new mass, called the Jesus Mass, was instituted by John Pinchbeck, the mayor, and in 1487 the Jesus Bell was hung in St Michael's and used only to summon the flock to the Jesus Mass. In 1478 it was also celebrated in Holy Trinity. In 1491 Thomas Bradmeadowe bequeathed money for its singing and it was suspended at St Michael's.

Bablake church, or the Chapel of Bablake, the chapel of the Guild of the Holy Trinity, had no public function. The records of the Trinity Guild for 1457 showed that the priest and clerks of St John's were paid 6s. 8d., plus 12d. for oblations, for celebrating St John's Day in the chapel and Guildhall. The players or waits, the city's musicians, played at the function and were paid 5d. The accounts of the Smiths' Company mention a harp player in 1456 receiving 14d. and, in 1467, two men, for minstrelling, two shillings.[45]

61 *A 14th-century carving of St Michael taken from the tower during restoration.*

CRIME AND PUNISHMENT

The Coventry Leet Book gives us a rare insight into the running of a medieval city and the legislative activity which took place. The Leet, or council which passed laws in the city from St Mary's Guildhall, consisted of up to 24 members, with an inner council of 12, headed by the mayor and Master of the Trinity Guild. There was also a Common Council, which in 1422 consisted of 48 members, that usually dealt with matters relating to common land and money. By 1503 this council numbered only 11, these men no doubt being controlled by the inner council. All had to agree with the 'majority' or suffer for their act of rebellion. A sheriff who opposed the council was fined and threatened with imprisonment, and lost his rank and the right to wear his scarlet robes at meetings and feasts. A mayor suffered a similar fate, being locked out of the council and warned that if anyone should 'comfort' him they would suffer the same fate. Order was kept by the justice and the city constables, 24 of whom were chosen at the Easter Leet of 1422. The constables were controlled by a sergeant, who could, 'take no brybe, a-pon the peyn of vjs. viijd.'.

The first 15th-century (September 1410) entry in the Leet Book contains the Metes and Bounds and acquaints us with some of the implements of law and order and those who dealt with them. In Coundon the prior is recorded as holding rights of frankpledge, gallows, pillory, and assize of bread and beer. Coundon Gallows were at the top of Keresley Heath, by the Tamworth road. They marked the boundary of the parish between Keresley and Coundon. Allesley and Corley Gallows served a similar function. As the boundary heads in the direction of Foleshill, there is mention of Gyb Lane, which is probably a corruption of Gibbet Lane. The Michaelmas Leet of 1423 ordained, 'Allso Þat Þer be a Cookestowle [ducking stool] made apon Chelsmore-grene [Greyfriars Green] to punyshe skolders and chiders as Þe lawe wyll.'[46]

At the Leet of 4 October 1414 it was ordained by 24 'honest and legal men … that whoever in future damages the enclosures of the Trinity Gild fields be taken and imprisoned, there to remain until he hath made amends fully according to the view of the then gild-master and six of his brethren without any grace'.[47] Thus was the Trinity Guild given the power to decide when someone had been sufficiently punished for a crime committed against themselves.

In 1421 the mayor, John Leder, made a proclamation fixing the price of bread. Those bakers who broke the law were first fined 13s. 4d., and if caught a second time 20s. A third offence earned the pillory and fourth exiled them from the city for 'a twelmonth and a day'. The price of wine was also fixed, with a 20s. fine for every trespass. Later, taverners who sold bad beer or wine would have their 'Taverne durre sealed Inne'.[48] Others laws dealt with the casting of muck about the streets, where corn was to be sold, and loose swine or ducks. Early poachers were warned that 'no man be so bold nor so hardy to go into the country to break no lords parks for to slay their deer, nor their coneys [rabbits], under pain of 100 shillings [fine], and their bodies to prison'.[49]

The use of weapons was also covered: 'Allso we commaund þat no man of town ne of countrey draw no swerd, ne knyfe, to odur, ne non othur wepon, up the peyn of xld. at euery trespass, but if hit be hymself defendant; and if he smyte with a swerd or a knyfe drawyn he schall pay half a mark for euery trespass.'[50] No butcher or craftsman was to carry around the streets, bills, staves or 'gysarnez', a broad-bladed axe. This could lead to confiscation of the weapon, imprisonment and a 20s. fine. Hostelers were told to warn their guests that if they ventured abroad they must leave their weapons at the inn, except 'if he be a knight or a Squyer'. It appears that the rules concerning the carrying of weapons within the city wall were issued following riots on Midsummer Eve and St Peter's Night in 1420, when individuals were badly injured by weapons. Nevertheless, in 1478 more riots broke out in the city.

Knights, lords and their servants were able to carry weapons and were the people most likely to cause trouble. In 1440 Sir Humphrey Stafford and his son Richard had been visiting Lady Shrewsbury, wife of John Talbot, in her lodgings in Coventry. As they crossed Broadgate at nightfall they were attacked by Sir Robert Harcourt and his men.[51] The fight, which ended with the wounding of Sir Humphrey, the death of his son and the deaths of two of Harcourt's men, was the result of an old quarrel. As the gentlemen involved were nobles, no arrest was made. Harcourt, the instigator, walked away, but was murdered some 22 years later by one of the Stafford family.

Coventry Gaol at this time would have consisted of one or two large open rooms, in which people slept on the floor. There were also dungeons, and rooms for wealthy prisoners who could pay for accommodation. Gaolers were not averse to taking bribes and it is recorded that they would release those condemned by the court for a 'consideration'.[52] The head gaoler was also receiving money for beds; the Leet Book of 1430 recorded that John Stoke was taking a penny a bed, and the Leet ordered alms to be given for the beds of those too poor to pay. Stoke was told to desist from the practice or lose his office. The city bailiffs were no better than the gaoler, for they took excess fines from offenders for certain favours. In 1435 it was ordained that prisoners, who could, should pay 4d. a week for their bed, and if they brought their own bed a penny a week for a chamber.

The Michaelmas Leet of 1432 forbade the gaoler from selling ale to the prisoners and told him to sell it in the town or be fined 20s. for the building of the city wall. The Leet ordained in 1450, 'that no person within the gaol of Coventry from this time forth cast no piss in to the highway, upon pain of the gaoler to lose at every default eleven pence'.[53] Mention is made of the Gaol Hall in 1434, when we are told that all the 'Strikes of the Cite', the official measures for liquids, cloth, etc., would be brought to St Mary's Hall, there to be checked

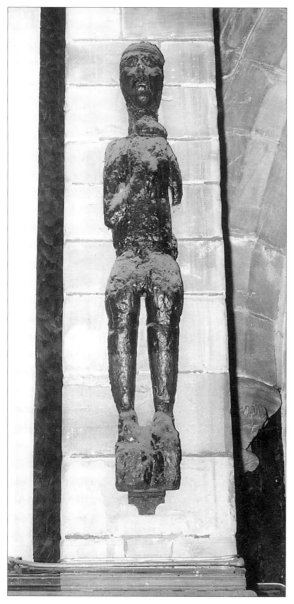

62   *The Knaves or whipping post.*

against the official strikes delivered to the city in the reign of King John, and then kept 'in the maiouris almery in the geyl-hall off Couentre'.[54] It is possible that the Gaol Hall was originally connected to the guilds in Wayley Lane, an earlier hall.

The Guildhall's Treasury was a secure room which held many chests and coffers. At meetings of the Leet the keys were issued to different people, making theft practically impossible. The first record of the issuing of keys is in the Leet Book of 1421, when five keys were issued to John Leder, mayor, Adam Hyton, Master of the Trinity Guild, William Belgrave, Richard Southam and Laurence Cook. By 1430 six keys were being issued and by 25 January 1445 seven in total, three for the door and four for the 'common measure and jewel chest'. The second largest chest, with three locks, is the only survivor today.

Those commiting minor offences, such as selling underweight bread, were put in the pillory or one of the many sets of stocks which could be found scattered around the city. Another common punishment was to be tied to the tail of a cart and flogged from the Knaves Post in Much Park Street to the cross in Cross Cheaping and back; in the following century this would be changed to the Mayors Parlour and back. Adultery had its own punishment, and the Leet Book records that, 'William Rowett, capper, and his paramour [were] carried and led through the town in a car, in example of punishment of sin [that anyone] from this time forward shall have the same pain.'[59]

DAILY LIFE IN LANCASTRIAN COVENTRY

Fifteenth-century Coventry witnessed the completion of the city wall and sat amidst fine open countryside full of oaks and elms. It must have presented a grand sight, set upon a hilltop in a valley, with the spires of St Michael, Holy Trinity, Greyfriars and Whitefriars visible for miles. Standing high and proud were the central tower of St Mary's, decorated with cupolas and pinnacles, and the great west entrance. The city gates would open with the ringing of the day-bell at 5 a.m. and the streets, cobbled with kidney stones and river pebbles, would spring to life. These narrow lanes, which were home to many courtyards, were lined with timbered daub-and-wattle and occasional stone buildings. At the beginning of the century many had thatch but later rules stipulated that, due to the risk of fire, buildings should be tiled. Likewise, chimneys made from hollowed-out tree trunks were abolished in 1493. Many of the two- or three-storeyed buildings jettied out, nearly touching at the top and blocking the light into the narrowest of streets.

The streets themselves were of dirt or cobbled with a central gutter. Often they were filled with rubbish, which also lay piled against the cross in Cross Cheaping; in 1480 the prior complained that he could not pass Priory Gate due to rubbish dumped there. But Leet laws were laid down as early as 1421 to control such problems, everyone being required to clean the pavement in front of their houses every Saturday: 'no man put no dung to his neighbour ... no man or his servants cast into the ditch of this city no manner of filth, by day or night ... Also that no man carry or lay no dung upon the high pavement leading from the New Gate.'[56] The Michaelmas Leet of 1426 ordered that no man should cast muck nor weed into 'the watir cald Shirburn' and that any sty, stable or house for beasts which lay near the water should have its drain to the river stopped up. In 1429 it was ordained that no earth or filth should be cast into the town ditch, and any who did so were fined 40d., the money to be used to repair the city wall.

It was also ordained, in 1421, that no beast except swine should be slaughtered within the city wall. This was changed in 1423 so that slaughter was permitted either within the butcher's own house or, in the case of pigs, at the common slaughter house. All offal was to be dumped in a large natural hollow at the Poddy Croft, off Warwick Road. At the Michaelmas Leet it was ordered that all bulls should be butchered after they had been baited at appointed places, such as outside the Priory Gatehouse, and no swine were to be kept in the city.

The market place had shrunk, largely due to the infilling of properties forming Great and Little Butcher Rows, Spicerstoke and one side of Cross Cheaping. In 1448 the Leet ordered poulterers to sell their wares outside the Priory door in the Bull Ring and as far as the end of Little Butchery, also known as the Poultery.

63   *A 19th-century view of Butcher Row and the Bull Ring (left foreground) where bulls were baited.*

Fish was sold from the middle of the road in Cross Cheaping, the Leet ordering fishmongers in 1459 to remove their boards within a yard of their house so that horses and carts could pass by. It was also ordained that no 'man shuld frohensfurth cutte stokfysshe ne saltfyshe vppon such borde as he cutte fflesh þe weke before'.[57] Anyone who sold bad fish was fined 12d. for his first and 1s. 8d. for his second offence, and for his third offence he would be placed in the stocks in the market place. Butchers who did likewise suffered on their fourth offence a day in the pillory, with their heads and hands clamped. If any foreigner, or person from outside the County of Coventry, came to sell in the market he would be allowed only to sell his goods within a set period of time, and if he wished to buy goods such as corn he had to wait until midday, three hours after locals had done their deals.

The city's other great attractions included the Mystery Plays and the Corpus Christi Procession and Fair. The fair is said to have drawn merchants selling coarse cloth from the West Country, Irishmen with druggets from Drogheda, Frenchmen selling cloth dyes, and traders from Bristol with wines from Guienne and Spain. Some of the 'foreign' merchants became members of the Trinity or Corpus Christi Guilds.

The annual riding of the Lammas Lands was led by the city chamberlains and selected gentlemen from each of the city's wards. This tradition was originally a public statement of the freemen's right to the land, but it began to get out of control when hundreds of 'unruly' individuals joined in. A similar thing happened at the torchlight processions at Corpus Christi, Midsummer's Eve and St Peter's Eve. The city fathers complained that 'great debate and manslaughter and other perils and sins' happened at these events because so great a multitude gathered 'that it lieth in no man's power ... for to please them all'.[58] In 1444 the tanners argued with the weavers, the argument erupted into a fist fight, and one Thomas Burdeaux was nearly beaten to death. The dispute was settled after great quantities of beer had been consumed.

Midsummer's Eve and St Peter's Eve were both celebrated with drinking and feasting. Streets and houses were decorated with boughs of greenery and bonfires were lit. Many of the guilds held feasts and St Mary's Hall was bedecked with lanterns. The torchlight procession on Midsummer's eve was spectacular, with the whole council on horseback followed by the guilds and the journeymen. Among them was the city watch, dressed in 'shining' armour and bearing swords and battleaxes, followed by minstrels and processions of men bearing pennants and torches. Giants with lighted torches in their heads glowed as they walked past the audience. At least one of these figures was the responsibility of the Cappers, for their accounts mention 9d. for a new skirt for the giant and 16d. for the mending of his head and arm.[59]

64   *A merchant's shop.*

One of the favourite sports of this period appears to have been roving, the stalking and shooting of moveable targets set up around the fields, which caused problems with landowners whose crops were damaged. At the Easter and Michaelmas Leets of 1468 it was decreed that 'butts around this city be made and no man from hence forth shoot at rovers, but at butts and standing targets'.[60] Those who continued with the former practice would face imprisonment and a 20s. fine. Complaints in 1474 led to a re-declaration of the earlier ordinance, although this time the fine was 11s. 8d. Six years later the prior complained that 'the people of this city yearly break the hedges and dikes ... in their shooting called roving and neither spare corn nor grass.'[61] He complained, too, of other sports: 'Also the people of the city hunt and hawk within the warren of the said Prior of Coventry, Whitmore, and many other places within the shire of Coventry and without.' He was referring to his ditched and fenced hunting park, which covered over 400 acres, bounded by Keresley and Holbrooks. The prior also complained that the people make 'severall grounds a sportyng place with shotyng and other games', and when challenged by his men the people give them 'short language', saying they will have their sporting place.

Another sport he complained of was fishing: the people 'hurten' the fish in Swanswell Pool by washing there, and fishing by night and day, and he lost fish yearly to the value of over £100. The council replied that the fish would probably grow fatter given the activity at the pool, and of the illegal fishermen they knew nothing, but if the prior gave their names they would be dealt with. Cockfighting gets one mention in the Leet Book and only in passing, William Oxton, sergeant-at-mace, being ordered to remove the butts by the muckhill in Little Park Street and build them elsewhere, 'prouiso quod nullus deinceps sagittet in le Cokfytyng place'[62] ('provided that no one shoot in the Cockfighting place').

The main trade since the 14th century had been wool production and weaving, and many of the city's rich merchants held interest in sheep, Coventry Priory and others such as Coombe keeping hundreds. The cloth from these sheep was sold at the Drapery in Bayley Lane and the south porch of St Michael's until the Leet forbade sales at the church in 1456. Next to the Drapery was the Wool Hall (both belonged to the Trinity Guild), where the wool was weighed. Wardens oversaw the weighing of wool and searchers checked it for cleanliness, and only then was it bagged and fastened with a lead seal bearing the elephant and castle, the symbol of quality Coventry wool. In 1439 the Leet ordered that certain duties had to be paid at the Wool Hall for weighing the wool, but the citizens saw this as a toll and resented it. In time some of the townspeople became more militant and leaders such as Laurence Saunders, city chamberlain, emerged.

In 1478 Coventry was stricken by the plague and 4,450 inhabitants of the city and county, out of a population estimated at around 14,000, died.

Four

TUDOR COVENTRY

HENRY TUDOR

After Henry Tudor's victory at Bosworth Field, he travelled via Leicester to Coventry, the City Annals recording that, 'The earl being proclaimed King in the Fields came to Coventry & the Citty gave him a hundred pounds and a Cup, & soe hee departed.' He stayed at the *Black Bull Inn* in Smithford Street, Coventry's most prestigious inn and home of the mayor, Robert Onley. The King held his council on St George's Day 1487 in Coventry Priory, where the Archbishop read out the papal bulls affirming his right to succession. He also threatened with excommunication and 'cursed by bell book and candle all such as would impugn King Henry's right'.[1]

At the Battle of Stoke, on 16 June 1487, a certain Martin Smart captured Thomas Harrington, of whom the annals record, 'On Wednesday, after St. Peter's day, Tho. Harrington was beheaded on ye Conduite by the Bull and buryed att the Grayfryers. He called himself the Duke of Clarence's son.' Lambert Simnel claimed to be a son of the Duke of Clarence, but he may have been brought to Coventry by Henry and the royal army, not for execution but to work in the royal kitchens. Thomas Harrington (or Hunington in the Flavel Manuscript) was most probably a notable Yorkist who met his fate on the Bull Conduit and during subsequent re-writings of the annals became confused with Simnel. Henry watched his execution from the window in Robert Onley's house. He also witnessed the Mystery Plays on 29 June, St Peter's Day, and before he left the city he knighted his host.[2]

In 1491 Henry borrowed £1,100 from the city to finance war with France, the first of many loans from the city. In 1493 the royal couple were staying at nearby Kenilworth Castle when the council complained to the King that the officers of Bristol had levied a toll on Coventry wares when they were supposed to be free from toll throughout the realm. The Bristol officers argued that their quay was new and therefore exempt.

In 1497 Henry asked for Coventry men to join him in his Scottish campaign and the crafts of the city supplied him with 40 men who then marched north. On 17 October 1498 the city was paid a visit by 12-year-old Arthur, Prince of Wales. The Leet Book records that he entered down a garnished Spon Street, where an actor dressed as King Arthur welcomed him with these words, 'Hayle,

65   *Henry VII (19th-century engraving).*

66   *An execution in the 15th century (19th-century engraving).*

prynce roiall, most amiable in sight.' In Cross Cheaping the Bakers' pageant
wagon was set up with the 'Queen of Fortune' and divers virgins, and on the
conduit stood St George in the act of killing the dragon. The Leet Book continues,
'And uppon Thursday in Þe mornyng the Maire with his Brethren cam unto Þe
princes Chambre [in the Priory] and there presented hym with a gilt Cup to Þe
value of x marc of gold therin.' Pleasantries over, on the following day the mayor
presented the Prince with a bill for 20 years' murage owed by the prior, and
asked him if he would speak to the prior about it, and also brought up the
problem of tolls or quayage. This was not settled until 1501.

   According to the City Annals in Dugdale's *Warwickshire* (Dr Thomas's edition),
in 1500 Henry made his final visit to the city, this time bringing Queen Elizabeth.
His popularity was at a low ebb, trade sanctions and high taxes causing rebellions
and riots in Coventry among other places. Henry, it is said, had 'lost the hearts
of his subjects by his insatiable greed for gold'.[3] Coventry was bonded, along
with all the towns and cities of the realm, to pay the Emperor Maximilian 50,000
gold ducats should a breach of the marital contract occur between Prince Charles
of Spain and his daughter. On 22 April 1509 Henry VII died and was succeeded
by his second son, Henry VIII, during whose reign England and Coventry would
change forever.

COVENTRY AND THE VENERATION OF HENRY VI

Throughout the Wars of the Roses the city of Coventry, as best it could, maintained its allegiance to the House of Lancaster. After Henry VI's death in the Tower his body lay in state at St Paul's and was quietly buried out of the way at Chertsey Abbey. Within a short space of time miracles were being recorded at the grave. Pilgrims started to flock to what quickly became the last resting place of 'Holy Henry of Windsor', and soon statues and paintings of the King were venerated as holy images. In 1479 the Archbishop of York issued a decree banning the veneration of images of Henry 'the Martyr'. But the decree did not stop the growing cult and Richard III had the body forcibly removed to where the remains of the popular priest saint, John Shorne, lay at Windsor. When the body was exhumed in 1474 it was said to be uncorrupted and smelling 'sweetly'.

Unlike his predecessors, Henry VII encouraged the veneration of Henry, who had prophesied his coming and legitimised his claim to the throne. He approached the Pope on the subject of his canonisation, and in 1494 a Commission of Enquiry was set up by Pope Alexander VI, which was continued by Julius II in 1504, who informed Henry that the process could be speeded up by an injection of cash. Henry, not noted for giving away money, chose to await the appropriate time.

The enquiry looked into the many miracles attributed to Henry, a long list of which still survives amongst the Harleian Manuscripts. Most of the 300 recorded miracles belonged to the end of the 15th century and were recorded in English. The 174 'wonders' attributed to Henry and written about in Latin were presumably destined for the Commission.[4] What became known as Henry VII's Chapel at Westminster Abbey was originally built by him to contain Henry's shrine,[5] but the translation of the sainted corpse was blocked by the church at Windsor eager to retain the money-spinning remains. Although entered into the record, the translation never took place, while Henry VII testified in his will it was his intention to move the body.

Hymns were dedicated to Henry, and books of hours, statues, panel paintings and stained glass were produced. Pilgrim badges showed him holding orb and sceptre and standing on a lion or antelope or sitting on a horse. By 1499 his cult had eclipsed that of the other great English saint, Thomas à Becket.[6] It was said that by 1500 the most venerated images in England were Henry VI and the Virgin. In 1529 it is recorded that Henry VIII made an offering at his 'shrine'.[7] But Henry VI's open veneration came to an end, as did the process of canonisation, following the Dissolution.

The earliest surviving evidence of the cult of Henry outside London was at York Minster, where his former secretary, Dean Richard Andrew, erected a screen bearing images of English kings from William the Conqueror to

67   *The King's Window in St Mary's Hall commemorating Henry VI and his ancestors (19th-century drawing).*

Henry VI, and Henry's statue was being venerated by 1473.[8] But survivals of the cult appear in Coventry to a greater extent than anywhere else. The great north window (once called the King's Window) of St Mary's Guildhall, was altered in the late 15th century and the present glass traditionally dates from 1492. It is the work of the King's Glaziers at the Westminster Works and contains images of Constantine the Great, King Arthur,[9] William the Conqueror, Richard I, Henry III, Edward III, Henry IV, Henry V and Henry VI. It mirrors the images at the shrine of Henry at York. All the kings depicted are Henry's direct ancestors or, in the case of Constantine and Arthur, certainly his claimed ancestors.[10] Four of the monarchs depicted were connected to the House of Anjou, a fact reflected in the scalloped 'M' of Margaret in the background, who could also claim connections through Henry's ancestors. There was originally an image of Henry VI in the east window too, but no description of it survives. On the outside of the building underneath the windows are decorative niches which once contained statues. What they were of is not recorded, but they probably mirrored the images in the window, with Henry VI in the centre. These statues were probably taken down during the Commonwealth.

Perhaps the greatest surviving relic of the veneration of Henry VI in England hangs below the north window in the Guildhall and is known simply as the Coventry Tapestry. The earliest reference to it dates from 1519, when 26s. 8d. was spent on two men, who 'take upon them to me'de ye cloth of aras, by advice of M' Meir and his bred'. In 1604 a further 40 shillings was spent on repairs. Sir William Dugdale, who was in the Guildhall in 1653 researching his *History and Antiquities of Warwickshire*, does not mention the tapestry because it contained too much religious imagery for Cromwellian England, although the windows were allowed to remain, for even Puritans considered images of kings and saints as good for keeping out draughts. The tapestry must have been cherished enough by the city fathers to be put safely away, probably for the first time in its history.

The first known written description of the tapestry is by Coventry's most notable late 17th- and early 18th-century historian and bibliophile, Humphrey Wanley, who mentions it in research documents written for his patron, Lord Harley, in 1719: 'The upper end of the Hall is adorned by a very large and fine piece of Arras, wherein are the Effigies of K. Henry VI, his Unkle the Cardinal of England, and the Chiefest of his Nobility are represented. Above are many of the Apostles and the Saints as St. George, etc. Against this King is his Queen Margaret, attended by her Ladies and protected by the Saints. Between them is the B.V.M. attended by many Saints and Angels, and Justitia above her.'[11] In the early to mid-19th century the noted antiquarians Thomas Sharp and William Reader also identified the figures as Henry VI and Margaret of Anjou, as did Poole, Fretton, Hutton, Strickland, and at least fifty later historians. All believed the tapestry depicted Henry holding mass at St Michael's. An unexpected mention is by novelist George Eliot, who uses the Hall for the courtroom scene in *Adam Bede*. She refers to the tapestry and Hall holding memories of 'old kings and queens, unhappy, discrowned, imprisoned', and knew them to be of Henry and Margaret.

Later in the 19th century it was realised by Sir George Scarf that the tapestry was wrought in the reign of Henry VII and the clothes belonged to that period.[12] A couple of late 19th-century historians naively assumed that if the figures were wearing clothes of Henry VII's reign, the scene must represent Henry VII. At the turn of the century the then Hall custodian, J.H. Welch, attacked Sir George's and Mary Dormer Harris's identification of the figures, stating that the king and queen were Henry VII and Elizabeth of York. He said, 'No public body would be insane enough to place the tapestry in the hall some years after to commemorate such a wretched period in the history of England.' He obviously knew nothing of the cult of Henry VI and the profusion of his images in Tudor England, or the important connection of the Lancastrian court with Coventry. Welch was also the first to note the Tudor roses on the tapestry and a mix of red and white roses in the border, claiming this fact alone was 'fatal to the Henry VI theory'.[13] But the tapestry includes no Tudor roses, and the white roses are in reality white daisy-like flowers, probably marguerites of Margaret of Anjou. The border contains

68   *A painting of the Coventry Tapestry in St Mary's Hall, first published in 1869. In the four corners of the actual tapestry the letters H & M, for Henry and Margaret, can be seen.*

red roses for the house of Lancaster and numerous red apples, which are symbolic of Anjou. Amongst the saints, Dorothea is depicted carrying a basket of apples which, by a miracle, are turned into red roses. All are symbolically associated with Henry VI and Margaret of Anjou.

The majority of historians continued to identify the figures as Henry and Margaret through the 20th century, then in 1948 the city archivist Joan Lancaster wrote a guidebook to the Hall which mentioned that Sir George Scarf identified the figures as Henry and Margaret, then stated, 'but in view of the probable date of its working, the tapestry is more likely to represent Henry VII and Elizabeth, while the costume supports the theory'.[14] In 1981 Miss Lancaster wrote a revised guide repeating that it was Henry VII, and adding that the tapestry was among 'well attested Tournai tapestries of c.1500',[15] whereas it was traditionally thought to be by Flemish weavers who were brought to Coventry. During conservation work in 2000 a Tapestry Conservation Officer, from the conservation department at Hampton Court, formed the opinion that it was

not crude enough for Tournai work and was most likely Flemish; certainly there were Flemish members of the Trinity Guild, such as the Purefoys.

There is also a Flemish painting which can be linked to the tapestry. Now in the University of Art in Ohio,[16] it bears remarkable similarities to the tapestry. Believed to date from the beginning of the 16th century, it is the work of a Flemish artist and depicts the marriage of Henry VI to Margaret of Anjou. In anticipation of Henry's sainthood the artist has placed a halo around the King's head. Figures in the painting can be matched with those in the tapestry. They are laid out in the same manner, with men on the left and women on the right, and above them can be seen architectural details and saints. I believe this is a cartoon, an early version of the tapestry, made by a Flemish artist, attached to a Flemish workshop of weavers in Coventry. The clothes are plain and few people are depicted, so the city fathers, who knew St Henry and the Lancastrian household well, told the artist to make the clothing more noble and the setting more spectacular. The rather outdated architectural details were added to divide the complicated scene.

69 & 70 *Henry VI as depicted on the Coventry Tapestry made to commemorate the royal court's attachment to Coventry and Henry's expected canonisation; and Margaret of Anjou as depicted on the Coventry Tapestry. (Craig Taylor)*

In the Guildhall ceiling there are numerous chained antelopes and lions, the badges of Henry VI, and chained swans, used as a badge by both the Lancastrian party and by Margaret and Edward, Prince of Wales.[17] What we have at St Mary's Guildhall is the greatest surviving 'shrine' to Henry VI in England. The whole of the north wall and its window were adapted to take the Henry glass and the tapestry in the late 15th century when his veneration was at a peak.[18] It might have been done at the time of the admission to the guild of Henry VII and Elizabeth, who would certainly have approved. Those years were dangerous ones for Henry, with 'much rising at Coventry', rebellion from Cornwall and a threatened invasion from Scotland by the pretender Perkin Warbeck. But probably it was simply part of the veneration of Henry VI and totally unconnected to any visit. The cult did in fact last for well over sixty years. The Coventry Tapestry, a record of the struggles of the House of Lancaster, could only have been produced by a city so closely associated with the royal family and court, and it is highly likely that everyone depicted, be they artist, writer, lord or lady, lived at some time in the city. The tapestry commemorates Coventry's greatest moment, when the city became the home of the royal court and of a saint.

LAURENCE SAUNDERS

Laurence Saunders was the son of ex-mayor, William Saunders, and came from a family of dyers who lived in Spon Street. In 1480 he became a chamberlain and member of the council, as well as a member of the city's two most powerful guilds, Holy Trinity and Corpus Christi. In his post of chamberlain he was responsible for the collection of murage, overseeing of common land and fining for stray cattle, but the mayor complained that he was overbearing and tried to subdue all those he dealt with. The trouble began when Saunders and fellow chamberlain William Hede refused to pay men who had been quarrying stone for repairs to the city wall. When murage receipts were poor, Hede and he were expected to make up the money, but Saunders refused, saying those who sent them to work should pay for them. The two men were imprisoned but released a week later when the mayor received a petition signed by Saunders' influential friends.

He found himself in trouble again when he and Hede were accused of taking excessive fines. Saunders had a disregard for the rules concerning common land, and in September 1480 he travelled alone to Ludlow Castle to present the Prince of Wales with a petition complaining that the mayor, prior, recorder and other powerful members of the council withheld from the citizens of Coventry half the commons, and that a favoured few kept whatever number of sheep they wished, while the common people were restricted.

The mayor and his men were summoned to Ludlow to answer the charges, the Prince found in their favour, and Saunders was ordered to pay their expenses of £15 11s. 11d. At St Mary's Hall Saunders was made to kneel before the mayor and his men and beg forgiveness for his wrongdoing. His response is not recorded but he quickly found himself in the city gaol again, where he stayed but a short time before friends aided his release.

In 1482 he was committed to gaol again for using 'untoward speech' on the question of enclosure. He was released after recanting his former 'speech' and warned that 'a third time in ward for such matters, it should cost him his head', and nothing is heard of him for 12 years. Then in early 1494 trouble arose over enclosures and tolls on weighing wool at the Wool Hall. Saunders was overheard saying before a group of people on Lammas Day, 'Sirs, hear me! We shall never have our rights till we have striken off three or four of these churls' heads that rule us and if thereafter it be asked who did that deed, it shall be said me.'[19] He also hit out at William Boteler, a member of the council and brother of late recorder Henry Boteler, who had a running vendetta with Saunders amongst others. William Boteler had sown oats on common land and Saunders told the people to take his crop for it was theirs by right. Saunders was imprisoned again, this time for seven months, with a massive £40 fine which he could not pay. His friends acted as surety for his fine and gained his release. In the meantime, the

Michaelmas Leet of 1494 under Mayor Green ordered that every craftsman in the city would have to pay 13d. for every apprentice they took on.

After his release, the Easter Leet ordained that Saunders 'be from henceforth discharged for ever from riding with the Chamberlains yearly on Lammas Day'. If he joined the ride he would face another £40 fine. It was also ordained that he be 'discharged from the Mayor's Council and the Common Council and all other councils, hereafter'.[20] But, not surprisingly, Saunders had a following amongst the common people, who saw the leaders of the city as a bunch of despots. As Friar Bredon had done years before, a message was nailed to the door of St Michael's Church. It warned the council that mob violence could break out at any time, especially at Lammas, and would probably be at the instigation of ex-City Chamberlain Laurence Saunders. At the meeting that followed in St Mary's Hall the council dropped his fine to £20. Half the remainder was in sureties and Laurence appealed to King Henry VII for help with the other £10. In 1496 he obtained a privy seal from the King, which asked the mayor to take the sureties and drop the £10 because of Saunders' age and poverty. The letter also alerted the mayor to the problem of common ground, which Saunders had informed him was in the city, although the council claimed it was not. The mayor was enraged by this and wrote to London informing the King of the 'great and many offences of the said Saunders'.[21]

On 20 July 1469 Saunders walked in on a meeting of the King's Bench at the Gaol Hall and said, 'Master Mayor, I have brought you a bill here [regarding enclosures], I pray you it may be read openly in court.' The mayor refused and told him to bring his bill to him on the morrow, to which Saunders replied, 'Master Mayor, hold up-right your sword, for as for Master Recorder I have reckoned with him before the king, and he shall be easy enough.' On the following day the bill was read and Saunders again found himself in prison, this time for sedition. During his confinement more verses were nailed to St Michael's door, including this one:

> Our comens that at Lamas open shuld be cast,
> They be closed in and hegged full fast,
> And he that speketh for our right is in the [gaol] hall,
> And that is shame for you and for us all;
> You can not denygh hit but he is yor brother,
> And to bothe Gilds he hath paid asmoch as another.

On 10 November Saunders was ordered to appear before the king and his council with his grievances. Four of the council came with the case against Saunders. John Rowley, Master of the Trinity Guild, Master Braytoft and John Boteler, steward, rode to London and, with Master Recorder Master Coke, Master Grene and William Pisford testified against Saunders at the Star Chamber. The case went against Saunders and he 'was then committed unto the Fleet [prison] there to abide unto the time the king's pleasure were known what further punishment he should have'. This is the last ever mention of Laurence Saunders and whether he ever came back to Coventry we do not know. The rising at Lammas never happened and the rebellion over commons, enclosure and hidden taxes in Coventry practically died with him.

RELIGIOUS REBELLION

As we have seen, Lollardism was well established in Coventry, and in the reign of Henry VIII, according to Dr Gairdner, the city was a 'special nest of heresy'.[22] In 1510, the year of Henry's visit, ten Lollards accused of heresy were forced to carry heavy bundles of faggots (symbolic of their death by fire) before the people in Cross Cheaping. All recanted except Joan Ward, who was burned at the stake in the Little Park at the Park Hollows. In 1519 the Bishop of Coventry, Geoffrey Blyth, ordered that Mrs Alice Lansdail, a widow, Thomas Lansdail, her brother-in-law, a hosier, Hosea Hawkins, a skinner, Thomas Wrexham (or Wrigsham), a glover, Robert Hockett and Thomas Bond, shoemakers, and Robert Silksby, should be purified by the church, and burned at the public stake in Little Park for saying their Ten Commandments, Creed and Lord's Prayer in English instead of Latin.

Alice Lansdail was discharged and Robert Silksby escaped, but on returning home Alice was searched and found to be carrying a copy of the Lord's Prayer and Ten Commandments in English. She was re-arrested and condemned to join the others. Two years later Robert Silksby was re-captured and suffered the same fate, burning in the sand hollow in the Little Park.

In 1527, still without his hoped-for son, Henry wanted to get out of his marriage and researchers discovered a biblical reference saying it was unclean to marry your brother's wife. He applied to the Pope to annul the marriage, but the Pope refused and Henry created himself head of the new independent Church of England. The Church declared the marriage null and void and Roland Lee, Bishop of Coventry and Lichfield, married the King to Anne Boleyn in a private ceremony. The Pope excommunicated Henry and within months Anne gave birth to Elizabeth. Then began the dissolution of the monasteries.

Henry died in 1547 and was succeeded by his son, Edward VI, who died aged sixteen. Lady Jane Grey was proclaimed queen in London. The Duke of Northumberland called for Coventry to proclaim her, and rode to the city hoping to find support, but found Henry's daughter Mary proclaimed queen there and the gates closed against him. For trying to place Lady Jane on the throne, Northumberland was executed and his land at Cheylesmore Park reverted to the crown. Mary was crowned in 1553 and it soon became apparent she wished the nation to return to the old religion. On 26 August the mayor of Coventry was ordered to apprehend Hugh Symonds, vicar of St Michael's, who had commented on the Queen's religion in a sermon. Symonds was examined by the council at

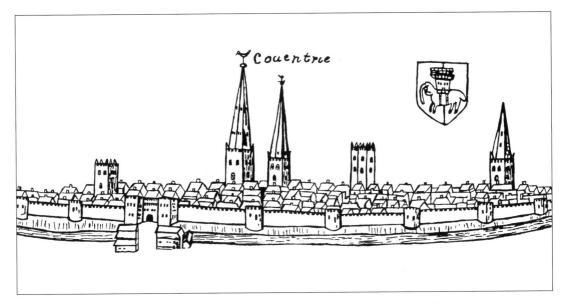

71   *Copy of Smyth's drawing of walled Coventry of 1576. (Neil Cowley)*

the same time as a commission was sent to the city ordering the punishment of anyone preaching against the Queen. If Symonds didn't recant, his 'Protestant tendancies' were to be dealt with, although how is not recorded. But a report that Symonds was married led the Bishop of Coventry to cast him from the church. The living at St Michael's lay vacant for four years.

The city magistrates were ordered to put down any Protestant services in the city, but few in Coventry were Catholic at heart and secret services went on in the fields until more tolerant times returned with the reign of Elizabeth. Coventry witnessed the persecution which would earn Mary the nickname ' Bloody Mary' at first hand, with the burning of another Lawrence Saunders in 1555. Saunders was born in Harrington in Northamptonshire in 1519. He was educated at Eton and King's College, Cambridge, and then apprenticed to a wealthy London merchant. He found the life not to his taste and his master cancelled his indentures, allowing him to return to King's College and continue his studies, especially the scriptures. In 1547 he was ordained, and he became the rector of All Hallows, Bread Street, London in 1553. Saunders preached at Northampton against 'popish doctrine' and later called the Church a 'papist serpent'. That afternoon he returned to his church but was stopped, arrested and commanded to appear before the Bishop of London. He was in prison for 15 months, charged with treason for breaking the Queen's proclamation and heresy for his sermon.

The Bishop told him, 'Notwithstanding the Queen's proclamation to the contrary, you have continued to preach.' Saunders replied that he had exhorted his flock to stand steadfastly in the doctrine which they had learned, and he only taught the 'purity of the word', which was now forbidden, and added that he would pray for the Bishop's conversion. He was returned to prison, during which time he kept in touch by letter with Cranmer, Ridley and Latimer, who themselves would later face the flames.

More than a year later he was again brought before the clergy, who offered him mercy if he would give up his 'abominable heresies and false doctrine'. Saunders repeated that what he did was a matter for his own conscience. At the end of the interview Bishop Bonner produced a document attacking the Catholic Church, accused Saunders of writing it and pronounced him a heretic. He was returned to prison, excommunicated and the Bishop of London came to 'degrade him'. When this was done Saunders said to him, 'I thank God I am not of your church.'[23] On the following day he was delivered to the Queen's Guard, who brought him to Coventry to be burned. Coventry was probably chosen because it was a notorious home of Lollardism and, apparently, Saunders was well known here. He was placed amongst the other prisoners in the common gaol and spent the night in prayer. On the morning of 8 February 1555, Foxe wrote, 'the fire being put to him, full sweetly he slept in the Lord'. Saunders was followed to the stake by Robert Glover.

72   *Burning Lawrence Saunders, from Foxe's* Book of Martyrs *(16th-century engraving).*

In November 1554 John Carelesse, a weaver who was described by his inquisitor as 'one of the pleasantest Protestants I have ever met',[24] spent two years in Coventry gaol, his wife and children staying with him. He was well liked by the gaolers and was allowed leave to play in the city pageants.[25] After two years he was sent to London and found guilty of heresy. While there he wrote in a letter, 'My friends in Coventry have put the Council in remembrance of me, not six days ago, saying, "I am more worthy to be burned than any that was burned yet." God's Blessing in their hearts for this good report.'[26] Carlesse escaped the stake by dying during his confinement. Jocelyn Palmer was the son of a Coventry mayor and Fellow of Magdalen College, Oxford. He spoke Latin and Greek and was a Catholic before witnessing the burning of Ridley and Latimer and changing faith. He lost his Fellowship and was thrown out of Oxford. He obtained a post as a schoolmaster in Reading but was marked and dismissed from his post. He was eventually burned at the stake in July 1557.

At the bottom of Little Park Street stands a monumental cross, unveiled in 1910 to the Coventry Martyrs. The actual site of execution, Park Hollows, stood south-east of the memorial and was in fact a shallow sandstone quarry used during the building of the city wall. By the 20th century the area called Martyrs Field was covered in factories and other buildings forming Mile Lane and Parkside.

DISSOLUTION

73 *King Henry VIII (19th-century engraving).*

By the 16th century many monastic houses had reputations for greed and ungodly acts, and the Church was accused of profiteering through the sale of indulgences to those anxious to avoid years in purgatory. It was the richest establishment in the land, often owning more than the reigning monarch. After Henry split from Rome and declared himself head of the Church of England. Bishop Roland Lee, the King's chaplain and later Bishop of Coventry, married him to Anne Boleyn and was ordered to persuade Sir Thomas More and Bishop Fisher to agree to changes in the church. Lee's negotiations failed and the men refusing to accept Henry's reformed Church were executed. Lee himself was later one of the main supporters of the Dissolution.

The Bible was officially translated into English for the first time, and with the destruction of the High Church there was no further need for monasteries and other religious houses. Their land and riches could be 'acquired' by the crown and kept, or in many cases sold off to enrich the royal coffers. In 1536 Henry decided on the 'Dissolution' of the monastic houses in England valued at less than £200 a year. He entrusted this job to his newly appointed Vicar-General, Thomas Cromwell. There was very little opposition to the Dissolution in Coventry, which was very much a monastic city.

It began with the forced closure and confiscation of 400 religious houses and the pensioning off of some, but not all, monks. Officers were sent around to make lists of all valuable church plate, but they found much had mysteriously disappeared, leaving only cheap latten and pewter ware for the commissioners. The first houses in Coventry to be dissolved were the Whitefriars and Greyfriars, which were not propertied organisations like the Benedictines, and the crown benefited only from the sale of the buildings, although the Whitefriars did have a yearly revenue of £7 13s. 8d. The Greyfriars were obliged to make their own surrender on 5 October 1538, sign it with their names and attach their seal. It read:

> For as much as we the Warden and the Friars of the House of Saint Francis ... commonly called the Grey Friars, in Coventry, in the County of Warwick ... with like mutual assent and consent do surrender and yield up into the hands of the same, all our said House of Saint Francis ... with all the lands and tenements,

74 *An occupant of Greyfriars' graveyard being unearthed in 1931. (Albert Peck)*

75 *Franciscan friar of Greyfriars.*

gardens, meadows, waters, ponds, fields, pastures, commons, rents, reversions, and all other our interest, rights and titles … Most humbly beseeching his most noble Grace to dispose of us … as best shall stand with his most gracious pleasure. And further, freely to grant unto everyone of us his licence, under writing and seal to change our habits into secular fashion and to receive such manner of livings as other secular priests. [27]

The document of surrender was signed by John Stafford, Guardian or Warden, and his ten brothers. Like the Warden and 13 brothers of Whitefriars, they were evicted from their houses with no pension, the King conceiving that as they had lived so long by begging they could subsist in that trade. Henry was so enriched by the first dissolution that in 1538/9 he decided on the second stage, the dissolution of the more valuable monastic houses. Cromwell sent agents to assess Coventry Priory and other local houses such as Coombe Abbey and Stoneleigh Abbey.

The Prior of Coventry pleaded for the Priory as did the Bishop, Roland Lee, who had done the King such good service. Lee was assured by Cromwell that the cathedral church would survive, but not the Priory buildings. Despite this assurance a commissioner came to Coventry with papers for its destruction and the Bishop again put pen to paper. The commissioner, Dr John Loudon or London, also wrote to his master Thomas Cromwell desiring instructions, 'that my Lorde may consider, as well in the Priory of Coventre of Black Monks as in all other lyk, what spoyle ys made in wodds, and what leasys and reversions be dayly graunted, etc. And bycause yt ys the see churche, whether hys Lordeshyppe

76 *Benedictine monk of the Priory.*   **77** *Carthusian monk of the Charterhouse.*

will have ytt suppressyd or alteryd to seculars'.[28] But Cromwell had made his mind up and Coventry Priory was taken by the crown on 15 January 1539. Loudon wrote to Cromwell saying that Thomas Camswell, the prior, was a 'sad honest priest as his neighbours do report him, and a Bachelor of Divinity. He gave his house unto the King's grace willingly, and in like manner did all his brethren.'[29] Loudon also compiled the list of relics in the cathedral which were to be sent to the Tower of London for destruction. He noted rather sarcastically that, 'among these reliques your lordship shall fynde a piece of the most holy jawbone of the asse that kylled Abell, and diverse like'.[30]

Pensions were issued for life to those at Coventry Priory, though most were never paid. The money would have come from the church's yearly income, which was £731 19s. 5d. a year.[31] The monks' expulsion may actually have been a blessing in disguise, Commissioner Richard, Bishop of Dover, having already written to Cromwell earlier to inform him that the monks were in such poverty they were selling leases to live. He had now confiscated the common seals, and before the year was out he believed the monks would be 'glad to leave and provide for themselves otherwise'.[32]

St Anne's was surrendered in 1539, the 12 friars pleading to stay or be moved to another house. They did so in vain, and on 27 June 1542 the King granted the land and buildings to Richard Andrews and Leonard Chamberlain, who passed it on to William Over. One friar, only, refused to accept the house's fate, Loudon writing to Cromwell that, 'I have also receyvid the unwise letters wryten by the monkes of the Chartre House in Coventrye … This Richard Wall wrote certen letters whiche be in my lorde of pryvie sealy's house, wich letters soundith daungerously toward hym, and I have nott appoyntede any pension to hym.'[33]

Greyfriars was given over to the mayor, bailiffs and commonalty of Coventry, and Sir Ralph Sadler acquired the prior's hunting park and moated grange at Whitmore Park and other property. He later sold on his Coventry acquisitions to John Hales, Clerk to the Hanaper, who turned Whitefriars (which cost him about £83) into his Coventry residence and called it 'Hales Place'. The Hospital of

78   *Carmelite friar of Whitefriars.*

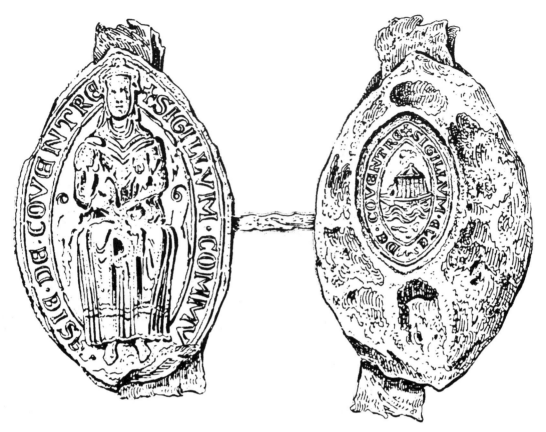

79   *The Common Seal, which appeared on the surrender document of Coventry Priory (19th-century engraving).*

St John was given a reprieve but closed in 1545. Hales acquired Whitmore Grange and Park for £250 3s. 4d. on 1 July 1547, and in 1586 his nephew, also called John Hales, built a splendid mansion called the New House by the site of the prior's grange.

The corporation fought to save the Cathedral and Priory of St Mary, arguing that the former could serve as a parish church, but Coventry already had two large parish churches and there was another cathedral at Lichfield, which held secular canons and not the Benedictines that Henry hated so much. In June 1545 the crown disposed of the Priory for £1,000.[34] On 28 July 1545 it passed to John Combe and Richard Stansfield, who afterwards passed it on to John Hales.[35] The Priory site later came into the hands of Hales' nephew, Charles, who sold it to the mayor and corporation for £400. The document of sale describes the remains as 'ye scite of ye late monasterie of our Ladie ye Virgine in Coventre aforesayed, together with the die house, water mill, and lete'.[36]

The actual destruction of the building may have begun under Combe and Stansfield but was continued by Hales. Abbot Gasquet informs us that lead valued

80   *Early 19th-century engraving showing remains of the Priory.*

at £647 was stripped from the roof and stored in the desecrated building.[37] A will surviving from the period mentions money made from melted down Priory lead being used to pay off debts. The author also left the 'coral beads' of his rosary to his daughters and stipulated that they must not go to his wife! Despite the Dissolution, his daughters, unlike his wife, were still good Catholics. By 1581 little remained, and a survey of that time informs us that, 'there is also upon the same ground stone which is left of the steeple and church there'.

Excavations in 1999-2001 showed for the first time how the building was systematically stripped. Broken glass around the great west entrance had been smashed from the outside, though some may have been taken away and re-used in other churches. After the lead was stripped, the roof tiles and timbers were probably removed and sold, leaving the west and central towers fairly intact while the main church building became a shell. Excavation of the crossing piers showed the estimated position of the tower had been slightly out and the nave was shorter than originally believed. The piers of the tower were Norman, *c*.1100, and some had been strengthened when the tower was heightened in the mid-14th century, so the original cathedral church was built shortly after Robert de Limesey moved the bishop's seat in 1102. The work could have continued into the reigns of Robert Peche and Roger de Clinton. Those stripping the building then started on the inside, removing stone, wood and floor tiles in their thousands. Heavy wagons and carts were pulled into the building by horses. Excavation work revealed that the semi-circular steps at the west entrance caused a problem and a ramp of dirt and broken stonework was built against them. Underneath the ramp the floor tiles had survived, but the cathedral floor below the steps resembled a ploughed field, churned up mud containing the odd broken tile, and the tracks of the wagons cutting deep into the floor between the undisturbed ones. Very few areas of tile survived elsewhere in the excavated building. What survived of the exterior walls stood only two or three courses high and just three column bases of the nine bays in the nave survived, one of which was carved from the rock.

A limestone tomb was excavated in a chantry chapel beyond the first pillar on the south side which had, apparently, been desecrated by the despoilers of the building. A piece of chainmail and a sword chape were unearthed in the 15th-century level, which may have been the remains of a knight's accoutrements, including war helm, mail shirt and sword, hung over his tomb. Later examination of the skull showed the main occupant had seen battle and received a sword cut to the head. The cut had began to heal, but a nearby hole showed an infection from which the knight later died. Dozens of bronze pins made archaeologists suspect someone had set up a workshop in the ruins, although an alternative explanation may have been the ritual at holy shrines of using pins to prick or scratch infected or injured limbs before pushing them into cracks or crevices in the shrine. Saint Osburg's shrine may have stood in the chantry, which would keep the pilgrims away from the monks' part of the church. Butchers dumped offal and animal by-products in the chantry area until it was stopped by the Leet; this brought semi-wild dogs into the ruins and, when part of the wall collapsed, it killed six of them, leaving their bodies for future discovery.

Archaeological investigation during the Phoenix Initiative showed that the outbuildings of the Priory ran down the hillside at different levels. These areas were pillaged too. Some parts have survived untouched since the 16th century, however, protected by tons of earth and rubble, such as the perfect spiral staircase near Hill Top leading down to a blocked doorway. Some of the most remarkable discoveries were made in 2000 when the undercrofts or cellars of the refectory and dorter were revealed. A large area of floor tiles was found intact in the former, untouched since the day the refectory floor collapsed into it. The tiles' design features the arms of England c.1340 and the debased arms of Richard Beauchamp c.1360. The pattern originally crossed the floor diagonally, covering an area estimated at 20 metres long. A number of beautifully

81 *Spiral staircase unearthed during the 1999-2001 excavations. (Margaret Rylatt/Coventry City Council)*

82 *Encaustic tiles from the Priory, probably made in Stoke. (Margaret Rylatt/Coventry City Council)*

83   *Carved head* in situ. *(Margaret Rylatt/Coventry City Council)*

84   *Dorter undercroft, originally filled with demolition rubble. (Margaret Rylatt/Coventry City Council)*

carved heads which once looked down on the monks were found amongst the mass of rubble that filled the cellar. The base of a statue of St Paul, showing bare feet, robes and the bottom of a sword chape, below which are three royal shields, suggests that the benefactor may have been Henry VI during his stay at the Priory.

The cellar under the refectory was found to be intact except for its vaulting. The building stood on a hillside and appears to have suffered from subsidence, the wall of the cellar having been thickened and limewashed. Under the wash are fragments of earlier paintings. A huge piece of the vaulted canopy from a pulpit was unearthed in the rubble of the cellar, which is believed to have fallen from the refectory and was used for preaching during meal times. It is decorated with leaf bosses and a green man with a single leaf exiting the corners of the mouth, the decorative bracing showing fragments of gold. Seven hundred pieces of carved stone were found on the site, including a piscina decorated with faces.

During filming for *Time Team* a stone-lined grave was found near the entrance to the Chapter House, which contained the body of either a bishop or prior. They were buried beneath the Chapter House because even in death their presence was thought important during meetings. By examining the bones it was discovered he was overweight and reaching middle age at the time of his death. As the coffin lid was missing and a broken one was found nearby one must assume that those who destroyed the building also ripped open the burials in the search for valuables.

Much of the stone of the cathedral and Priory would have been sold by the yard and carted away from the city, although some would have been re-used in local buildings, or possibly in repairs to ageing sections of the city wall. In 1554 the Chamberlains Accounts state, 'for getting stone in the p'orie to the broid well, xxd.' Also, there is a reference to 'hewing stone in the p'orie'. After the main sale of building material, locals may also have helped themselves. Over the centuries parts of the Priory were incorporated into such things as the Coventry Cross and St Mary's Hall and fireplaces have been discovered in the city made from columned priory stonework. The most notable building constructed from re-used ancient timber is Lych Gate Cottage, butting onto one of the west towers and said in most sources, including the Trinity Deeds (193) of 1650,[38] to have been built by the Rev. John Bryan at that time. This building has recently been re-dated by dendrochronology to the 15th century, although tradition insists it re-used old timber, one beam once bearing a brass plaque which stated that the oak timbers came from 'the palace of Leofric and Godiva'.[39]

There is a reference from the late 14th century to the Priory's library. The illuminated books included two missals of prior Roger Cotton, a book of charters, a 'Palladium of Agriculture', a book of experiments, the 'Merlinus' (probably the prophecies of Merlin) and many more. The document listing them can be found in the Bodleian Library and begins with these words, 'These are the books

85   *Excavations of the undercroft off Hill Top, July 2001. (David McGrory)*

which John of Bruges, a monk of Coventry, wrote for the use of the Church of
Coventry: whosoever take these away from the Church without the consent of
the convent may he be accursed.' John's curse meant little at the time of the
Dissolution, and over the following years the library was destroyed. John Bale
wrote in 1549 of the fate of England's monastic libraries, which were used 'to
scoure candelstyckes, and some to rubbe their bootes. Some they solde to the
grosser and sopsellers, and some they sent oversee to the bokebynders, not in
small nombre, but at tymes whole shyppes full, to the wondering of the foren
naycons.'[40]

The main survivors from the Priory appear to be the arbour, once in Palace
Yard, which may have began life as a tomb or shrine, and, possibly, the so-called
'Guild Chair' in St Mary's Hall. The chair, one of the finest of its type in the
country, has since the mid-19th century been claimed to date to 1450 and to
be where the mayor and master of the guild sat together at council functions.
Fittings for a screen whereby the chair could be attached to a choirstall, however,
suggest an alternative origin as a bishop's throne, a notion which dates from at
least the 18th century, but which modern study of the chair might confirm.
The Decorated arches with quarter-foils on the back date the chair to the late
1200s,[41] although it is likely the design could have been in use in the provinces

up to the mid-1350s. Decoration on the chair includes the grapevine, the body of Christ, the three acorns, symbolic of the Holy Trinity, and roses representing the 15 mysteries of the Catholic faith. On one arm a now headless 14th-century huntsman with pouch and dagger scabbard pins down a now headless deer, while on the other arm can be seen a hunting dog (a second dog is now gone). The back, amid foliage, depicts a huntsman and his dog and various animals, including deer and hawk, which reflects the bishops' favourite pastime, Coventry's bishops having their own hunting park at Whitmore. The *Pilgrims Rest*, the Priory guesthouse, was also decorated with hunting scenes and religious themes.[42]

On the left-hand side of the chair is a carving of the Virgin seated and holding the baby Jesus in her right arm, as shown on the seal of St Mary's Priory. On top of the chair on the right is Coventry's elephant and castle. On the right of the chair are two lions holding what appears to be a crown, the top of which has been deliberately chiselled off. There would have been no reason to remove the crown, but a bishop's mitre might have become redundant when the chair changed its role. The crown-mitre symbol and lions attached represented bishops of Lichfield and Coventry up to the 17th century. Worked into the foliage below the lions is a Staffordshire Knot. Bishop's thrones also had built in or detachable canopies and this chair still has *in situ* the metal lugs for the canopy.

The earliest record of the chair is in the City Accounts for 1579, 'Item, paid for carage of the chere from S' Nicholas Hall to St. Mary Hall, vjd.' Despite there being no record of its ever leaving the Hall, it was always assumed the chair was being returned, but it was possibly being brought to the Hall for the first time, St Nicholas Hall standing just a stone's throw from the Priory. There are good reasons to look upon the 'Guild Chair' as a survivor of the Priory, 'the Bishop's seat in the quire'.[43]

86 *The state chair in St Mary's Hall probably originated as the bishop's or prior's throne.*

87 *Remains of the Priory mill survived into the 1930s.*

Another survivor up until the early 19th century was a decorative timbered building in Palmer Lane (originally Marshalls Lane), known as the *Pilgrims Rest* and traditionally identified as the Priory guesthouse. It stood within the shadow of the Priory but no reference to it has ever been identified amongst the buildings owned by the Priory, although the Trinity Guild maintained a 'common lodging-house of thirteen beds' to receive poor travellers on pilgrimage or other pious business.[44]

In 1542 it appears that St Anne's (Charterhouse) began to be demolished. In the Chamberlains Accounts, 2s. 6d. was paid for transporting ten wagon loads of stone from the site. Within a short time it was recorded that the 'hole howse, besides the churche, ys in moche ruyne'. The Hospital of St John was finally surrendered on 4 March 1544 and the document, signed by its master William Wall, granted the church, hospital and its lands to 'the most illustrious and most invincible Prince our Lord King Henry'.

The sale and destruction of Coventry's monastic houses had a major effect on the city. Dugdale wrote,

> 'to so low an ebbe did their trading soon after grow, for want of such concourse of people that numerously resorted thither before that fatal dissolution, that many thousands of the inhabitants to seek better livelyhoods, were constrained to forsake the City: insomuch, as in the 3. E. 6. [third year of the reign of Edward VI] it was represented unto the D. of Somerset … by John Hales … that there were not at that time above 3000 inhabitants, whereas within memory there had been 15000.'

Although there was a major drop in the population, it is believed Hales may have overestimated the former total, which was nearer to 7,000. In 1520 the mayor caused a census to be made and the population was recorded at 6,601, although a letter to the crown in 1545 states, ' Whereas formerly the city has been wealthy and famous it had of late years been brought into decay and poverty; and though numbering 11,000 or 12,000 houseling [householders] people, had but two churches where God's service could be done.' The only thing we can state for sure is that after the Dissolution there was a drop in population of between 1,000 and 12,000 people.

Religious reform continued under Edward VI. In 1547 the City Annals record that, 'the Lord Protector and the rest of the Councell sent Commissions unto all parts of the Realme willing them to take all images out of the Churches for the avoiding of Idolatry. With them were sent divers preachers to persuade the people to avoid beads [rosaries] and such like Ceremonies.' In the same year copes of red and green velvet, as well as other costly vestments and banners that belonged to Holy Trinity Church, were sold to laymen, and an Act of Parliament ordered the suppression of chantries and guilds. Bablake College, followed by the Guild of the Holy Trinity and Corpus Christi, was taken by the crown because its funds had been used for superstitious practices. The church of St John the Baptist was suppressed and ceased to function as a church until 1734. St Nicholas's Church, possibly one of the city's most ancient, was used as a storehouse before being demolished, shortly after 1610.[45] The council purchased the guild and chantry lands for £1,315 1s. 8d. with money supplied by Sir Thomas White, and the rentals brought in £200 a year. The sale of some properties soon paid for various others, including the old Guildhall, which from this time became simply the Council House. The investment in land helped the city through difficult times and the money provided by Sir Thomas White still today brings in an annual income.

The surviving churches suffered destruction and poverty. The vicar of Holy Trinity found the church so in want in 1550 that he leased the vicarage and other church property to pay the wages of an assistant curate.[46] In 1559 and 1560 the churchwardens accounts of Holy Trinity record, 'For taking down ye rode, & Marie & John, iiijs. iiijd. To ye carpenter for pullinge downe ye rode loft, iiijs. viijd.' The church plate was sold and the high altar decoration was taken down, and popish symbols painted out or defaced. In 1560 the annals record that, 'This year the mass was put down, all images and Popish reliques beaten down, and burnt in the streets.' At Holy Trinity in 1564 four pence was paid for the blotting out of Trinity images, and in 1582 sixpence was paid for 'pullige downe the Idols'. In the 1590s there are numerous entries in the accounts for painting, whitewashing and panelling the church, destroying what was left of its pre-reformation painting. Luckily, the beautiful 15th-century eagle lectern survived since it bore no popish images. The rectory of St Michael's with its advowson passed to the crown and was sold to the corporation in 1565. In 1522 St Michael's had its vicar selected by the prior, 18 priests and six chantry priests. By 1553 the last of them, Thomas Ellyson, had been pensioned off for £5 a year.

Doomsday of the Mystery Plays

Like York, Chester and Wakefield, Coventry had it own famous cycle of Corpus Christi or Mystery Plays, known commonly as Pageants. An anonymous verse from Hones Table Book of 1827 attests to their popularity:

> The state and reverence and show
> Were so attractive, folks would go,
> From all parts, every year to see
> These pageant plays at Coventry.

At Shrewsbury the Mercers Guild threatened to fine any of its members who found occasion 'to ride to Coventrie Faire' on the feast of Corpus Christi and missed their own procession at Shrewsbury.[47] It is believed by some that the Coventry Plays were the most popular in the kingdom and the name 'Coventry Play' became a more general term; the *Ludus Coventriae* from Lincoln is an example of such usage.

The Mystery Plays were normally performed by the city's trade guilds on Corpus Christi day, and appear to have been linked with Coventry Fair. After the early morning torchlight procession, the first section of the Pageants began with the Creation, followed by the Deluge and then the Birth of Christ. During the Shearmen and Taylors' pageant Mary complains that the child is cold and Joseph takes him and says, 'Now in my arms I will Him fold, King of all Kings, Lord of all who live; He might have had better, if He Himself would, Than the breathing of the beasts to warm Him.' Joseph returns him to Mary and the famous Coventry Carol, 'Lully, Lullay, thou little tiny child', would be sung.

Until Doomsday, at nightfall, the various crafts would perform on pageants, huge wagons which were basically stages on wheels with a dressing and prop room underneath. These were dragged around the city to the appointed play stations at Broadgate, Much Park Street (near the corner), Gosford Street, Cross Cheaping, St Michael's churchyard and by New Gate, Greyfriars, Bishop and

88 *Pageant wagon in Broadgate just above the Cross. (Merridew & Son, 1825)*

Spon Gates. Each of the crafts provided its own wagon and props, which were kept in pageant houses, the Drapers having one such building in Little Park Street in 1392. The Cappers and several other companies kept theirs in Mill Lane, and a deed of 1503 refers to the pageant house of the Shearmen and Taylors, betwixt those of the Pinners and the Weavers in Mill Lane. The Trial and Execution of Christ and the Death of Judas were played by the Smiths, and the Resurrection and Harrowing of Hell by the Cardmakers and Cappers. Rehearsals were held in places such as St Nicholas Hall, St Mary's Guildhall, the Bishop's Palace and the Park, and real actors were also hired by the guilds. They painted their faces to exaggerate their expressions, and figures such as Christ and St Peter wore golden wigs.

Other popular figures were the devils. In John Heywood's *The Four Ps* the Pardoner relates that as soon as he found a female friend of his had gone to hell he would go there and bring her back, 'Not as who saithe by authoritie, But by the way on intreatie. And first to the devil that kept the gate I came, He knew me well For oft, in the play of Corpus Christi He hath play'd a devil at Coventrie.'[48] This devil may have been accompanied by an attendant called 'the vice', who constantly belaboured him with 'a dagger of lathe',[49] the comic duo bringing hilarity to the final proceedings.

During the last pageant of the day, the 'saved' souls wore white leather while the 'doomed' had blackened faces and wore yellow clothes painted with flames. Accompanied by the cries of the crowd, each was dragged or driven into a giant 'hells mouth' by a black devil with a wool-filled club. Doomsday was presented by the Drapers, whose record of what was used in their pageant included, 'Hell mouth, with fire kept at it; a windlass and three fathoms of cord; a barrel for the earthquake … Three worlds painted … A link to set the worlds on fire.'[50]

The accounts of 1557 also mention, 'payed to Robart Crowe for making of the boke for the paggen, 20s.' Crow acted as well as wrote, and a payment for 1560 notes, 'payed Robert Cro for pleayng God, 3s. 4d.'. Crow rewrote the Weavers Pageant and that of the Shearmen and Taylors, the original document bearing the inscription, 'Thys matter newly correcte' be Robart Crow the xiiij day of Marche, fenysschid in the yere of owre lord god MCCCCC & XXXiiij [1534].'[51] Crow appears to have made considerable alterations to the old text adding many 'coarse jests and piquant observations'. He also supplied props for the pageant, including the giants for the Corpus Christi procession.

Many records survive of the various expenses for these spectacular plays, such as the following in the *Antiquarian Magazine* of 1906 taken from the Drapers' accounts:

> Paid for four pair of Angel's wings 2s. 8d.
> Paid for painting and making new hell head 12d.
> Paid for keeping hell head 8d.
> Paid for a pair of new hose and mending of the old for the white souls 18d.
> Paid for a pound of hemp to mend the Angels heads 4d.
> To Fawston for hanging Judas 4d.
> To Fawston for cock crowing 4d.
> Item. To reward Mistress Grimsby for lending of her gear to Pilates wife.
> Starch to make a storm.
> The barrel for the earthquake.
> Pulpits for the Angels, etc.

Many of the craft guilds tried to pull out of their pageant because of growing expense, but the Leet forced them to continue by imposing heavy fines.[52] The first major problems occurred in 1494, when the Leet ordered that 'diverse charges have been continued … for the worship of the … pageants … which have been borne by diverse crafts, which crafts at the beginning of such charges were more wealthy, rich and more in number than now'.[53] To aid the established crafts, the Dyers, Skinners, Fishmongers, Cappers, Corvisers, Butchers and others were required to contribute towards the cost or be fined. The wealthier crafts, such as the Drapers and Mercers, were able to continue unaided. Because of a decline in trade in 1529, the Weavers were unable to continue and their role was taken over by the Cappers Company. They failed in turn, and in 1531 the Fullers and Skinners were ordered to continue with the Weavers Pageant,[54] and many other smaller companies were forced to bail out the established ones. The Butchers were required to join the Whittawers but disregarded the order and the Leet ordered them to join again in 1509, although the Butchers appear not to have got involved in the pageant until 1552 when they assisted the Tanners, who seem to have fallen on hard times.[55]

By the 1580s Coventry was becoming more puritanical. Many saw the plays as 'papist' and calls were made for their abolition. The crafts were in agreement because of the financial burden, but many of the city traders and the council felt that for centuries the plays had brought the city prestige and drawn thousands bringing with them great wealth. It was decided to replace the Mysteries with a more 'politically correct' pageant, and the new work, known as the 'Destruction of Jerusalem', was written by John Smythe of Oxford. It played for the first time in 1584. Amongst the actors was Reginald Headle, who was paid 5s. for playing Simon and Phynea, Gabriel Foster, who received 6s. 8d. for playing Justus, and Henry Chamberlain, who received 3s. 4d. for playing Pritus.[56] But it was thought by many to have been a complete failure as it lacked the spectacle and humour of the old Mysteries.

The last cycle of Mystery Plays was performed in 1589, and in 1591 the Common Council Book records, 'It is agreed by the whole consent of this house that the Destruction of Jerusalem, the Conquest of the Danes, or the historie of K. E. the X. [Edward the Confessor], at the request of the Comons of the Cittie shalbe plaid on the pagens on Midsomer daye & St. Peters daye next in this Citte & non other playe.'[57] The Smiths paid 20 shillings to be excused from taking part. The play was another failure. The Coventry Mystery Plays fell into obscurity until their revival in the late 20th century.

The *Ludus Coventriae*, which was thought to represent the complete text of the Coventry plays, is now believed to belong to Lincoln and not Coventry.[58] The only surviving local texts are the Shearmen and Taylors and the Weavers pageants.

THE COVENTRY CROSS

The deeds of Holy Trinity Church contain the first reference to a cross in Coventry. It is mentioned in a document dated 1300 as standing on the corner of Broadgate, on a messuage in the occupation of one Richard de Spycer, 'illud messuagium quod est in foro prioris de Coventria ante crucem',[59] which is by Spicer Stoke, a small lane leading into Butcher Row.

The cartulary of St Mary's Priory, compiled around 1400, also contains a reference to this early cross while describing the bounds of Broadgate. It notes that the messuage of Spycer now belongs to Robert Shippley (mayor in 1402 and 1416) and is 'near the cross in the market place'. The cross no doubt stood on the boundary between Broadgate and Cross Cheaping and would have been of local red sandstone, consisting of a tall shaft bearing a simple cross upon a plinth of three or four steps, very much in the style of other crosses scattered around the city and surrounding districts. On 24 May 1423 the Leet ordered that 'all arrears in the late mayor's hands, with the chamberlains distrained goods, be placed with the mayor [Henry Peyto] to make a new cross, and clean the ditches'. On the Thursday after St Matthias Day 1423, Henry Peyto led a great meeting in St Mary's Hall which officially sanctioned a new cross to be built in Cross Cheaping.[60] At the Michaelmas Leet held on 6 October that year £50 was put aside for building it and Henry Peyto made a personal contribution.

According to the City Annals, the new cross stood on eight pillars. It remained for over a hundred years, but part of the upper section had to be dismantled in 1537 when it became unsafe. The lower section stood forlorn for a number of years and there was much talk about a replacement. In 1506 Thomas Bond gave £6 13s. 4d. towards it, which sum was added to in 1518 when Thomas Haddon gave another £20 towards the fund. In 1541 Stoke-born Sir William Hollis, former mayor of London and son of Thomas Hollis of Stoke, Coventry, left a will directing that, 'I give and bequeath unto the Mayor and Aldermen of the City of Coventry, and to the Commons of the same, £200 sterling, to the intent and purpose here- after ensuing, that is to say, to make a new Cross with-in the City.' An indenture was made with exact details as to how the cross, which was based on the one at Abingdon in Berkshire, was to be constructed. It should be made of 'seasonable free-stone of the quarries of Attleborough and Rowington'. A more hard-wearing stone was to come 'from the late Priory of the said city'. It was to be erected where the old cross stood and to have on every pinnacle of the lower storey 'a beast or fowl holding a fan', and of the second storey 'the image of a naked boy with a target and holding up a fan'. The 'six or eight old images to be set in the said cross' were said to have been taken from Whitefriars. Three of these survive: that of Henry VI in the museum and the two upper smaller figures in the oriel window of St Mary's Guildhall.

The City Annals record that Cuthbert Joyner, the mayor, laid the first stone of the new cross in 1541. It rose to a height of 57 feet, excelling all expectations. In the lower section stood statues of Henry VI, King John, Edward I, Henry II, Richard I and Henry V. In the second storey were Edward III, Henry II, Richard III, St Michael and St George. The top had figures of two monks, St Peter, St James and St Christopher and, above them, a lantern holding figures of Liberty and Justice. After its completion in 1544 an entry in the Treasurers Accounts for 1545 stated, 'Pd. to Matthew Gilder and John Adkins for gildyng ye Cross', though no entry for payment was made. An entry below has, 'To Matthew Gilder for gildyng the crosse £8 6s. 8d.'[61]

89 *Coventry Cross, completed in 1544 (19th-century engraving).*

Sir William Dugdale wrote, 'It is one of the chief things wherein this city most glories, which for workmanship and beauty is inferior to non in England', but it was little appreciated by those who lived near it. In 1544, the year of its completion, the Leet Book notes, 'whereas the inhabitants of the Cross Cheaping in times past have not only commonly used to lay dung and other filth nigh unto the cross there to the great incommodity of the market place and to the great danger of infection of the plague ... it is now inacted ... that no inhabitants ... shall from henceforth lay any dung or filth in the Cross Cheaping.'[62]

In 1609, the annals inform us, the cross contained an image of Christ which offended the puritanical strain in the city, so it was removed and replaced with a figure of Godiva. A pamplet published in 1613, of a sermon made by Francis Holyoak at Holy Trinity Church, reads,

> If the whole citty should be governed by men of that faction there would be an odd government. It appeared a year or two since, when some of them were in special authority, one of them pulled downe the picture of Christ from the market cross as a monument of superstition, having been there many hundred years, and placed in the rome the picture of a naked woman without superstition, til many grave ancients of the citty seeing the absurdity, caused it to be taken down and the princes armes to be set in the place.

In 1626 Thomas Sargenson, stone mason, and Bartholomew Bewdley, plumber, were engaged by the council to make an assessment of the cross's condition. They reported that it was 'now in some parts thereof decayed, shall be repaired and newly laid in oyle and colours, and such parts thereof gilded as shall be thought fitting for the more credit of this Cittee'.

During the Commonwealth the cross came under threat from puritanical fanatics, and had the 'good hap to stand', according to Dugdale, 'by favour and protection of the butchers chiefly, who have been its best protectors'. Despite the butchers' protection, with meat cleavers presumably, Colonel Purefoy ordered the cross's demolition but it appears to have been saved by Puritan mayor, Robert Beake. He got Purefoy to agree to a compromise by removing six sets of royal arms from the cross on 27 December 1650.

The cross was still in good condition when John Evelyn came to the city and wrote in his diary, 'August 3rd, 1654, The Cross is remarkable for Gothic work and rich gilding, comparable to any I have ever seen, except that of Cheapside in London, now demolished.' The cross still had a national reputation in 1662, Edward Browne, physician to Charles II, writing after a visit to the city, 'Wee likewise saw that famous structure, Coventry crosse.'[63] In 1688 it received a major restoration, having suffered 'injury of time or otherwise much defaced'. The total outlay for the work was £323 4s. 6d. and 15,403 books of gold leaf were used, alone costing £68 15s. The re-gilding was not of selected features but covered most of the cross, and Britton said of this cross, in his *Antiquities of English Cities*, it was so bright country people could 'hardly bear to look upon it when the sun was shining'.

Guillem's *Heraldry* states, 'No place compares with this city for a most beautiful cross of large dimensions and height, adorned with beautiful statues, figures and sculptures laid out in gold and set out with becoming colours.' Celia Fiennes, who saw the cross during her horseback tour of England in 1697, wrote,

> the Crosse is noted and the finest building in England for such a thing, and in my phancy it very much resembles the picture of the Tower of Babel, is all stone carv'd very curiously and there are 4 divisions, each being less than another, to the top, and so its Piramidy forme … there is variety quite up to the top which is finely carv'd and gilt.[64]

The cross features in an old rhyme which is said by some to be older than the Banbury Cross rhyme:

> Ride a cock horse to Coventry Cross,
> To see what Emma can buy,
> A penny white cake,
> I'll buy for her sake,
> And a two penny tart or a pie.[65]

By 1703 it was once more in need of repair and Sir William Wilson, a noted sculptor, was paid to come to Coventry to assess the work. The cost must have been great for the council left the work undone, possibly because of financial problems with law suits relating to Sir Thomas White's charity. In 1753 the upper part of the cross was so ruinous it was in danger of falling and was taken down, and in 1755 mayor John Hewitt further reduced the height so it was level with the surrounding rooftops. The Common Council Book entry of 27 September 1771 reads: 'Agreed by the House that the inhabitants of Cross Cheaping be at liberty, and they are hereby authorised if they see fit to take down the cross there, provided that they permit the Corporation to take away such stones and materials as they Choose for their own use ...' In 1772, however, the *Coventry Mercury* records that the cross was still standing, and in 1778 an anonymous writer wrote, 'The cross heretofore so famous for its workmanship, has no longer anything to please. It was erected in the time of Henry VIII with the stone of the country, which is sandy and porous; and being much decayed, all the upper part was taken down about twenty years ago.'[66] The cross was probably demolished some time between 1778 and 1782, when traveller and naturalist Thomas Pennent visited the city but did not mention it. Many of the figures which decorated the cross found their way to the home of a certain Alderman Buckle at Redfin, near Berkswell, which became known as the 'Image House'. It is said that he willed the figures of Henry VI and two other saints to be returned to Coventry and placed in St Mary's Hall on his death. A fourth figure, St Peter, is now lost. Other parts of the cross were spread around the city, the base finding its way into the garden of Keresley House.

ELIZABETH AND MARY

Queen Elizabeth made her one and only visit to Coventry on Saturday 17 August 1565, during one of her state tours around the realm. John Throckmorton, the recorder, gave a speech of welcome, informing her of the city's connection to the Black Prince and Henry VI and of her father's 'bountiful' dealings with the city, pointing out that the city was not as prosperous now as it once was.[67] The retinue entered the city through Bishop Gate and the Queen was informed that the Grammar School was set up by order of her late father. She entered the

90   *Queen Elizabeth I (19th-century engraving).*

building and made it a gift of monies, then continued up Cross Cheaping and into Broadgate where crowds gathered to welcome her.

Elizabeth stayed for two days with John Hales at Whitefriars (Hales Place) and on the Sunday was entertained with a special performance of the Mystery Plays. The Tanners played their pageant at Spon Gate, the Drapers in Cross Cheaping, the Smiths at Little Park Street and the Weavers at Much Park Street. In the evening the mayor and council dined with her at Whitefriars.

Elizabeth's host, John Hales, made his first acquaintance with the city when he accompanied Henry VIII's commissioners at the time of the Dissolution. During Henry's reign he held the post of Clerk of the Hanaper and received all the king's monies connected with seals of patent, charters, commissions and fees for enrollings. Soon after Elizabeth's accession, Hales was said to have written a pamphlet supporting the house of Suffolk's claim to the throne should the Queen die without issue, and was arrested in Coventry, brought to London and placed in the Tower. He procured his release with the help of William Cecil, who proved it was not Hales who had written the pamphlet but Sir Nicholas Bacon. Hales spent his latter years in Coventry and was no doubt officially forgiven by the Queen by the time he entertained her.

In November 1569 Elizabeth ordered that Mary Queen of Scots be brought to the safety of walled Coventry. On 25 November Sir Ralph Sadler wrote, 'Yesterday the Queen of Scots was removed from Tutbury to Ashby and we make assured account she shall be in Coventry this night.'[68] Four hundred troops entered Coventry as night closed in and Mary was lodged in the *Bull Inn* in Smithford Street. The following morning the Earl of Shrewsbury wrote to the Queen's secretary, Sir William Cecil, informing him he would keep her from view as long as they were in Coventry, for the more she was seen the greater the danger. He added that Nottingham Castle would have been a much better choice since it was difficult to keep her apart from her followers in an inn, and notes, 'At conspiracy Mary was an adept, at acting a consummate performer, and she took care during her checkered life never to allow these gifts to rust for want of using.'

Huntingdon also wrote to Cecil stating that he was uneasy with the situation and found Mary none too closely kept from 'sight and conference'. He continued, 'She lieth at an inn, where for me there is no lodging; her men also lie in the town, and go where they will.'[69] Elizabeth ordered Mary to be moved from the 'common inn' to somewhere more secure, such as Coventry Castle (then little more than a ruin) or a rich merchant's house. Shrewsbury complained there was no appropriate lodging for Mary in the city, stating,

91   *Mary Queen of Scots (19th-century engraving).*

> And where your Majesty doth mislike with the lodging of this Queen at an inn, it may please you to understand that upon Mr. Skipwith's coming, by whom your Highness did send your commandment for the purpose of bringing her hither, we did immediately send our men to prepare a lodging for her, and gave them in charge to get either Mr. Hales' house or some merchants which by no means on so short warning could be obtained, and since our coming hitherto we have done the best we could to prepare a lodging which till this day could not be made ready for want of the necessary stuff.[70]

Having failed to obtain Whitefriars or a merchant's house, the 'lodging' they acquired on such short notice is likely to have been St Mary's Hall. A chamber in Caesar's Tower is usually identified as her cell, although this tradition only dates from the mid-19th century. The City Annals record that the Old Mayoress's Parlour (now called the Draper's Room) was the real room. The Hall, however, had no domestic furniture for the Queen or her ladies, and the following day a letter reports that she was moved again, this time to Whitefriars, the home of the former Lord Chief Baron, John Hales. There she was kept out of 'sight and view of the people', until Elizabeth ordered her return to Tutbury on 2 January 1570.

In 1583 Henry Goodere, whose seat was at Polesworth but who also kept a house in Much Park Street and spent much of his time in Coventry, was sent to the Tower. Patron of poet Michael Drayton, who lived in his Coventry house, and friend of John Donne and Ben Jonson, Goodere was also a great admirer of Mary Queen of Scots. While she was held in Coventry he visited her a number of times and was said to have carried messages for her. For his loyalty Mary gave him a set of gold buttons, which he wore sewn onto his hat, and for this he was sent to the Tower 'for the Queen of Scots sake'. In the same year another Coventry man, John Somerfield, was examined over his dealing with Goodere and the messages sent by the Queen of Scots.

But by 1587 Mary was executed and Henry Goodere had returned to favour. In 1589, with the threat of invasion from Spain, Goodere and his colleagues raised huge sums in Coventry and Warwickshire to equip up to 600 men, and in 1599 he was knighted.

EDUCATION

Before the 16th century education was in the hands of the Church and the guilds, who kept small grammar schools to educate deserving 'aumbrey' boys and the children of guild members. It was during the reign of Henry VIII, amid the destruction of religious houses and the fall of the old educational system, that a new Free School or Grammar School was set up in the city. Henry himself was indirectly the founder of the school although John Hales carried out the King's wishes. A surviving document reads,

> After his return from Coventry to London he desired his intimate acquaintance, Lord Cromwell and Sir Anthony Dennis, to move the King, that he might have leave to purchase some of his Majesty's lands, lying in and about Coventry. The King was easily prevailed upon to hearken to any notions of this kind; but understanding there was no Free-school in the said city, he told Sir Anthony that he should be well pleased to meet with a purchaser who would give something towards the foundation of a school, whereby others might be encouraged to promote so good a work. Sir Anthony answered, that his Majesty knew John Hales to be a very good scholar and a lover of learning and learned men; and could not therefore meet with a purchaser more fit for the purpose. Hereupon, the King sent for Mr. Hales, and asked him, whether, in the case of a purchase, he would be willing to do something towards the erection of a Free-school in Coventry. Mr. Hales answered that he should be very well pleased to do so; and that, since the motion was made by his Majesty, the school which he would found should be called King Henry VIII's school.[71]

Hales established the school and paid a minimum yearly stipend for its upkeep. Some believed that Hales also received lands from the King for the school's maintenance and that a fuller endowment was promised. John Throckmorton's oration to Queen Elizabeth noted that her father had intended to found a free

92 *John Hales, Baronet, speculator and founder of the Grammar School (late 18th-century watercolour based on 16th-century original in St Mary's Hall).*

school but certain lands of great value meant for establishing the school were withheld by Hales from the city. The Queen ordered Sir William Cecil to investigate the allegation but no evidence could be found and 'upon examination of Mr. Hales patent, no mention was made in it, of any houses or lands thereby given or reserved for the foundation and maintenance of a school'.[72] Sharp refers to a petition in the Council Treasury (which may or may not still exist) which informs us of John Hales' personal involvement in the dissolution of the Hospital of St John. It states that in 1545 Hales dissolved and defaced the hospital and that he had all the provision for the poor carted away. It accused him of reducing the value of the building and properties 'by his corrupt means', and therefore acquiring it at a cheaper price. It then adds that he obtained licence of mortmain for 200 marks of land per year to the corporation, noting that 'Hales hath not yet assigned any part of the said possessions, or any other land, towards the said foundation.'[73]

It appears that after his acquisition of St John's the city fathers were under the impression that Hales would found the free school in his own property. But he asked the council for permission to set it up in council property, namely the church of the Whitefriars behind his house. The council granted permission and, as the latter document states, Hales 'pretended to establish the said school'. He appointed a schoolmaster who appears not to have exercised his office, and the school was soon closed when the council retook possession of it. Hales then set up a school in the chapel of the Hospital of St John, placing along its walls the choirstalls from Whitefriars as seats and benches for the pupils, where they still remain. Hales decided before his death actually to endow his school, and in a will dated 17 December 1572 he left by indenture certain houses, lands, mills and rents to pay for 'the maintenance of one perpetual Free-school within the City of Coventry', with a learned schoolmaster, usher and master of music.

After his death, however, the indenture was found to be invalid since there had been no delivery of possession. The corporation petitioned the Queen for an Act of Parliament to give the indenture force of law, claiming that the 'invaliditie of the said dede, the said schole, and the godly purpose of the said John Hales may be hereafter called into question and utterly overthrown'.[74] The Act was passed and the lands thereafter were given over to the school. In his lifetime Hales appears to have had few admirers in the city and Leland wrote of the school, 'Hales with the clubbe Foot, hath gotten an Interest in this Colledge, and none ['but the Devell' added in a different hand] can get hym out.' He may have been a speculator in property and the school simply a means to an end, but testimonies against him would have been written by those who didn't approve of the 'foreigner' who made himself into the city's most powerful citizen. The 'club foot' appellation was due to an injury suffered as a young man, when he accidentally stood on his own dagger.

In its period at Whitefriars and, initially, at St John's the first master of the school was called Sherwyn. He was followed by John Tovey, who the City Accounts of 1599 state was paid 40 shillings to go to Oxford to take his degree as Master of Arts. Tovey would lead the new school successfully into the new century.

It is said that after Thomas Wheatley had sent his agent to Spain to obtain steel wedges and found they were actually silver he used his unexpected riches to found Bablake School in 1560. Wheatley actually endowed rather than founded the school, which was already established on this site. Records show that Bonds Hospital was added onto an existing school by Thomas Bond in 1507, and a list of members of the Corpus Christi Guild in 1522 includes one 'John Bedull, Skolmayster of Bablake'.[75] After the suppression of the Trinity Guild in 1547, the council petitioned the crown to give them the buildings, which in the following year were granted at a peppercorn rent of one penny a year. The church was allowed to fall into decay but Bablake may have continued in some form as a school.

A 16th-century document which used to hang in the headmaster's office read, 'In the year of our Lord God 1560, then being Mayor of the city of Coventry

93 *The Free Grammar School by Florence Weston. (Coventry City Libraries, Local Studies/Mrs Spragg)*

Mr. Richard Smith, the hospital of Bablake was erected. And then was taken into the house the number of 41 children; their overseer the schoolmaster, and two women to keep them.'[76] Thomas Wheatley's bequest to the school was made on 7 April 1563 and in 1566 that bequest brought the school its first annual sum of £49.

The school which Wheatley endowed had shrunk to 21 pupils, which unlike those at the Grammar School were from poor backgrounds and were especially picked because of their deserving character. The boys were given free board, uniforms and an education, which was still a rare thing in England. Lasting but two short years, it would set them up to be apprenticed to a craftsman, in Coventry or elsewhere. An interesting entry in the Leet Book of 1563 records the will of William Locker, 'Citizen & Plommer of London'.[77] He gave ten shillings a year to Bablake School, and one assumes he attended in the years before its re-foundation.

CRIME AND PUNISHMENT

One of the best sources for crimes commited during the 16th century is the City Annals. Although they are not always accurate with regard to dating, in 1523, during the mayoralty of Julius Nethermill, they record that,

> In this year Pratt and Slouth were arrested in Coventry for Treason and their Confession was to put the Mayor and his brethren to Death to have Robed St. Mary's Hall and to have taken St. Mary Hall, Kenilworth Castle, they were had to London for judgement but Executed at Coventry, they were drawn on a slead to the Gallows and were hanged, drawn and quartered, the head of Slouth was set on New Gate with a leg and a shoulder and the Rest of him was bestowed on Bishop Gate and the Head of Pratt was set on Babblake Gate with a leg and a shoulder and the rest of him was bestowed on Grayfrier Gate.[78]

Another ambitious crime was recorded in 1526, when 'Pickering Clarke of the King's Larder and Anthony Manville, gentlemen intended to have taken the King's Treasure off his Subsidue as the Collectors of the same came towards London, therewith to have raised men and to have taken Kenilworth Castle, then to have made Battle against the King for which they were hanged, drawn and Quartered at Tiburn, the other of the Conspirators were Executed at Coventry.'

94   *Bayley Lane with all its original timbered cottages around the Guildhall (19th-century engraving).*

The arguments over common land were ongoing and in 1524 the annals record that the commoners pulled down the enclosures which had encroached on the land at Whitley, something that had taken place in 1480, too. In the following year things got more serious:

> The last Lammas Day on which rose the Comons of Coventre and pulled down ye gates and hedges of ye grounds inclosed, and they that were in the Citty shutt ye New Gate against ye Chamberlains and their Company. The Mayor was almost smothered in ye throng. He held with the Comons for which he was carried prisoner to London. He was put out of office, and Mr. John Humphrey served out his year.[79]

Sir Edmund Knightly, the city recorder, was personally ordered to remove the mayor from his office and send him with the leaders of the revolt to Cardinal Wolsey for examination. That Christmas Knightly informed those involved of their punishment and forty were imprisoned. At the next meeting of the Leet it was ordered that the commons which had recently been enclosed should be opened again.

In 1547 the annals record that, 'the stews was putt down by the King's Commandment', the suppression of brothels being part of a nationwide attack on immorality. An entry for 1561 reads, 'One Moor, faining himself to be Christ, was whipd', which may refer to a moor, or black man, whipped for calling himself Christ, and therefore be the earliest reference to race in Coventry; or it could refer to someone whose surname was Moore.

The year 1569 saw a murder committed in the city by the reigning mayor, John Harford. Harford was walking his two greyhounds in the fields when he came upon William Heely walking his spaniel with his wife and mother. Harford's greyhounds attacked the single dog and Heely tried to beat them off, on seeing which Harford ran over to Heely and 'struck him outrageously over the Back'. After two weeks of pain Heely died and at the coroner's inquest Harford was found guilty of manslaughter. The Queen ordered that Harford be removed from office, but it appears he was pardoned on the authority of Heely's wife after he had paid her an unspecified large sum.

Another scandal took place in the city in 1588, during which year Knightly, the nephew of John Hales II, borrowed Whitefriars, for the Hales now lived at New House in Keresley. During his time there he secretly brought in a printing press and produced what were known generally as the 'Martin Marprelate Tracts' – outlawed pamphlets of a 'violent and abusive' nature which have been described as extreme Puritanism. Other printers captured in Lancashire confessed to the existence of the press in Coventry, which was smashed. Hales appears to have known nothing of what was happening in his property, but was under suspicion and fined £1,500. It was later agreed that he was in fact innocent, but the Queen insisted that as his property was used a £500 fine should be paid. It was finally paid by his grandson, another John Hales, in the reign of James I.

95   *Set of stocks by St Mary's Hall.*

Crimes of a lesser degree were devised by the Leet, that of Easter 1525 recording,

> Wher-as in tyme past dyvers & meny of the Inhabitants within the Citie disposed to Idleness not having xis. of freholde by yeire inordinatlie have vsed to hawke & to hunt, kepyng haukes, greyhounds & hounds, spanielles, ferretes, heyes [rabbit nets], Targes & other engennes, wherby all manner of fowles & beastes of waren & of chace be excessyvelie taken & destroyed.

The Leet ordained that anyone within the city and county who owned less than 11 shillings freehold was for-bidden to own any of the above; those who did would be fined 6s. 8d. by the sheriffs.[80] Game needed protection, and the Leet of 1549 safeguarded the king's deer, which appeared to be escaping from the Great Park into the Little Park. The chamberlains were ordered to make a wall in the Little Park at their own cost to stop the problem and protect the deer.

Local records reflect the national problem of beggars following the Dissolution. In 1517 the Leet ordered every alderman in the city with men to search for 'vacaboundes and lusty beggers' and make them leave their wards on threat of imprisonment. And in the following year,

> And these bygge beggars, that wil-not worke well to gete ther levying, but lye in the feldes & breke hedges & stele mennys fruyte in somour, let them be banysshed the town, Or els ponyssh theym so without fauour that they schal-be wery to byde therin.

But the problem did not go away, and in 1521 the Leet enacted that every alderman was to search his ward for beggars, and those who were deemed acceptable, probably Coventry born, were given a badge which bore the city arms, the 'Olyfaunt'; others were told to leave within a night and day. In 1524 the Leet ordered that, 'no begger of this Citie fromhensfurthe shall begge within the two parishe Churches of this Citie in the tyme of Goddes service used ther, upon peyn to be punysshed by imprisonment of the stokes by the space of a day and a nyght.'[81]

There were stocks within the city at Mill Lane, Bishop Gate, Well-street Gate, New Street, Greyfriars Gate, Little Park Gate, New Gate, by St George's Chapel, Bablake and by the Chapel of St Christopher and St James at the end of Spon Street. Various documents in the city archives mention stocks in St Michael's churchyard from 1574, and new ones being erected in the Bullring at the bottom of Butcher Row in 1583; a suspended iron cage is mentioned in Cross Cheaping in 1575. The following Leet entry from 1529 warns of the consequences of not learning the lesson of the stocks:

> Every person that hereafter shal-be founde or takyn Brekyng of hegges or cuttyng of mennes woodes or trees shal-be brought unto the next stokkes within this Citie & ther to continue by the space of ij dayes with bred & water & non other sustinaunce, and if he or they be takyn the seconde tyme with like offence then the same persone to be banysshed the Citie for ever.[82]

In 1598 it was ordered that the mothers and fathers of illegitimate children were to be publicly whipped, in 1597 women classed as scolds, brawlers or disturbers of the peace were put to the 'cooke-stool'.

DAILY LIFE IN SIXTEENTH-CENTURY COVENTRY

The Dissolution of Coventry's many monastic houses was not entirely responsible for the city's declining fortunes. As early as 1523 there were 565 empty houses counted in the city. Much of this is believed to be due to the decline in the cloth and cap trade. Production of the famed 'Coventry true blue' cloth and dark blue thread noted for its permanence lasted from the 15th to the end of the 16th centuries. The colour came from the woad plant, which was imported via Southampton. That Coventry blue was better than most is often attributed to the local water, but other old sources suggest that woad was being mixed with madder and sloe berries which once grew prolifically in the area.

Coventry's exquisite 'true blue' was so popular that it is mentioned numerous times in various works of the 16th century. Michael Drayton, in his *Shepherds Garland* of 1593, wrote,

> His tar-box on his broad belt hung,
> His breech of Cointree blue.

Production of the cloth made Coventry the fourth richest provincial city in England.[83] John Hales wrote, 'I have heard say that the chief trade of Coventry was heretofore in making of blue threade, and then the towne was riche, even in that trade in maner onely, and now our thredde comes all from beyonde sea. Whereforto that Trade of Coventry is decaied, and thereby the town likewise.'[84]

At the beginning of the century all the wool woven in the city was placed in the Searching House next to the Wool Hall in Bayley Lane. The quality of the weaving was checked by two weavers and fullers especially appointed for the task.

If it met the approved quality standards a lead seal bearing the elephant and castle and the length of the cloth on the back would be attached to the bale and the merchandise taken into the Wool Hall for sale. By the seal 'men schall perceive and see it is true Coventry cloth, ffor of suerte ther is in London & other places that sell false & untrewe made cloth, & name it true Coventre cloth'.[85] Merchandise which did not meet the required standard was returned. When, in 1529, a new dye became popular locally which was not as durable as Coventry blue, the Leet enacted that, 'no person or persons … fromhensfurth die or colour within this Citie eny woll or Cloith with the new or disceivable Coloures … latelie invented & begone in this Citie by a frenche-man.' All such cloth that bore the seal of Coventry should have the seal removed, thereby 'avoydyng the gret sclander that myght happen to this Citie'.[86]

In the 1520s there were 90 separate trades in the city and a survey of 1522 considered the leading ones were Cappers, Weavers, Shearmen, Butchers, Shoemakers, Drapers, Dyers, Bakers, Mercers, Tailors, Tanners and Smiths.[87] Julius Nethermill, a draper, was the second richest man in Coventry. A grocer, Richard Marler, who paid for the Marler's Chapel in Holy Trinity, was considered the third or fourth richest merchant in England. In 1524 Marler alone paid one-ninth of the city's subsidy.[88]

At the other extreme, almshouses were founded for the poor. In 1507 ex-mayor Thomas Bond founded Bond's Hospital for the reception of 'ten poor men and one poor woman to prepare their meat and drink'. His will stipulated that every inmate should wear a hooded black gown and attend nearby St John's every day for matins, mass and evensong. Each was required, 'daily after they had supped, to go into the church, and there kneeling, every man to say fifteen paternosters and fifteen aves, and three creeds, in the worship of the passion of Christ, and then to drink and go to bed'.[89] And, with the assistance of a priest, they were to pray daily for the souls of their founder Thomas Bond and 'his father, grandfather and all Christian souls'.

The inmates were chosen at a meeting of the Trinity Guild, and during their daily service they prayed for the guild brothers and sisters. Bond's will gave land and tenements in the city centre, in Coundon, Bulkington, Arley and Fillongley, and in Leicestershire with which to pay for the inmates, a priest, a bailiff, and the yearly distribution of alms to the poor. When the guilds and their chantries were suppressed in 1547 the lands of the hospital were confiscated, although the next year they were returned to the council to continue the good work.

The city's second important (and surviving) almshouse was Ford's Hospital in Greyfriars Lane. It appears to have been built upon the site of a former chapel within the Greyfriars Friary, for when Shelton explored the building following bomb damage in 1940 he discovered under the present floor encaustic tiles such as would be found in a chapel building. The hospital was founded by William Ford, a merchant. The executor of his will of 1509, William Pisford senior,

96 *Courtyard of Ford's Hospital (mid-19th-century engraving).*

considerably enlarged the original endowment, and it is likely that Pisford was William Ford's father and that the younger William shortened his name for obvious reasons. Pisford senior erected the present building using a large quantity of teak, a building material usually found only on the coast. With the money left by his son he purchased, as directed, land to maintain the house for five aged men and one aged woman and look after their needs. These inmates, too, were chosen by members of the Trinity Guild.

When Pisford senior died he willed that into the almshouse should be placed

six poor men and their wives, being nigh to the age of three score years or above, and such as were of good name and fame, and had been of good honesty, and kept household within the said city, and were decayed and come to poverty and great need, in the same city, and that every of the said six poor men and his wife to be admitted into the said almshouse should have seven and a half penny a week as long as the said poor man and his wife lived together in the said almshouse.[90]

Should the wife die the man would get the whole sum to himself but anyone misbehaving in any way, such as 'haunting alehouses, making strife, or other notable offences', would be put out on the third or fourth warning by the master of the Trinity Guild. Should the husband die the wife could continue to stay but only on half of the said sum.

William Pisford also willed that a priest live within the complex and say mass for the souls of the founders in the hospital's chapel and in the guild chapel in St. Michael's. He should also lead the inmates in prayers for the souls of those involved in the hospital's foundation. No inmate was allowed to stay out overnight without permission from the priest or the master of the guild. By the 18th century the hospital had become exclusively female, and by 1867 it held 17 aged women, each with their own room and a weekly income of four shillings; a further 20 women received a weekly pension from the trust set up by William Pisford and his son. The hospital is still used today and the complex was extended in the 1970s.

In 1547 the Leet ordered the aldermen of the city to make a census of their wards to find out how many were unemployed and who could employ them. Anyone who didn't work was to be punished and, if that didn't work, banished from the city. Anyone who for good reason could not sustain his family was to be 'releved by the Comon almes of the City'. It was also enacted that all those who employed workers should pay them in ready money and not in 'wares or vitayle'. Many local tradesmen were out of work and the Leet ordered in 1553 that

> all carpenters, masons, tilers, dawbers and also all kind of labourers within this city lacking work shall assemble themselves at five o'clock in the morning in the summer time with their tools in their hands at the Broadgate, according as in times past ... and that none of them be found idle at home or in any ale house, upon pain of imprisonment.[91]

The Leet clamped down on alehouses in 1547, closing many. In the same year it was ordained that no labourer 'of the pooreste sort doo sytte all daye in the halehouse drynkynge & playnge at the Cardes and tables and spend all that they can gett prodigally upon themselfes to the highe displeasure of God'. The time would be better spent with wife and family. No labourer, journeyman or apprentice was to go to an inn on any work day upon pain of imprisonment of one day and one night. The Leet also controlled the sale of ale at the 'sextary' (which must have been the disused sextry of the old cathedral) and ordered that no brewer sell his best ale at higher than one penny a gallon. By 1551 best ale was priced at 4d. a gallon, and in 1552 the Leet Book refers to the excessive number of alewives and to 'Typlers' increasing vice in the city. In 1553 craftsmen, tradesmen, journeymen and apprentices were forbidden from eating and drinking in an alehouse unless it were a market day or fair day and the drinker were in the company of a stranger, presumably sealing a deal, and the price of ale sold at the

97 *Old Malt House in Gosford Street, by Florence Weston. (Coventry City Libraries, Local Studies)*

sextry was reduced to 3d. a gallon. Despite the efforts to control drinking within the city, however, John Platter who visited in 1599 wrote, the city

> hath abundance of ale houses, taverns and innes whiche are so frought with maltworms noghte and daye that you shal wunder to see them. You shal have them ther sitting at the wine and good ale all daye longe and nighte too, even a whole week as longe as money is lefte.

Fines had outlawed roving but men were required to practise the long bow every 'feast day' at the archery butts. Many broke this law, enacted in the reign of Edward IV, and played bowls and quoits instead. In 1517 the Leet ordained that anyone found using the latter should be reported to the sheriff and fined 6d. It also ordered that 'no person cast no bowle in the streets within this Citie' or be fined 6d. Much of this bowling took place in the fields by 'seynt Anny's' by the Charterhouse, and the Leet ordered that no one was to bowl there before six o'clock in the morning, nor after six o'clock in the evening, unless 'they be honest persones that will make litell noyse'.

98   *William Shakespeare, now thought to have played St Mary's Hall.*

Other pastimes were cock-fighting and animal baiting. The baiting of badgers, dogs, bulls and bears was a pastime enjoyed by all classes, and special places were set up in the city where the 'sport' could take place, such as the Bullring outside the Priory gate. Bear baiting was conducted by the 'bearward', a man often connected to some noble household whose livelihood this was. The bearwards of Sir Henry Compton and the Earl of Derby were both in the city six times in the 1570s and '80s. Robert Dudley, Earl of Leicester, allowed his bearward into the city on three occasions between 1573 and 1577.

During the 16th century Coventry was one of the most important centres for visiting players, including the best in the land such as the King's Men, the Queen's Men, the Chamberlain's Men and those of the Earls of Derby, Leicester, Oxford and Shrewsbury. Between 1594 and '95 the city was visited by Baron Chandos's Men, Lord Darcy's Men, Lord Monteagle's Men, Lord Morley's Men, Lord Ogle's Men, the Queen's Men (Elizabeth I) and the Earl of Shrewsbury's Men. Amongst the players was one William Shakespeare, who played in Coventry with the Queen's Men every year between 1585 and '91. In 1594 he joined the Chamberlain's Men and his last tour as a player was with the King's Men in 1603, when the company again played Coventry.[92] There is no actual record of the venues for these companies, but the most likely is St Mary's Guildhall,[93] which at the time served as both council house and stage for any notable event within the city.

The city waits were musicians who played at the feast held by the city fathers and guilds in St Mary's Hall. Festivals included the May Day celebrations around the city's giant maypole, which probably stood in the Broadgate/Cross Cheaping area, as well as those in other parts of the city. These maypoles would have been a permanent fixtures before the rise of Puritanism and the destruction of 'pagan idols'. In 1591 the Common Council Book records, 'And that all the may poles that nowe are standing in this Citte shalbe taken downe before Whit-sonday next & non hereafter to be sett up in this Citte.'

Five

SEVENTEENTH-CENTURY COVENTRY

ROYAL VISITS

During the journey of James VI of Scotland to London he was invited to stay at Exton Hall, the main seat of Sir John Harington of Exton and Coombe Abbey, on the outskirts of Coventry. Sir John was given the title of baron and made ward of the King's eight-year-old daughter, Elizabeth, who was sent to Coombe Abbey to be educated with other noble ladies by John Tovey, who had resigned his mastership of the Grammar School. Lord and Lady Harington had created at Coombe a wonderland where miniature horses and cattle wandered amid follies and aviaries of exotic birds. The City Annals of 1604 record her arrival in Coventry.[1]

The Gunpowder Plot of 1605 was hatched in Warwickshire, home to many notable Catholic families. The intention was to place the Princess Elizabeth on the throne, marry her to a Catholic prince and reinstate Catholic rule in England. Robert Catesby of Lapworth was a gentleman, soldier and religious zealot. He introduced Thomas Winter of Worcestershire to the plot and he in turn brought in his elder brother Robert and the notorious soldier, Guido (Guy) Fawkes. When a cellar directly beneath the Great Chamber of Parliament became available to rent it was quickly acquired by the plotters, who placed within its depths 36 barrels of gunpowder.

99 *King James I (18th-century engraving).*

149

100   *Palace Yard in Earl Street.*

Among others joining the plot was Sir Everard Digby, who took up residence at Coughton Court, promised money towards the rebellion, and invited like-minded friends to join. Clandestine meetings were held at the *White Lion*, Dunchurch and the *Bull Inn* in Smithford Street. During these meetings it was agreed that after Fawkes had done the deed in London a large force of men gathered on Dunsmore Heath in the guise of a hunting party would ride on Coombe and take the Princess by force.

On the afternoon of 4 November Catesby and Wright left London for Warwickshire to join the 'hunt' now gathering there. But news of Fawkes' arrest spread quickly and Percy and Christopher Wright headed for Warwickshire to inform the others, leaving Ambrose Rokewood behind awaiting any last minute news. Rokewood left later in the day, overtook his fellow conspirators and informed the rest of the plot's failure. The 'hunting party' began to break up, although many wanted to continue with the rebellion. The Princess was no longer at Coombe, however, but lodged within the safety of walled Coventry, Lord Harington having received a letter from Mr Bentock, a horse-trainer from Warwick, earlier that day saying some of his horses had been taken by John Grant of Norwood. Fearing a Catholic rising was at hand, Harington had sent the Princess to Coventry under the protection of Sir Thomas Holcroft, and she was lodged in the Hopkins' mansion, later known as the Palace Yard. Armour and weapons were issued from St Mary's Hall and soldiers guarded the city gates and the body of the Princess.

In the morning the county was up in arms and Sir Fulke Greville, the Earl of Warwick, rode on Catholic houses and confiscated horses and weapons and placed men to guard the roads. The Sheriff of Warwickshire and others raised a *posse comitatis* of over fifty men and pursued the main conspirators across three counties. They were eventually surrounded at Holbeach Hall in Staffordshire and the house was put to the torch. Those conspirators not killed were taken. On 30 January 1606 Sir Everard Digby, who was not involved in the last stand, Robert Winter, John Grant and Thomas Bates were hanged, drawn and quartered before a vast throng by St Paul's, London. The following day Fawkes, Thomas Winter, Ambrose Rokewood and Keyes suffered the same fate. Afterwards Sir John Harington wrote of the event:

101 *Sir John Harington of Coombe Abbey (19th-century engraving).*

> I am not yet recovered from the fever occasioned by the disturbances. I went with Sir Fulk Greville, to alarm the neighbourhood and surprise the villains who came to Holbeach, and was out five days in peril of death. If their wickedness had taken place in London, some of them say she [Elizabeth] would have been proclaimed Queen. Her Highness doth often say, 'What a Queen should I have been by this measure!' and, 'I had rather been with my father in the Parliament House than wear his crown on such terms'.[2]

Princess Elizabeth remained at Coombe Abbey under the guidance of Sir John until 1608, when she moved to Kew. Her expensive lifestyle continued to be paid for by Sir John and in 1613 she married Frederick, Elector of Palatine. Later that year Sir John Harington died leaving over £40,000 in debts. Elizabeth encouraged her new husband to take the crown of Bohemia, but Frederick found himself dragged into a war. Catholic Spanish forces attacked Protestant Bohemia and English troops were sent to help under the direction of Coombe Abbey's new master William, Lord Craven. Craven fought many campaigns in defence of

102   *Princess Elizabeth, daughter of James I.*

Bohemia and swore his devoted service to Elizabeth, its queen. Things began to turn against them, however, and in 1629 Frederick died a broken man aged only 39. Elizabeth devoted herself to her 13 children, the most notable of whom was the later Prince Rupert of the Rhine, who attacked Coventry during the Civil War. In 1662 Elizabeth, erstwhile Queen of Bohemia, died, and Craven had her buried at Westminster Abbey, bearing her crown before her coffin.[3]

On 2 September 1617 the King himself came to the city.[4] He was presented with a golden cup containing £100 in gold and kept in a crimson velvet and taffeta-lined case. The entertainment amounted to £220 14s. 8d., of which £47 17s. 7d. was spent on the supper alone. The Leet Book of that year records that 25 citizens should make up the common council, and that on the death or removal from office of any member the mayor, aldermen and Leet members alone would chose a replacement. This radical reform replaced the ancient rights of certain citizens of Coventry, acquired in the reign of Edward III, to elect members of the council. The closed council was confirmed in King James' charter of 1621, known as the 'Governing Charter', which gave the right of self-election to a 'Grand Council' of 31 members made up of men who had previously held the office of mayor, bailiff, chamberlain or warden. An extract from it reads:

And for the better performance and execution of our will and pleasure ... we ... appoint our well beloved Henry Sewell, for the governing of the said ward called Bayley Lane Ward; Richard Butler, for the governing of the said ward called Jordan-Well Ward; Christopher Davenport for ... Bishop-street Ward; William Hancock for ... Broad Gate Ward; Sampson Hopkins for ... Earl-Street Ward; Henry Smith for ... Cross Cheaping Ward; John Herring for ... Spon Street Ward; Henry Davenport for ... Smithford-street Ward; John Barker for ... Much Park-street Ward and Samuel Miles for ... Gosford-street Ward, to be and shall be modern Aldermen of the said City, to continue in the said office ... during their several natural lives.[5]

The charter was obtained by Sampson Hopkins for the sum of £187 12s. 6d. and was confirmed only after James had received evidence from the Bishop of Coventry that the people of the city were receiving the sacrament on their knees as he had ordered in 1611. With the establishment of a closed council the Leet became redundant, and it wasn't until 1835 that any form of open election took place again.

The future Charles I quarrelled with the city in 1612 over a rental of former Priory land. The argument was settled at the Court of the Chancery in Coventry's favour. Things did not end there, and in 1626 Charles, now King, tried to raise forced loans from cities, including Coventry, without Parliament's permission, in order to pay for a Scottish war. Those who failed to pay answered for their misdeeds before the Privy Council at Whitehall, and in the following year a number of Coventrians were committed to prison for refusing to pay money to the King's commissioners. When the King taxed inland

103 *Coventry Cup presented to James I.* (Gentleman's Magazine, *1825*)

towns and cities for the 'Ship Money' needed to build up the royal fleet, many in Coventry refused to pay. In 1637 only £65 5s. 4d. was raised. In 1639 the city was ordered to pay £500 but wrote to the King and got the sum reduced to £266 13s. 4d.[6] Taxes such as these combined with local Puritanism meant the King would find the city uncooperative in the coming Civil War.

GREAT REBELLION AND GLORIOUS REVOLUTION

Charles' wife Henrietta was a practising Catholic and many believed the King a secret follower of the old faith. Archbishop Laud attacked Puritanism and William Prynne, a Puritan lawyer, wrote a book entitled *Histriomastix* condemning stage plays, although some thought it a covert insult to the Queen, who enjoyed taking part in masques. Prynne was found guilty of seditious writings, imprisoned, and sentenced to be pilloried and have his ears removed, but as he was being transported through Coventry the mayor and citizens took the opportunity to show their solidarity with the unfortunate lawyer. He was made welcome and even attended a service held in St Michael's in his honour. For this show of defiance Archbishop Laud summoned the mayor to London and the city was fined £200 by the Privy Council. In 1640 Prynne's sentence was found to be unjust and some of his Coventry friends escorted him back home from London.

A record was made of the city's armoury at St Mary's Hall on 19 December 1640. It contained 16 headpieces, 24 pieces of armour, 77 muskets (50 of which arrived from London in September), 29 Caleevers, 50 musket rests, 65 pairs of bandoliers, 24 pikes (10 of them new), five bows, 20 halbeards and gleaves, 36 poleaxes, 28 bills, nine swords, two brass serpentine (cannon), two iron cannon, 'a little short brass peece mounted on wheels', a similar iron cannon (brought to the city in 1450 during the Jack Cade scare) and a short iron piece mounted on a stock, namely a 15th-century hand cannon. It was also noted that 20 bills were stored in the Mayor's Parlour in Cross Cheaping.[7] Over the following year the armoury was extended by private donation, bills and poleaxes were repaired and new ones were made. The five old bows in the inventory were horned, shaved, rosined and strung at the cost of 5d. Over 200 weight of lead was cast into bullets and over 800 weight of lead pigs stored in the undercroft of the Guildhall.

104 *Entrance to St Mary's Guildhall, used after 1547 mainly as the Council House.*

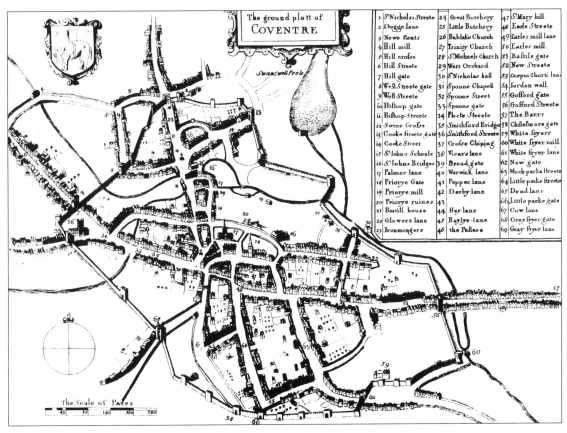

The ground plott of COVENTRE

1	St Nicholas Streete	24	Great Butchery	47	St Mary hill
2	Dogge lane	25	Little Butchery	48	Earle Streete
3	Newe Rents	26	Bablake Church	49	Earles mill lane
4	Hill mill	27	Trinity Church	50	Earles mill
5	Hill crosse	28	St Michaels Church	51	Bastile gate
6	Hill Streete	29	West Orchard	52	New Streete
7	Hill gate	30	St Nicholas hall	53	Corpus Christi lan
8	Well Streete gate	31	Spoune Chapell	54	Jordan well
9	Well Streete	32	Spoune Street	55	Gofford gate
10	Bishop gate	33	Spoune gate	56	Gofford Streete
11	Bishop Streete	34	Fleete Streete	57	The Barrs
12	Swine Crosse	35	Smithford Bridge	58	Chilesmore gate
13	Cooke streete gate	36	Smithford Streete	59	White fryers
14	Cooke Street	37	Crosse Chiping	60	White fryer mill
15	St Johns Schoole	38	Vicars lane	61	White fryer lane
16	St Johns Bridges	39	Broad gate	62	New gate
17	Palmer lane	40	Warwick lane	63	Much parke streete
18	Prioryе Gate	41	Pepper lane	64	Little parke streete
19	Prioryе mill	42	Derby lane	65	Dead lane
20	Prioryе ruines	43		66	Little parke gate
21	Bastill house	44	Hay lane	67	Cow lane
22	Glowers lane	45	Baylyе-lane	68	Gray fryer gate
23	Ironmongers	46	the Pallace	69	Gray fryer lane

Swanswell Poole

The Scale of Paces

105   *Coventry in 1610, published by John Speed.*

In January 1642 chains designed to obstruct large groups of horsemen were ordered to be hung at the ends of West Orchard, Broadgate, Greyfriars Lane, Pepper Lane, Little Park Street, Hay Lane, Bayley Lane, Much Park Street and Dead Lane. In the same month Christopher Davenport, the mayor, ordered that,

> for the better defence of the Citie, some great pieces of ordnance be ordered from Bristol or elsewhere, and that every house-holder and person of ability of this Citie, shall find and provide himself with such a proportion of musketts compleatly furnished, so this City maie have in reddyness, upon any suddaine occasion, at least five hundred muskets for its defence and safeguard.[8]

The aldermen of each ward were ordered to supply a suitable person to watch the city wall from 9 p.m. to 5 a.m., as long as 'no common or ordinarie watchman be accepted or allowed in theise troublesome times, but that the watch be perform'd by able men both of estate and persons'. On 12 March 1642 the Common Council ordered William Jesson, M.P. for Coventry, to purchase while he was in London four new pieces of ordnance for the city as the existing ordnance was somewhat antiquated.

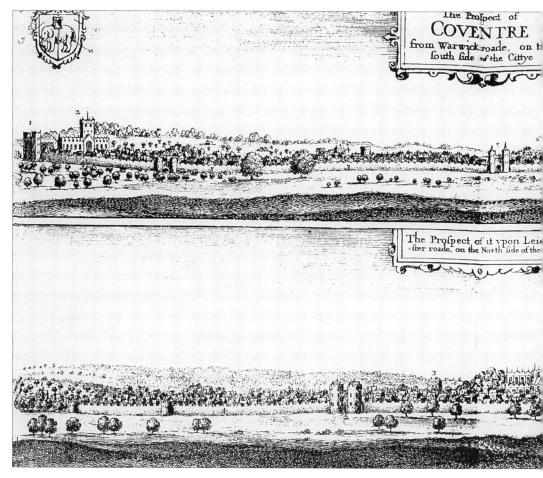

The Prospect of COVENTRE from Warwick roade, on the south side of the Cittye

The Prospect of it vpon Leicester roade, on the North side of the

England was beginning to fracture into supporters of either the King or Parliament and, locally, Lord Northampton, the City Recorder, and Lord Brooke, the Lord Lieutenant of Warwick, held great animosity towards each other. Brooke is recorded as stating that Northampton ought to be 'translated to Warwick Castle, there to stand sentry to fright crows and kites', and on 14 June 1642 a Cavalier supporter of Northampton hit back at Brooke by smashing up his family chapel at Warwick. Things were starting to get personal and Civil War drew nearer.

In May the mayor received a letter from Sergeant Wightwick, Steward of Coventry Court in Leicester, directing him and his sheriffs to attend the King there. The Council agreed to 'give satisfaction to his majesty, that no prejudice shall happen against the city, or the liberties thereof'. Afraid of the royal hand, they were prepared to do the King's bidding, but the citizens of Coventry tried by force of numbers to prevent the mayor and sheriffs leaving the city. Two days later it was ordered that 'each inhabitant of this citie (being of abilitie) shall provide him and themselves of arms of his and their owne wt all convenient

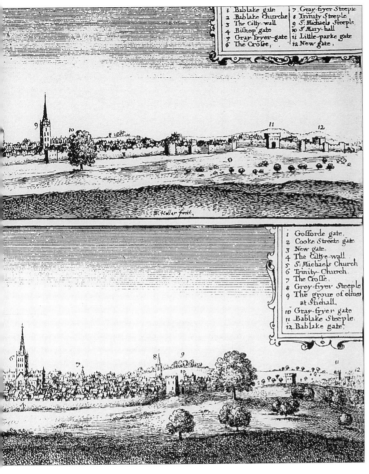

1 Bablake gate	7 Gray-fryer Steeple
2 Bablake Churche	8 Trinity Steeple
3 The City-wall	9 S. Michaels Steeple
4 Bishop gate	10 S. Mary-hall
5 Gray-fryer-gate	11 Little-parke gate
6 The Crosse,	12 New gate.

1 Gosforde gate,	
2 Cooke Streete gate	
3 New gate.	
4 The Cittye-wall	
5 S. Michaels Church	
6 Trinity-Church	
7 The Crosse,	
8 Grey-fryer Steeple	
9 The groue of elmes at Stichall.	
10 Gray-fryer gate	
11 Bablake Steeple	
12 Bablake gate.	

106 *A prospect of walled Coventry, engraved by Hollar, dated 1649.*

speed', and alderman were to call on every household to check this had been carried out. On 30 July 40 men were appointed to watch the walls every night and 12 men to watch the wards every day, two guarding port-gates and two at Hill Street Gate and Well Street Gate.

The city fathers decided that if the King and Prince Charles did visit, 'a purse containing 200 pieces [of gold] shall be presented to the King; and another purse with 100 pieces in it to the Prince',[9] and on 19 August the King arrived at Stoneleigh Abbey, home of Lord Leigh. City Recorder Spencer Compton, Earl of Northampton, informed the King he would hold Coventry for him and secured the powder magazine in Spon Gate, but Sergeant Wightwick, Alderman Bassett and Barker retook it and moved the powder to Warwick, as there was probably a shortage of powder at the castle. Northampton had 400 followers in the city and worked to raise more, but 400 armed men from Birmingham began to arrive. As Northampton tried to raise support in the *Bull Inn* in Smithford Street, he was forced to flee for his life through the Bull Yard and out of Greyfriars Gate. He headed straight for Stoneleigh to inform the King of the state of play.

The following day Charles wrote to the city demanding its subjugation, the King's Herald, Sir William Dugdale, bringing his demand. After a short consultation he was informed by Dr Robert Phillips that, 'his Majesty's royal person should be most respectfully welcomed, but we could not with safety permit his cavaliers to enter the town,' although it was agreed the King could enter with only 200 followers. Charles was not a man to be dictated to and, deciding to take the city by force, he sent to Northampton for siege weapons and set his cannon up on Park Hill on the brow of Little Park Quarry.

A Parliamentary pamphlet of the time entitled 'Certain Special and Remarkable Passages, from both Houses of Parliament' says,

'The Houses also received letters informing them of the true state of things at Coventry. That his Majesty continued his siege and battered against the town from Saturday till Monday last. That the cavaliers, with their pieces of ordnance, having battered down one of the gates, the townsmen, to prevent their entrance, stopped up the passage with harrows, carts and pieces of timber, and with great courage forced the cavaliers (notwithstanding their ordnance) upon every attempt towards the gate soon to retreat, and that with the same loss.[10]

107 *King Charles I (19th-century engraving).*

Other reports suggest that 70 royalists were killed, John Rous claiming but one among the city's defenders. He adds that, 'If bookes be true, and if Coventry men at Sturbridge fayre say true, that the king was not there, but the army was, and did not enter the town but shot into it, yet kild only one man ... the town issued out and slue diverse.' The rest of Rous's account matches that given above, which appears to be the truth behind the siege of Coventry.

The attack lasted from Saturday until Monday morning, when the King decided on a strategic withdrawal knowing Lord Brooke of Warwick and Colonel Hampden had entered the county with a superior force and were only ten miles away. Nehemiah Wharton (sometimes called Nicholas), a subaltern officer in Essex's army, was among them and wrote to his master in London of the events:

108 *Re-enactment of a Parliamentary musket volley. (Barry Denton of the Sealed Knot)*

In the morninge early our enemies, consistinge of about eight hundred horse, and three hundred foote, with ordnance, led by the Earle of Northampton, the Lord of Carnarvan, and the Lord Compton, and Captain Legge, and other, intended to set upon us before wee could gather our companies together, but being ready all night, early in the morning wee went to meet them we marched thorow the corne and got the hill of them, whereupon they played upon us with their ordnances, but they came short. Our gunner took their own bullet, and sent it to them againe, and killed a horse and man. After wee gave them eight shot more, whereupon all their foote companies fled, and offered their armes in the towne adjacent for twelve pence apeece. Their troopes whelinge about, took up their dead bodies and fled; the number of men slaine, as themselves reported, was fifty, besides horse.[11]

The troops the Parliamentarians encountered in the Southam area were in fact the King's army, which had left Coventry. Charles realised things were not working to his advantage and left the main force to hold off the Parliamentarians while he rode on to Nottingham with a number of lords. On his way he left two companies of foot and one of dragoons to hold Kenilworth Castle. He arrived in Nottingham that evening and raised the royal standard. The English Civil War had officially begun.

109 *Robert Greville, Lord Brooke (19th-century engraving).*

110 *Spencer Compton, Earl of Northampton (19th-century engraving).*

Nehemiah Wharton wrote from Coventry on 30 August:

> My last was unto you from Coventry, August the 26th, which place is still our quarter; a city environed with a wall co-equal, if not exceedinge, that of London for breadth and height; the compass of it is near three miles, of free stone. Thursday August 26th our soldiers pillaged a malignant fellowes house in this City, and the Lord Brook immediately proclaimed that whosoever should for the future offend in that kind should have martiall law. Fryday several of our soldiers, both horse and foote, sallied out of the City unto the Lord Dunsmore's Parke and brought from thence great store of venison, which is as good as ever I tasted, and ever since they make it their dayly practise, so that venison is almost as common with us as beef is with you.

Fearing his men in Kenilworth Castle may be placed under siege, Charles sent two further troops of horse and one of dragoons to bring them to safety. Because of his knowledge of the countryside, William Dugdale led the expedition which, for safety's sake, used the minor lanes of the Warwickshire countryside. Anthony Wood, in his *Life of Sir William Dugdale*, wrote of the event:

> ... they came about ten of the clock at night to Kenilworth and though they made such haste in getting carriages for their ammunition, as that they marcht out of that castle by seven of the clock the next morning; Nevertheless by intelligence given to the rebels in Coventry, such numbers of those with Horse and Foot pursued them, as that they were constrayn'd to make a stop in Curdworth Field to encounter them, when they chardged these rebels (though five to one in number) so stoutly that they put them to the rout and took some of them prisoner.

Wharton, a Parliamentarian, wrote of the same incident that, 'This even we had tidings that Killingworth Castle in Warwickshire … was taken with stores of ammunition and money, and some prisoners … the rest fled, and the country pursued them, and wanted but the assistance of Coventry to have destroyed them all.'

Coventry was now under military rule and a permanent garrison established in the city. The Earl of Northampton was thrown out of office and Robert Devereux, Earl of Essex and Parliamentarian general, was made City Recorder in a ceremony in St Mary's Hall.

111 *Robert Devereux, Earl of Essex.*

Trading was suspended and a governor appointed to control the garrison. Another siege was feared and Essex ordered more men and cannon to a city which now held over 4,000 troops and had formed its own citizen's militia. Known Royalists were arrested and secured and those who had chosen to flee had their property confiscated. Samuel Hinton, who in 1640 had called noted Parliamentarian William Pym a collier because he held coal pits on the outskirts of Coventry, wrote in his diary,

> For upon Saturday ye — of August [1642] I was not allowed [by Barker, a draper and a Parliamentarian] to carry anie more goods with mee for myself, wife and six children, than would be conteyned in one cloake bagg, and my goods must bee left behinde when I have leave to goe, and goinge I was sett upon by a companie of foote, and sent back yere. My wife and children pluckt off there horse and manie other barbarous usages and rude language.

The King's nephew, Prince Rupert of the Rhine, was harrying the county and had already made an abortive attempt on Caldecote House before being moved on by Wharton's regiment. On 14 October 1642 a letter delivered to the city asked the Council to hand it over in Charles's name to Prince Rupert. The city replied that, because of the 'inhuman acts of the Cavaliers … how they had ransackt, pillaged, and tooke away by force all that they could laye their handes upon', the city was 'forced to denye his Majesty's desires'!¹²

Rupert appears to have attacked with a small group of horse and was quickly repelled when he found '26 pieces of cannon waiting to play on him'.¹³ Rupert

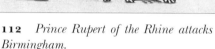

112 *Prince Rupert of the Rhine attacks Birmingham.*

113 *Spon Gate.*

and his men fled back into the countryside to rejoin the King's army, which within a few days fought an inconclusive but bloody battle at Edgehill. As the retiring Parliamentarian forces passed through Coventry, prisoners were left here and 18 wagon-loads of provisions allotted to them.

Alderman Barker was promoted to governor of the city in 1643, and made colonel of the regiment which had been raised to keep the city permanently garrisoned. At the beginning of March Lord Brooke passed through on his way to Lichfield, intent on destroying the cathedral, where he was killed. On 3 April Prince Rupert attacked Birmingham, putting many to the sword and burning down 80 houses, and after the attack he was reported as saying, 'Where's your Coventry now? Where's your God Brooke now? You may see how God fights against you!'[14] A letter published in a tract shortly afterwards states, 'Sir, Though I can write you but the same lamentation which I believe you have already heard; yet I cannot be silent to acquaint you of the truth as neere as I can: If Coventry had sent us what helpe it might, I believe the Enemy dost not have assaulted us ...'[15]

The City Annals for 1643 record that many houses were pulled down outside Bishop Gate, Well Street Gate, Hill Street Gate, Spon Gate, New Gate and Gosford Gate and were quickly replaced by 'many built in the Priory, now called New Buildings', by Governor Barker, and others in St Agnes Lane and Greyfriars churchyard.

The town was full of people that fled in here for safety. Very deep trenches made around the outside of the walls and sluices where the two rivers enter into the town to stop the water and to flood all the ground without at their Pleasure. All the gates stopped up except Newgate, Spongate, Bishopgate and Gosfordgate; only Greyfriars was open for a little time. Deep trenches made before these gates, and half moons made without three of them, which were very strong bulwarks, and drawbridges to pass out of them. A piece of ordnance reddy charged within the gates, ordnance planted on all the considerable houses. Barrs Hill fortified with works, and a line drew to pass to it from the Citty, which was demolished after a time as being to far off.[16]

114 *Basil Fielding, Earl of Denbigh.*

After Brooke's death, Basil Fielding, Earl of Denbigh (Recorder of Coventry in 1647) became Major-General of Coventry and Commander in Chief of Warwickshire, Worcestershire, Staffordshire and Shropshire. During the winter of 1643-4 he wintered his troops in Coventry but many were disorderly and brawled continually with the local garrison. Richard Baxter, a notable clergyman who was based in Coventry, wrote later of that time, 'We that lived quietly in Coventry did keep to our own principles, and thought all others had done so too, except a few inconsiderable persons.'[17]

In 1644 we are informed by the annals that,

> The king's side prevailing this Citty was in danger of being besieged, and the people were numbered to make provision, and they were about 9,500 souls. A new tower built betwixt Newgate and Little Park Street gate at the turning of the wall, which was five square, and it had in each square a porthole below and another above it, and it had great guns planted in it both below and above. Also this year a great number of Hercules Clubbs provided against a siege.

With more and more people seeking the safety of its walls, Coventry was getting overcrowded. Food was running short, and on 24 July it was noted,

> Forasmuch as this Citie is now filled with people, especially of strangers, amongst which some are separatists, and refuse to come to Church, and divers of them single women that work at their own hands. It is order'd that each Alderman of this Citie … shall speedily inform themselves what and how many strangers in his Ward are now come to this Citie, and in whose houses and how employ'd; and also what separatists that come not to Church, and likewise of the single women as aforesaid to the end that such of them as shall be thought fit may be expelled the Cittie.

The annals for the year 1645 read, 'The King taking Leicester caused the City to expect a siege, and the next Saboath day morning all the Citty was called to make a strong outwork without Gosford Gate compassed round with a river, which was done, but the king's army being beat at Naseby put them out of fear.' What the annals don't mention is the visit that year of Oliver Cromwell. He wrote a letter from the city dated 18 May 1645, intending to join forces with the Scots, Fairfax and Brereton and attack the King. After this had taken place he wrote, 'Then I know not why we might [not] be in as hopeful a posture as ever we were, having the King's army between us, with the blessing of God to bring him into great straights'.[18] Cromwell's second and third visits were also unrecorded in the City Annals, references to him being deliberately removed by those 'royalist' writers who later copied and extended the records. Cromwell's New Model Army had been formed recently and Parliament wanted to change its leaders. Coventry's Recorder, the Earl of Essex, resigned his post, and on 14 July Cromwell's 'Ironsides' defeated the King's forces at Naseby and Charles fled westwards.

In 1646, 11 regiments of Scots encamped on King's Field by Gosford Green, where provisions were sent out to them. Parliament ordered 100 barrels of powder, with match and ball, be supplied to them from the armouries of Coventry and Warwick. They remained until January of the following year, when a part payment of their wages convinced them to return north. The Earl of Essex died on 14 September, and on 1 November the Earl of Denbigh was made the city's new Recorder in St Mary's Hall; he held the post for four years. Denbigh fought against his own Royalist father at Edgehill, a case of divided family loyalty which was echoed throughout the land.

In March William Jesson M.P. expressed a desire for Parliament to dismiss the garrison in Coventry and to slight the recent fortifications. The House voted by a majority of 12 to do so, but the Committee of Coventry petitioned against this measure and it was agreed to continue the garrison with only 200 men under Colonel Willoughby. The remainder of the garrison was sent to Ireland.

In April 1648 Royalist uprisings in Kent and Wales where put down by Fairfax and Cromwell. In August a Scottish Royalist army heading south was defeated at Preston and half the army fled back to Scotland, but the remainder was forced to surrender. Several hundred prisoners were brought to Coventry and imprisoned in St John's Church, the Leather Hall (St Nicholas), Spon Gate, Greyfriars Gate and other unidentified places. It has been said that when these prisoners were exercised in the street they were snubbed, giving rise to the 'Sent to Coventry' expression, but there have been alternative explanations for its origins. As we have seen already, those sent to Coventry for execution were unlikely ever to be spoken to again.

It is said that Dr Grew of St Michael expressed his concerns for the King's life to Cromwell next time he was in Coventry, and Cromwell assured him Charles would not die. When Cromwell and the army took control of Parliament it was

115 *The church of St John the Baptist was used as a prison during the Civil War (19th-century engraving).*

decided to try the King, and Grew is said to have written to Cromwell reminding him of their conversation, but Cromwell did not reply. When Charles was tried and executed for tyranny, one of his judges was ex-Commander and later Recorder of Coventry, Colonel William Purefoy of Caldecote Hall. Purefoy took a prominent role, attending all but one sitting. He sat in court when Charles was sentenced and signed the death warrant. He was later quoted as saying, 'I bless God that I have lived to see the ruin of Monarchy, and also that I have been instrumental in upsetting it, for I do here acknowledge that such was my design ever since I was at Geneva, thirty years ago.'[19]

Purefoy was made City Recorder in October 1651 and declared that his fee should be used to repair the windows at St John's Church (then used by the Independents), which were broken by the Scottish prisoners. Purefoy became Lord of the Admiralty under the Commonwealth and it is believed that at the threat of the Restoration he, like others of the regicides, chose simply to disappear.

It was reported in the annals of 1651 that Prince Charles had led a Scottish army into England and was heading south. Coventry was re-fortified and a regiment of foot raised to defend it. On 25 August Oliver Cromwell arrived in the city, followed by an army under Generals Lambert and Harrison. As Charles approached he gained intelligence of the massive Parliamentarian force at

116 *Colonel William Purefoy, Recorder and M.P. for Coventry.*

Coventry and his army veered off towards Worcester, where Cromwell led the New Model Army and destroyed the Royalist force. Coventry was on the receiving end of hundreds of prisoners again, and the English Civil War finally came to an end.

It wasn't until September 1682 that a member of the royal family came to Coventry again. James, Duke of Monmouth was the illegitimate son of Charles II, and a popular rival for the throne to the Duke of York, who was disliked as a Catholic. He was met outside the city by hundreds of people and his entrance was heralded by the ringing of bells and fires lighting the way to the *Star Inn* in Earl Street, where he was staying. The mayor refused or chose not to attend so Monmouth spent the night feasting with ex-Parliamentarians in the *Star*. A letter to James reported one incident among many involving fires:

> There was one at the Cross, which Alderman Nathaniell Harriman perceiving, went and threw doune the faggots, dispercing the company, charging them in the King's name peaceably to depart; but they soon rallyed, and began a second bonfire lower in the same street, which the said Alderman likewise put out and commanded them again to depart in peace, but they flocked about him, shouting, 'A Monmouth, No Yorke.' And some offered violence to him, but he defended himselfe so that he had not much hurt; so likewise a third and fourth fire extinguished.

The following morning Monmouth, surrounded by a multitude shouting 'A Monmouth, No York!', called on the Mayor's Parlour in Cross Cheaping. Here he drank a glass of wine and passed some time in conversation with the mayor before leaving. The Duke of York was crowned James II and in 1686 the Duke of Monmouth was beheaded after leading a rebellion in the south in an unsuccessful attempt to gain the throne.

The 'Mayor List' informs us that, 'On the first of September this year [1687], King James the Second came to Coventry. The Mayor and Aldermen having notice of his Intention provided a Cup of Massy Gold, weighing about 3lb., and is said to be worth about £200, to present to the king.'[20] But the 'Mayor List' does not tell us that the visit was not a success and for more than one reason. After James was presented with the traditional Coventry Cup he insulted the mayor and Council by immediately giving it to George Legge, Lord Dartmouth, declaring, 'I would have your Lordship receive this gift as a mark

117 *James, Duke of Monmouth (1903 engraving).*

118 *King James II (1903 engraving).*

of the City of Coventry's concern for your father in times past.' Colonel William Legge had spent a short time imprisoned in the city after a skirmish at Southam and again after the Battle of Worcester.[21] He escaped this second imprisonment by slipping past the gaolers dressed in his wife's clothes. The King's insult meant no more Coventry Cups were given to visiting monarchs. James was expected to stay at Whitefriars, which was prepared for him, but he wanted to support local Whigs so chose instead to stay at the home of Richard Hopkins, Palace Yard, where he entertained local nobility and gentry. Hopkins was offered a knighthood but refused the King's offer, knowing it would not go down well in the city.

In order to gratify the Dissenters, on 28 November 1687 James ordered the sheriffs and a number of aldermen to be removed from office and replaced with men more acceptable to the former. In the morning he visited the mayor, and during his 'touching' at St Michael's it is recorded that there was 'so great a throng, that the very galleries crackt again'.[22] He suffered a certain amount of indignity when the table collapsed on him during the breakfast in St Mary's Hall, spilling, it is said, 'Corporation Custard' and other foodstuffs over his fine clothes. When the huge portrait of James was cleaned in 1999 two repaired holes were observed in the portrait, not unlike those pistol or musket fire would make. The idea of an angry ex-sheriff or alderman putting two shots through his image isn't so difficult to imagine.

After William of Orange's landing, Princess Anne, the second daughter of James II, publicly declared her disapproval of her father and joined William's supporters at Nottingham. She came to Coventry on 11 December 1688 and her visit is recorded in William Hinton's diary:

> The Princess Ann, of Denmark, flying from Queen Mary, came most nobly attended to Coventry, with many lords, knights, esquires, and gentlemen, and many hundred horse, and was met by Mr. Mayor and his brethren, and the companies, as they did before to King James at Bishopgate. She lay at the aforesaid Esquire Hopkins his house, and was soon conducted to Warwick.

In 1690 thousands of English, Dutch, German and French troops passed through Coventry on their way to Ireland, where James was trying to raise support. King William himself passed through on 3 June on his way to join the army. His coach was met at Willenhall Bridge by the sheriffs, and at New Gate by the mayor, aldermen and city companies. He did not stop in the city but continued to Packington Hall where he had dinner but, according to the Common Council book, no cup was given. After their defeat at the Boyne 150 of James's officers were imprisoned in Coventry and great celebrations were held in the city.

RELIGION

One of the main features of early Presbyterianism was the religious meetings known as 'Prophesyings', at which religious texts were discussed. Those who attended these meetings were frowned upon by the Church, and finally the Court of High Commission put a stop to them. But amongst their number were many members of the established church, the Rev. Humphrey Fenn of Holy Trinity (1577-90) being imprisoned several times by order of Archbishop Whitgift for 'prophesying' in his own church. Sir Robert Dudley brought pressure to gain his release and return him to his Coventry flock, for Puritanism would not be suppressed so easily and was gradually infiltrating the establishment.

The Puritan practice of 'Lectureship' allowed biblical verse to be read or lectures on God's word given, and many preachers were created by the Church. In 1589 Lord Burleigh accused it of making too many 'rude and unlearned ministers'. Bishop Overton of Coventry and Lichfield had made 70 new ministers in one day from shoemakers and craftsmen. Many lecturers were university taught, however, and had taken deacons' orders. They dressed in a Geneva Gown and took no part in the church service, but they preached the sermon. After opposition to the liturgy grew the lecturer waited outside until his moment came. Samuel Clark was appointed lecturer of St John's Church but during one of his sermons he gave offence to the vicar of St Michael and was compelled to vacate the office. In 1608 William Hancox, the mayor, hired a lecturer to preach in St John's every Saturday afternoon for the 'better fitting of the people for the Sabbath'. Puritan lecturing came to an end in Coventry in 1629 because Archbishop Laud believed

119 *The interior of St John's in the 19th century retained its 17th-century pews.*

its practitioners were disloyal to the Church and would no longer license them, and they did not reappear until 1641. By 1642 the Long Parliament had passed an Act giving local authorities the right to appoint lecturers without the consent of the Church.

Proof of just how well established Puritanism was in Coventry is provided by a letter James I wrote to the city dated 4 February 1611:

> The said disorder noted with you is that you refuse to receive the Blessed Sacraments of the body and blood of Christ kneeling, but receive it for the most parte standing or sitting. We have hereof given especiall Charge to our servant, the Bishop of that diocese, to see this abuse reformed.[23]

James's order was carried out, 'to the grief of many', before he granted the 'Governing Charter' in 1621. But between 1621 and 1631 Puritans were the majority in Coventry's ruling elite. In 1633, the year of Archbishop Laud's

120   *An early 19th-century engraving of the remains of the west tower made into a dwelling in the late 18th century.*

advancement to the primacy, those who followed his beliefs dominated the Council and the Rev. William Panting, an Anglican, was made vicar of St Michael. He ordered all the middle aisle seats to be removed, and the City Annals inform us that, in 1636, 'the High Altar sett up in Trinity Church, and cost a deal of money. Also the Communion Tables altered ... and that which is worst of all, three steps made to go to the Communion Table, altar fashion. God grant it continueth not long.'[24]

A great many things were forced upon the puritanical-minded congregation, including the persecution of individuals who wrote against Laud's church, such as William Prynne, until things began to change in 1642 when the Puritans held sway in the city. Panting was replaced by Dr Obadiah Grew and within a short time he became a pauper and, to add to his misery, began to go blind. He tried to sell his library to Grew who refused but, out of kindness, gave Panting the money he so badly needed. Occasional payments were also later made by the Corporation. Grew remained at St Michael until the Restoration and resigned his benefice after the Act of Uniformity was passed in 1661. Because of the fear of plague in 1665, he held open-air meetings until the Oxford Act forced him to leave the city. He returned in 1672 and was allowed to preach under licence. He held his meetings at St Nicholas Hall, also known as the Leather Hall, in West Orchard. In 1682 his licence was revoked under James II and Grew found himself imprisoned in the city gaol for six months. He left the city and, because he too was going blind, dictated his weekly sermon for reading to small groups. After the 'Glorious Revolution' Grew returned to Coventry, where he continued to preach until a month before his death in 1689, aged 82.

In 1644 John Bryan, ex-treasurer to Warwickshire's Parliamentarian forces, was made vicar of Holy Trinity. Six teams of horse were sent to Barford to bring his goods. Bryan was initially resented by the city as he was Parliament's choice, not theirs, but he quickly grew to be one of the city's most respected clergy. Within three years his stipend was raised to match that of his former parish. In 1650 he built houses on the former west towers of the cathedral and his own 'Tower House' on the cross aisle, at the central tower. He also cleared much of the surviving ruins of nave and aisles to make a garden, which would explain why little was found in this area when it was excavated. Bryan used old timbers for the buildings, either from the old Priory or, possibly, the timbers stored in the church which are mentioned in the Churchwardens Accounts of 1643: 'Payments for taking downe diverse houses and buildings without Bishops gate & Spon gate ... & bringing the tiles and Timber into Trinitie Church.' John Bryan held his benefice until the Restoration. He continued to live in Coventry until his death in 1675.

A number of other Presbyterians took refuge in the city in 1644, including the celebrated Richard Baxter, who later wrote, 'How happy was I to abide two years in Coventry.' Baxter ministered to both inhabitants and soldiers, and during his time in the city came across Anabaptists, of whom he wrote,

> The Anabaptists sent to Bedford for one Benjamin Cox, an old minister of their persuasion, and no contemptible scholar, the son of a bishop. He and I had first a dispute by word of mouth, and afterwards in writing. In conclusion about a dozen poor townsmen were carried away [by the faith]; but the soldiers and the rest of the city were kept sound from all infection of sectaries and dividers.[25]

Cox set up the first Baptist church in Coventry and stood minister for it until Baxter had him imprisoned for refusing to comply with an order to leave the city. The Baptists survived but other sects were put down completely, like the Ranters who filled Coventry Gaol in 1650. George Fox, informed of the Ranters on a visit that year, went to visit them and wrote, 'When I came into the gaol, where the prisoners were, a great power of darkness struck at me, and I sate still, having my spirit gathered in the love of God. At last these prisoners began to rant and blaspheme, at which my soul was greatly grieved.'

121   *Richard Baxter (18th-century engraving).*

More acceptable to the Puritans were the Independents, whose beliefs were also based on Calvinistic views which first emerged in Geneva. Samuel Basnet, son of a city alderman, set up an Independent or Congregationalist group in Coventry which was eventually given use of the redundant church of St John the Baptist in Fleet Street. City leaders belonging to this group included Colonel William Purefoy, Robert Beake and John Barker. Basil Fielding, who became City Recorder in 1646, took the covenant in St Michael in 1644 and ordered his officers to do likewise. He ordered all his troops to attend Sunday morning sermon, to fast, 'Refraine from swearing, excessive drunkenesse and do noe thing that which is offensive to God.'[26] This belief, 'God with Us', was shared by the Parliamentarian army.

Baxter also indicates just how the war was perceived in Coventry. Shortly after leaving to become chaplain to Cromwell's regiment he wrote,

> We that live quietly in Coventry did keep to our old principles. We were unfeignedly for King and Parliament. We believed that the war was only to save the Parliament and kingdom from papists and delinquents, and to remove the dividers, that the King might again return to his Parliament; and that no changes might be made in religion. But when I came to the army among Cromwell's soldiers, I found a new face of things, which intimated their intention to subvert both church and state. I was loath to leave my studies, and friends, and the quietness of Coventry, to go into the army so contrary to my judgement.[27]

He spoke not only for himself but for many others, including John Bryan of Holy Trinity and Obadiah Grew of St Michael.

Changing religious beliefs affected the fabric of the city's churches. In 1526 the churchwardens of Holy Trinity had agreed with two London organ manufacturers on an organ for the church bearing an image of the Holy Trinity. Following the Reformation the image was removed, and in 1570 the bellows were sold. The organ fell from use until Laud's ascendancy, when it was again in fashion and was repaired. An organist was also employed who received a salary of £10 a year, but in 1640 this was reduced to £4. In June 1641 it was ordered that no salary be paid to the organist for the church was in 'decay and ruyn' and the money was to be used instead for the building and not for things 'of lesser moment'. On 16 November it was ordered that the organ be removed into the vestry until it could be sold. The Puritans had at last silenced the 'squeaky abomination'. The organ wasn't reinstated until 1684.

The Puritans also found offensive the old (and present) font, despite its simplicity, and had it removed in 1645. The new font appears to have been made of painted and gilded wood. After the Restoration the old font was replaced in its present position, and the stone for its steps is traditionally said to have been the original base of Swine's Cross in Bishop Street. Trinity's fine 15th-century eagle lectern, which occupied a prominent place within the church, also suffered. During the reign of Elizabeth it was placed in the quire, but the Puritans placed it out of sight in the vestry. The Vestry Book for 13 July 1654 informs us of the church's intention to sell this important piece of church furniture, noting, 'Mr. Abraham Watts made a motion that whereas he was informed that this House had an intention to sell the brazen Eagle standing in the vestrie, that he might have the refusal thereof.'[28] On the restoration of the monarchy the lectern was replaced in the main building next to the pulpit.

The Churchwardens Accounts during the 1650s show much time and money being spent on the church fabric, especially the steeple and spire. But, despite this, the steeple fell during a storm on 24 January 1665, killing a small boy. It also did much damage to the building. Work on the church was quickly followed by work on the spire, which the City Annals state was finished in 1668. In 1674 we learn the top half was taken down and made 'stronger'. In 1647 we learn that one Hope was paid 3s. 6d. for defacing the king's arms, and four years later the arms of the Commonwealth were set up in the church. Hope was back in 1660, receiving £6 to emblazon the church with the arms of Charles II.

St Michael's church accounts for 1645 note that, 'pd for levellinge & paveinge, where ye old font stood, 2s.' The new font, which cost £1 12s. to gild and paint, was probably made of wood. The church celebrated with the ringing of bells in 1642, at a cost of 3s. 6d., 'when the Lo' Brooke came in with his army'. In 1650 three of the king's arms were washed from the church walls and the following year the arms of the Commonwealth were painted. The accounts of 1656 contain an unusual entry, 'A collection for Paul Isaiah, a converted Jew, for his reliefe, £1 10s.', which is followed the following year by the equally curious, 'Feb. 20, a day of solemn Thanksgiving, for discovery of a wicked design to kill the Lord Protector, collected £1.' With the Restoration came the return of the king's arms, again costing £6. No doubt Mr Hope was again at work.

The earliest known nonconformist church in Coventry was built in Hill Street by the Quakers and was known as the Friends Meeting House. It is believed to have stood a little below the present ring road, and below it was a burial ground, now the site of the present Meeting House. When James II visited Coventry in 1687 the noted Quaker and founder of Pennsylvania, William Penn, was in the royal retinue and he worshipped with his fellow Quakers.

CRIME AND PUNISHMENT

122   *Cook Street Gate.*

In 1639 the problem with rights over common land was raised again. The annals tells us that 'The Commons of Coventry arose & Spoyled a field of oats called Barnsfield and threw down a wall att Newgate [and] att Harbors Quarry, 5 of the Rable was putt in Gaole, but the same night 3 or 400 with Clubbes and Crows of Iron came to Break down the Gaol whereupon they were let out.'[29] The city fathers had no means of stopping an armed mob of such size. Around 1641 an inmate in Bond's Hospital in Hill Street, a man referred to as Johnson, managed to poison 12 inmates of the hospital who 'displeased' him before being discovered, whereupon Johnson administered poison to himself. He was buried at Holy Trinity, but after objections was disinterred and buried as a suicide at the road junctions outside Cook Street Gate.

In 1649, 'On Christmas Eve the Butchers rose, and Howes, one of the principal of the Companie killed a souldier that came to gather excise, for which many of them were imprisoned, and Howes tried for his life, but was found guilty of manslaughter. He lived above forty years after, and died an old man in Bablake Hospital but never prospered after ye aforesaid fact.'[30] A later entry states,

Fryday, Oct. 18th 1695, between 12 and one in the morning, one Nicholas Lambe, an Excise man, Will. Whitaker, & Saml. Wickes, two Corporalls of Captain Porter's troop came from the Star Inn [Earl Street] and went through Much Parke Street, Dead Lane, Little Parke Street, High Street & to the Crosse, all the way breaking the windows, & at the Crosse, one William Bennet, dyer, being Constable, & the Watch came from the Mayors Parlor into the street to the assistance of one they were beating, & upon the Constable requiring them to be Civill. Hee was immediately killed by a wound he received under his left arme which came out between his Necke and Shoulder. The three persons first named all fled, but being pursued was taken and committed in the morning to Gaole.[31]

The city constable was buried at St Michael's with all honours before the mayor and Council, and on 30 March 1696 the three men were tried in the city and found guilty of his murder. William Whitaker was pardoned and Samuel Nicks and Nicholas Lambe were found guilty and hanged. The gallows was by now a permanent structure at the corner of Whitley Common by Howes Lane. The men would have been brought in a cart, sitting on their own coffins.

A pillory is recorded in 1629 placed on top of Cross Cheaping Conduit, and in that same year the wife of one Overton was ordered to be placed in it four times a year on market day. In 1619 a set of stocks to add to the existing ones was placed in Vicar Lane off the top of Smithford Street. Another set was placed outside the Gaol Hall, which probably stood on the site of the old Governor's House in Bayley Lane. An entry for 1640 reads, 'Paid for making new irons for the stocks at the Bullring, which the Souldiers broke and took away, weighing 36 lbs, and crab nails 4s.'

Perhaps the best record of antisocial behaviour in 17th-century Coventry was kept in a pocket book by draper Robert Beake, ex-major in the Parliamentarian army, city alderman, sheriff and M.P. for the city on four occasions. Beake was mayor of Coventry in 1655-6, and during this short period he kept a record of his daily dealings with the innocently challenged, extracts from which speak for themselves:

> 17th November. I walked to observe what order the streets were in, and gave a special charge to remove muckhills, viz. in the Butcherow, Welstreete and Sponstreete.
>
> 18th November. A man for travelling from Alsley, being the Lord's day, was set in the stocks.
>
> 19th November. 3 quakers for travelling on the Lord's day were set in the cage. Memorandum: it grieved me that this poore deluded people should undergoe punishment of such a nature.
>
> 2nd December. A souldier that came out of Scotland from travelling on the Lord's day was putt in the house of correction. The same day 3 carriers men loitering at their Inne in tyme of publique worship were sent to the stocks. Major General Whaley [Coventry's governer], being first in the church, sate above me upon a mistake, supposing he had given me the right hand.
>
> 13th December. I sate in the parloure with other Justices about the ministers maintenance, suppressing alehouses, etc. in which latter we made a progress to suppress many, and ordered to send 6 or 7 to the house of correction for terror to others. The wife of Nicholas Unit sent to the house of correction for scoldring and fighting at the Beare … Widow Chantry bound to the good behaviour for being of an ill fame in entertaining of sugar [soldiers] in her house.
>
> 5th January 1656. I sent for the master of the bakers to go with me to weigh the bread.
>
> 17th January. The bedle cryed that all should sweepe their streets, which was dun universally throughout the citty.

21st January. I signed a warrant for a hue and cry after Mr. Warden Phillips his man who ran away with some of his masters clothes. John Berry's man also before me for confederating with Clifton's boy to run away.

26th January. This night I granted a ticket to Goody Raby to travel the next Lord's day to Ffolshill to a dieing woman.

8th March. A warrant to Much Park streete constables to bring the body of Anthony Robinson tyler to show cause why he departs not the towne.

27/28th April. Being the Lord's day, I went to the parke and observed who idly walked there.[32]

Commonwealth Coventry had strict rules regarding the observance of religion. They did not cease with the Restoration, however, and in the Coventry Constables Presentments of 7 June 1675 we find one James Holt before the court for 'keeping a disorderly house upon the Sabbath day'. In 1679 John Budd and his wife faced the same court for failing to attend church for a month.

In the presentments of 7 January 1683 there was a purge on non-attendance of church and the court dealt with 39 individuals, such as David Gee, cooper, Brigit Suthwarn, spinster, and John Murdock, baker, for missing '3 Sondays'. All three were in court again a year later for non-attendance, and in April 1684 Suthwarn and Gee were again indicted, with 29 others. Some people at this time regarded the church as too high or low, supporters of the High Church including city notables such as Frances Harryman, city alderman and ex-mayor. With seven others he was brought before the court for 'irreverence and disorderly behaviour in the church during the tyme of divine service and sermon'.[33] Some of the city's most notable inhabitants stayed away in protest. The split came to a head in the 1690s. For many years the High Church party held power in the city. But in 1695 the Low Church Thomas Glover held the senior post and, the following year, all High Church members of the Council were issued with false invitations to dinner. While they were absent a meeting was held in St Mary's Hall at which eight new Low Church members were illegally elected to the Council and a new mayor was chosen. On discovering the deception, the missing members held their own meeting and chose another mayor, but when the standing mayor retired in November he chose the Low Church candidate, Edward Owen, as his successor. On the same morning, Alderman Harryman and others took their man before the Mayor's Parlour and swore him in. Eventually, at a cost of £500, Owen obtained the office and he was sworn in later for a second time.

The main home for Coventry's Quarter Sessions in the 17th century was the Gaol Hall and the Guildhall. Typical cases include Ann Lines of Styvechale, indicted for brewing without a licence and selling ale contrary to statute, Richard Aston for setting up a dog kennel next to the town wall, Richard Kevitt for leaving a cart outside his door for three weeks, Thomas Middleton for not railing off a deep hole in Whitley mill brook, Samuel Gravenor for keeping swine in Palmer

Lane (outlawed over 200 years earlier), and William Webster, for keeping a mastiff unmuzzled. Richard Heycock, Richard Hollis and John Oldhams, who appear to have built their cottages on common land at Radford in 1675, were brought before the court again in 1680 for 'continueing cottages at Radford'.

In 1696 a plot to assassinate King William III and restore James II to the throne was discovered. A large number of buried new weapons had been unearthed at the home of Sir William Perkins of Marston in Warwickshire, which had previously been kept at Caludon, Coventry, the home of a certain Mr Hayward. They were brought to Coventry and the plotters were imprisoned. Hayward won his freedom by turning king's evidence against Sir William.

EDUCATION

The main source of education at this time was the city's Free School in Bishop Street, set up in the old church of St John by John Hales for the education of freemen's sons (12d. admission) and those others who wished to pay. The City Annals record that in 1602, 'at the earnest suit of Mr. Tony [Tovey], schoolmaster, the library was begun, and he with Mr. Arnold the usher, made such request to gentlemen, that it was quickly furnished with books'. Tovey later took up the post of tutor to Princess Elizabeth at Coombe, and *Nugae Antiquae* records of Lord Harington's son that, 'his noble father sent him to travel in France and Italy … and for a guide and tutor for him in his travels he chose on Mr. Tovey, a grave, learned and religious man, and formerly Headmaster of the Free School at Coventry.'[34] During this trip Tovey's and the earl's son's 'protestant zeal' was noted by some Jesuits who, aware of Lord Harington's part in foiling the Gunpowder Plot, administered a slow poison to both men. Both returned immediately, but Tovey soon died and was quickly followed by Lord Harington's son, then only 22 years of age.

Tovey's own son, Nathaniel, followed in his father's footsteps and was taken under the patronage of Lord Harington's daughter, Lucy, Countess of Bedford. He took a degree as Bachelor of Divinity at Christ's College, Cambridge. John Aubrey, in his *Lives of Eminent Men*, states that while there John Milton was under his care. Nathaniel Tovey became rector of Lutterworth until ejected for his support of Charles I.

After John Tovey left the Coventry Free School, usher Jeremiah Arnold became master, and he was succeeded on 7 March 1611 by James Cranford or Crawford, under whose mastership Sir William Dugdale was educated. In 1615 the will of Alderman William Wheate left land rental at the Bastill Meadows near Gosford Gate to pay for someone to look after the school's library, a post previously taken by a senior scholar. This originally amounted to 13s. 4d., but by 1615 it had risen to £57 6s. 8d., which enabled the school to raise the master's salary from £20 to £30 and the usher's wage from £10 to £15 a year.[35]

The famed Doctor Philemon Holland was elected new master of the school on 23 January 1628. Holland was born in Chelmsford, the son of a divine. He studied at Trinity College, Cambridge, gaining a degree in medicine, and at Oxford, where in 1587 he gained his M.A. Holland is thought to have moved to Coventry at this time, and studied and practised medicine. He moved into a house by the Grammar School around 1595, so his connection with the school may have begun then.

It was in Coventry that he began the task for which he is famed, the translation of many of the classics. In 1600 he dedicated his translation of Livy to Queen Elizabeth and in 1601 dedicated his translation of Pliny's *Natural History* to Sir Robert Cecil. In 1603 he dedicated Plutarch's *Morals* to James I, and in 1606 Suetonius was dedicated to Lady Harington. This particular translation was not written in Coventry for Holland had been forced to leave his post temporarily as plague raged through the city.

In 1609 he dedicated his translation of *Ammianus Marcellinus* to 'The Right Worshipfull the Maior and his Brethren, the Aldermen, etc, of the Citie of Coventrie.' His reasons for the dedication are, firstly,

> for your wise and moderate government of the place, wherein I have so many yeares conversed, hath afforded unto me both quiet repose and meanes, also to follow my studies. Secondly, the affectionate love that yee have always borne to good literature, testified by courteous entertainment of learned men; by competent salaries allowed from time to time to such professors as have peaceably and with discreet carriage bestowed their talents among you; by exhibition given to poore schollers in the Universitie, by erecting also of late, and maintaining of a fare Librarie, not exampled in many Cities of the Realm. Lastly, the experience I have already of your kind acceptance of my former Labours, though not exhibited to you at the first hand.[36]

For his work and praise the mayor presented Holland with £4 pounds, and in November 1609 the Council granted him a lease for 21 years on his house in Bishop Street. In 1621 an adjoining house was granted to him for 61 years at a rent of 6s. a year.

In 1610 Holland published what is thought to be his greatest work, a translation of Camden's *Britannia*. Among the first to buy a copy was the City Council, and the Treasurers Accounts record, 'paid to Mr. Doctor Holland, the xxx of may, 1610, for a boke called Camden's Britanya, vl.[£6]' A letter from Holland to Camden still in the British Museum is signed 'Your loving & affectionate ffriend.'[37]

Holland was made a Freeman of the City in St Mary's Hall on 30 September 1612. He made a long oration to King James I on his visit to the city in 1617, and the following year John Taylor, the Water Poet, visited the city and wrote, 'Through splashes, puddles, thick, thin, wet and dry I travell'd to the City of Coventry; There master Doctor Holland caused me to stay The day of Saturn and the Sabbath day.'

Rule 12. It is also ordered, that the Singing Schoole, shall be taught in the place for that purpose appointed, on Thurdaies and Saturdaies, and halfe Holy days in the Afternoone from One of the clock 'till Three. Ffreemans sonnes are to be taught gratis.

Rule 15. That there shall be dictionaries, chained in the Schoole, for the generall use of the schollars there.

Rule 17. The best scholler of the highest Forme in the Lowe Schoole, shall be taken up into the higher Schoole, leaving the worser or weaker behinde, as is and hath been the custom of all Schools.

Rule 18. The Heade Schoole Maister, and Usher, shall teach and instruct all the Schollers impartially (yet preferring the Sons of Citizens).

Rule 20. The Head Schoole Maister and Usher, shall use fit correction, not beating with the hand or fist about the head, or pulling children by the haire, eares or suchlike, but with the rod only.[39]

Philemon Holland was succeeded by Phineas White, who requested an assistant for the school which was so overcrowded that many were behind others in their learning. If he didn't have help he would have to put some pupils back, 'which might displease the parents and would discourage the scholars'.[40] White resigned and was replaced by Samuel Frankland in 1651. In 1671 Frankland was also complaining about overcrowding, to the detriment of the school, but he was successful in gaining an assistant for the wage of £10 a year. This did not improve the situation and the school went into decline, the scholars becoming unruly and at one time locking the masters out of the building, causing much damage in the process. The cost of the repairs was taken from Frankland's wages.

In 1685 a Council Order records the state of affairs at the school:

> This House taking into consideration the former flourishing condition of the Free School, and now sad declining state, almost brought to nothing; arising as they conceive, from the 'idleness and unfitness' of Mr. Frankland, who since he has been assisted by Mr. Orton, scarce ever comes into the School until 10 o'clock, considering also the great disturbances made by the scholars shutting out their Masters of late years; order that Mr. Frankland and Mr. Orton be not continued as Master and Assistant after Lady Day.

The order was only partly complied with and Frankland appears to have served the school well for forty years, leaving money for scholarships. Humphrey Wanley recorded his final night:

> Between two and three o'clock in the morning died Mr. Frankland, the Schoolmaster of this citty, and was buried July 23, at night [in Holy Trinity] … That night before he died he gave one of his scollars a great deal of good advice … And to another young gentleman, who came to see him as soon as the other was gone; he said (after some good counsel given him), Oportet Episcopum mori proedicantem; meaning I believe, that it was fit a Schoolmaster should die teaching.[41]

124   *The Free Grammar School in the late 18th century. The half-timbered section was demolished to build Hales Street.*

In 1691 Samuel Carte took charge. Carte was the son of a clothier who himself had been educated in the school. In 1668 he was appointed the school's librarian and in the following year took two degrees at Oxford. He took religious orders and served two benefices before becoming Master of the Free School in 1691 for the 'better education of his children'. He continued to hold church benefices and resigned his mastership in 1700 to concentrate on the church.

The Free School library was one of the first in the country to loan books to borrowers. In 1655 it was noted that a book in Italian by Dante was overdue. It had been borrowed by Sir John Skeffington, an ex-pupil, who 'promised under his hand to restore it by the 10th of March'. He had been asked numerous times to return the book but refused and the school intended to sue him. An interesting letter to Samuel Frankland from Dr Ralph Bathurst, Vice-Chancellor of Oxford University, concerns a donation of books: 'Worthy, Sir, I herewith send a parcel of books (being eleven in number) to be placed in your publique library, at the

Free School, as a small testimony of the kind remembrance I retain for that place where I received some part of my education.'[42] The City Council wrote to Bathurst praising his 'bountifull gift' and informing him that his 'honourable' name should be added to the list of benefactors to the library. The munificence of Mr Bathurst was even exceeded by others and the Free School library grew into one of the finest in 17th-century England, although the diligence of its upkeep would begin to falter in the 18th century.

For those less fortunate than the sons of freemen and the wealthy there was the chance of an education in Bablake School in Hill Street. It survived on endowments and in 1611 Nicholas Chambers gave two tenements in Smithford Street for the 'maintenance and relief of the poor children of the hospital of Bablack'. In 1625 Abraham Bowne gave the rents from pasture land near Radford, and in 1653 the Council leased a tenement in Cuckoo Lane, a watermill, a spring and a building in the Prior's Orchard and Swanswell Pool, the income from which was given for the upkeep of the 'Bablake Boys'. It appears that the tenement in Cuckoo Lane also housed an ancient 'waterworks' which was sold in 1829 so that the gaol could be enlarged. Compensation of £200 was awarded to the trustees of the school. The watercourse leading through Trinity churchyard was almost certainly the original water source for St Mary's Priory, which lay about 100 feet below it.

Various payments were given on a yearly basis to the Corporation, who were the trustees of Bablake. The origin of 'Hunton's Gift' is recorded in the Common Council Book under the date of 7 March 1682. It reads:

> His father and mother being dead, and himself between nine and ten years old, he was cast upon the care of the mayor and his brethren, who put him into the hospital of Bablake, where he was taught the knowledge and fear of God, and afterwards sent to London to be an apprentice.[43]

The scholars at Bablake wore a uniform which consisted of a dark blue tunic reaching to the ankles, tied at the midriff with a thick leather belt. Around their necks was a wide white collar and on their heads a round black cap with a yellow tassle in the centre. A yellow petticoat and stockings were worn underneath and brown buckled shoes. The City Annals record that in 1681 the Blue Coat Boys Hospital was altered, 'from a Fullsome Ugley Place to what it is'.

In 1690 one Samuel Barker granted to Robert Beck and six other inhabitants of Coventry an annual payment of £8 from rents on properties in London. This group would meet together and pick eight needy male children, aged between four and six, to be educated at Barker's expense in a school in the city. They were to be taught to read the Bible well. By another will of 1695 the number of children was increased to twelve. A further £20 a year was added to the gift and a house was purchased and converted into a schoolhouse.

125   *The home of Orlando Bridgeman, M.P. for Coventry, in Little Park Street (19th-century engraving).*

EVERYDAY LIFE IN SEVENTEENTH-CENTURY COVENTRY

During the Civil War period the City Governor and Committee overlooked and administered the city of Coventry. On 23 December 1653 Oliver Cromwell was proclaimed Lord Protector of the Commonwealth of England, Scotland and Ireland, and in Coventry the proclamation was read out to the sound of trumpets and drums and all the city bells were rung. A bonfire was lit in Cross Cheaping and cakes and ale were doled out from the nearby Mayor's Parlour.

Cromwell died in 1658 and was succeeded by his son Richard, who was proclaimed in Coventry to the sound of drums. Ninety-four addresses affirmed their various senders' allegiance, Coventry's, which was dated 11 November, reading, 'Now that he is exalted to be head of the tribes of the land, they desire the wisdom of Solomon, the integrity of David, and the zeal of good Josiah, for a reformation may centre in him, and being satisfied with his unquestionable authority and right to govern these nations, they declare they are resolved to stand by and adhere to him in his person and government, with their lives and estates.'[44]

The following year Richard Cromwell's protectorate was in difficulties and Sir George Booth raised a rebellion in Cheshire in support of a Free Parliament. Five companies of infantry stationed in Coventry were sent north and Booth was captured. When the companies headed back south they were complemented in case of more trouble by two more troops of infantry and two of cavalry. The city also armed its own militia of 340 men from the armoury in St Mary's Hall.

On 26 December 1659 Alderman Major Beake, accompanied by a large number of armed citizens, declared for a Free Parliament. They were joined by another 160 men and gathered in St Michael's churchyard, from where they marched to the cross in Cross Cheaping and demanded that the city guard join them. Whereupon, say the City Annals, 'a Company of Redcoatts marched away, and they took their place for Parliament, ordering the King's Declaration from Breda to be read'. On 29 May 1660 Charles II landed in England and was celebrated in Coventry with 'joy'. In October James Compton, son of Coventry's pre-war Recorder, rode into the city 'attended by almost all the nobility and gentry of the County'. They were entertained in St Mary's Hall and exercised regiments of horse and foot in the Great Park, no doubt in order to impress on the population what the new order was. On 22 July 1662 Compton returned, this time to 'slight' the city wall so it could never again stand against the sovereign. The ritual slighting started at the New Gate which Charles I had attacked some twenty years earlier and was followed by the destruction of over half of Coventry's ancient wall.

Charles was crowned on St George's Day 1661 and two of the city conduits ran with claret. A feast was held at the Guildhall and bonfires burned in the streets. It is said that a maypole brought into the city and set up by Gosford Gate was a symbol of idolatry too far for the mayor, who had it removed. In the following year Coventry's new mayor, Thomas Pidgeon, had a huge maypole erected outside the Mayor's Parlour itself. It is said he frowned on 'pious good ministers' and put a stop to the weekly 'lectures'. He wished to restore some of the entertainment so frowned upon during the Commonwealth.

The annals for 1678 states that, 'Att the Great Fair several Companys found a streamer of the Armes of their Companyes & each paraded a follower & the Lady Godiva Rode before the Mayor to proclaim the Fair.' Another version of the incident states that James Swinnerton's son acted as Godiva in the first recorded Godiva Procession, although in 1659 a certain John Warren had written in his copy of Camden's *Britannia*, 'Beeing in Couentry in the yer 1659, and at the end of the stret going to the Cross out of the window stands a statu of a man. I asked one of the cittezens what it ment [and he] related this story [of Godiva].'[45] Perhaps the procession had taken place since the end of the Commonwealth but with no mention in the annals.

The late 1600s saw some unexplained extremes in the weather. In 1674 the annals record that,

> Last year so wet that it rained more or less every day for many months together ... So great snow in Februarie which was alsoe driven with the wind that travailers could not pass, so were frozen to death, and others lost in the snow. Winter continued so long that oats and barley could not be sowed, and the summer following was such a backward harvest that they had very little.

The year 1684 saw 'Ye Great Frost. It began to freeze in September. The Great Frost began Nov. 20, 1683, and continued till Ladyday 1684.' Despite the fact that many people and animals died and no spade or plough could penetrate the ground, nothing further is said. The ice was so thick that, in London, fairs were held on the Thames. In 1686 the annals record that, '3,000 inhabitants died, the food having been spoiled by the hot summer and long frost'. This is likely to be an exaggeration, but clearly many died of starvation in that year.

Fruit was scarce in 1693, and in 1696 the annals note, 'The poorer sort of people beginning to murmure for want of bread, corn & malt'. The King had called in all clipped coins and made their use illegal until they were replaced. The result was a shortage of usable coinage. It is said that a charitable Mr Hill of the Charterhouse sold the 'poorer sort' of grain at market price and accepted the old money, which he could afford to sit on until it was exchanged by the King's Commissioners.

Six

Everyday Life in Eighteenth-Century Coventry

At the end of the 17th century Coventry was a prosperous city with a population estimated at around 9,000 souls. This was lower than before the Dissolution and at times during the Civil War, but by 1748 new industries had caused the population to rise to 12,177 and the city contained 2,065 houses.[1] Unlike in its heyday, Coventry no longer received royal visitors or played any major part in national events. Despite the fact that it was a city, it had grown somewhat quiet and comfortable and taken on the feel of a market town. Things changed when the city became a garrison town.

The beginning of the 18th century saw the decline of the wool trade and the Drapery was demolished in 1727. New industries included the manufacture of worsted cloth, silk ribbon weaving and the production of cloth tammies, camblets, shalloons and calimancoes. Trade secrets were closely guarded and in 1780 William Newey, a worsted weaver, published an apology in the *Coventry Mercury* for having instructed some Spanish prisoners held in the city in the art and 'mystery of worsted manufacture'.

Mayor William Bird set up a silk ribbon works in 1705, probably with the help of French Huguenots skilled in this work. By 1756 he employed 2,000 handloom weavers. Many other works sprang up and Coventry became the centre of ribbon weaving in the Midlands, producing at first black ribbons, although a rainbow of colours later poured from the city's looms. In 1782 Thomas Pennant described the trade: 'About eighty years ago the manufacture of ribands was introduced here, and for the first thirty years remained in the hands of a few people who acquired vast fortunes; since it has extended … and is supposed to employ at least 10,000 people.'[2]

The first reference to the growing trade of watch making is in 1727, when George Porter, mayor, was described as a watchmaker. By the middle of the century watch making had become firmly established in the city. Samuel Vale began trading in 1747 and later became Vale, Howlett and Carr. Vale later became a partner of Richard Rotherham, who would survive alone into the 20th century. In 1764 a certain Mr Arnold, late of Coventry, exhibited to George III a repeating watch so small it would fit into a ring. Others who manufactured in Coventry were Thomas Heath, Thomas Hales and Henry Harding, who started in 1783.

126   *The west side of Broadgate in the 18th century (19th-century engraving).*

He appears to be the only casemaker submitting work for assay between 1783 and 1792 and is thought to have acted as a sole agent,[3] for between 1783 and the end of the century there were many watchmakers in the city, including Vale & Howlett, Bradshaw & Ryley, Mann & Wall, Howlett & Carr, Wall & Dumelow and Vale, Howlett, Carr & Rotherham. Lone producers included Edward Archer, James Patterson and Thomas Swift.[4]

By the 18th century Coventry no longer had a closed Council and the city also held parliamentary elections, M.P.s being chosen by the freemen of the city, who earned the right by working a seven-year apprenticeship. Elections could be boisterous to say the least. Coventry's first M.P.s of the new century were Tories Thomas Hopkins and Sir Christopher Hales, the latter born at Whitefriars in 1676. It is said the pair lost the next election because of 'bribery, corruption and intimidation', as the Whigs outspent their opponents. The Whigs in question were Edward Hopkins and Henry Neale of Allesley Hall, who was related through his wife to Oliver Cromwell. Neale lost his seat when a committee of enquiry claimed his election null and void because of 'bribery, threats and rioting'. Sir Christopher Hales retook and held the seat until he was ousted in March 1715, when the city sheriffs supported the Whigs and stopped many Tories from entering the Gaol Hall to vote. They also dismissed many Tory votes and even imprisoned some supporters for crying 'Hales and Skipwith' in the street.

There was much corruption in the Council for a good part of the 18th century, members acquiring land for peppercorn rents and lining their own pockets. In 1711 the mayor and Council were accused of embezzling £2,000 from the Thomas White charity estate. All the city's civic plate had to be sold to pay the debt and the St Mary's Hall was taken out of Council hands for six years. Elections remained corrupt throughout the century with some, such as the first 'Bludgeon Fight', which took place in September 1780, getting violent. The mayor secretly swore in 66 new freemen on the understanding they would vote for the Whig candidate, and several hundred colliers, roughs and prize-fighters were also brought in by the Whigs, who took control of the election booth. Lord Craven of Coombe Abbey, a Tory, hired hundreds of 'ruffians and clodhoppers' and armed them with clubs and bludgeons. They marched on the election booth and a pitched battle ensued which ended with a group of Whig supporters being chased into St Mary's Hall and bricks being thrown through the ancient stained glass. During the eight days of the election, intimidation meant that only 96 out of over 3,000 voters managed to vote.

On 12 March 1781 the 'Coventry Election Act' was introduced, which was meant to stop the illegal swearing in of unserved freeman. In 1784, during a particularly close fought contest, 'mushroom' voters, those who had been sworn in illegally and had still to be removed from the list, were brought in by the Corporation to vote. The election turned riotous, and on 13 April a group of men pretending to be voters marched on the booth with axes and saws under the coats and totally destroyed the very large tent. The Easter Assize of 1785 dealt with another incident which took place during this election and George Harris, Joseph Atkins and Thomas Goode were sentenced to six months' imprisonment for 'inhumanely beating and afterwards tarring and feathering, Richard Oldham'. Oldham, servant to a clergyman and acquaintance of two of the election candidates, was standing near the *Rose and Crown* (now the *Courtyard*) in the High Street when a mob of about thirty dragged him by his hair into the stables of the *White Bear* (*Craven Arms*) and beat him. He was dragged through Broadgate into Butcher Row, his clothes were torn from him and then he was tarred and feathered.

One of Coventry's most extraordinary mayors took office in 1755. Alderman John Hewitt junior was a silkman who kept a journal concerning various events, dealing mainly with his pursuit of the criminal fraternity, but also describing military matters. He recorded in 1756 the arrival of 600 troops he had to billet. The men belonged to General Stewart's 37th Regiment of Foot. During their stay 47 pressed men joined them. In May 1779 the arrival of the press gang was described as an occasion 'which no doubt must have given very painful sensations to every stickler for English liberty; a number of impressed men to the amount of twenty, chained, two and two, with one continuous chain … driven … like a gang of galley slaves.'[5] In 1760 it was reported that Colonel Hales' regiment had

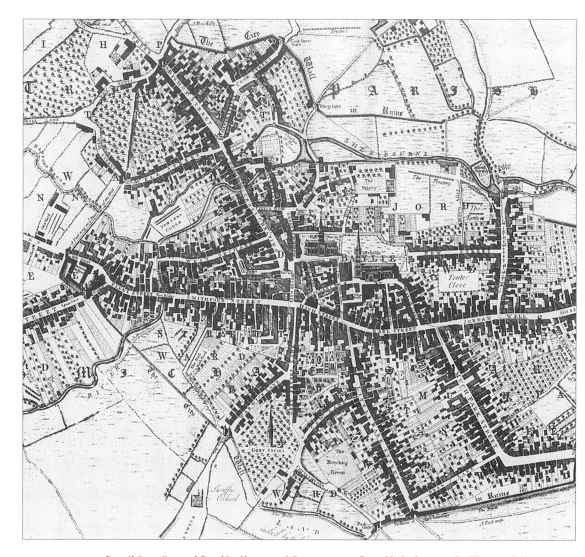

127   *Detail from Samuel Bradford's map of Coventry 1748, published 1750, by Thomas Jeffreys.*

kept their horses at the new riding school outside Bishop Gate. The riding school, which was thatched, caught fire while soldiers fired carbines to condition their horses, and was burned to the ground.[6] In 1757 an affray occurred in a public house during which a cavalry soldier slashed a man with a sword, putting his life in danger. The watchman was called and the soldier attacked him, cutting off one of his fingers.

In April of that year it was reported that a soldier was shot for desertion in Coventry Park, at the bottom of Little Park Street.[7] The *Coventry Mercury* also reported in June that, 'On Wednesday morning last a soldier belonging to General Stewart's Regiment received a thousand lashes and was afterwards drummed out of the Regiment, with a halter about his neck for desertion.' During June, George Robinson of the same regiment was shot for desertion and died very 'penitent', a warning to other soldiers to beware 'lewd women'. A soldier in custody who should have been shot the previous month received a reprieve but deserted again and was now waiting for the regiment to return to carry out his execution.[8] Shooting was considered a soldier's death, and in April 1765 the mayor had the Scots Greys reviewed in the Park by the Duke of Argyll because two soldiers, Drury and Leslie, were being hanged on Gibbet Hill for the murder of a Stoneleigh farmer and there were fears the soldiers would interfere, regarding the mode of execution as inappropriate.

With the threat of invasion by Napoleon Bonaparte, permanent army camps were established throughout the land. In Coventry the medieval *Black Bull Inn* in Smithford Street and its extensive grounds were purchased for £2,025 and converted into a military barracks, which then remained until the First World War. The first occupants were the newly formed Coventry Volunteers, consisting of two troops of horse and three of infantry. All were householders in the City and County of Coventry, sons of householders, or men approved by the committee. The Rev. Joseph Rann of Holy Trinity was chaplain of the Volunteers, who drilled regularly in the Park. From the late 1790s the barracks were occupied by dragoons, hussars and lancers, and the troops became part of daily life in the city. They were often watched by young ladies while taking exercise on Greyfriars Green or in the Great Park.

The Lammas Lands of the freemen, which surrounded the city, continued to be a bone of contention. People continued to encroach upon them, fence them off, graze on them or even grow crops. On 3 January 1793 a proclamation stated that the freemen 'intend to take possession of all those Lammas Grounds that have any sort of grain standing at the time'. The freemen did not always take action, however, and were said in this century to have lost the Lammas grounds at Kingfield in Stoke, which included Gosford Green.

The first regular stagecoach from Coventry to London ran from 6 August 1750. The journey, which began from the *Cross Keys* in Smithford Street, took two days initially and 14½ hours by the end of the century. With the coaches came road improvements and the development of turnpikes, maintained roads paid for at toll-houses. More coaches in the city streets meant bottlenecks had to be dealt with, and the entrance to Greyfriars Lane was widened. In 1762 many streets were cobbled, with central gutters, and each householder was ordered to keep clean the area before their house and to keep a lighted lantern outside their door at night.

In 1768 the Coventry Canal Company was formed and in May of that year the first sod was cut in Longford/Foleshill. James Brindley completed the job quickly and on 10 August 1769 the city celebrated when two coal barges from Bedworth entered the Canal Basin.

Education and Religion

Eighteenth-century Coventry still had its Henry VIII and Bablake schools, but the period saw the creation of various charity schools for the ordinary child. During the first half of the century an elementary education movement resulted in the foundation of 2,000 charity schools in England. Unlike the endowed schools, which relied purely on land or money bequeathed in wills, the charity schools also accepted donations and collected large quantities of money after special regular charity sermons given in the city's churches. This paid not only for the schools but also for the children's clothes and placement in an apprenticeship.

The first of these schools was Baker, Billing and Crow's school, which eventually settled in Cow Lane in 1703 and became known as Cow Lane School.[9] It was named originally after its founder and two benefactors. Although it was a non-sectarian school, the boys were required to attend services at the Great Meeting House in Vicar Lane. It became generally known as the 'Black Gift School' owing to the boys' uniforms consisting of coarse black suits. The school amalgamated with Bablake in 1900.

Blue Coat Girls School was founded in 1714. It supported a number of girls and provided a sound education, plus training in domestic service. It was maintained by benefactions and by charity sermons at Holy Trinity, where the girls worshipped. Bayley's Charity School, also known as the 'Blue Gift', was founded by spinster Katherine Bayley in 1723. It was not until her death in 1733, however, that the school came into being in Bayley Lane. When it opened, it had 16 scholars, eight boys and eight girls, but became exclusively for boys as the century progressed. The original foundation was augmented by charity sermons at St Michael's Church. The boys were taught the three R's and were carefully guided in the doctrine of the Church of England. They attended St Michael's twice every Sunday.

The Fairfax or Green Gift School was founded in Spon Street and the children attended St John's. In 1769 the school contained 12 boys and 12 girls and the schoolmaster was a cobbler who, apparently, made the children's shoes while teaching them. By 1780 the school had become exclusively for boys and taken its name from the boys' green collar and green tuft set in their hats. On leaving the school the children would be given a full suit of clothes and two shirts, a Bible and Prayer Book, and an apprenticeship, all at the charity's expense.[10] A girls' charity school for Quakers was set up in Vicar Lane by Brigit Southern and Frances Craner in 1723. With an income of £110 a year, the school educated and clothed 36 girls, although none were Quakers as Coventry's Quaker community appeared not to be in need of charity.

Other charities set up in the city for the poor and elderly included Crow's Charity in 1707, Moore's Charity in 1729, and Smith's Charity in 1724. Much of

128 *Girls of the Blue Coat School, set up in 1714.*

129 *The Blue Coat School, built on the Priory entrance in 1856.*

their work was designed to instil the religious beliefs of those involved. In 18th-century Coventry the Church of England was pre-eminent, with often exemplary clergy such as the Rev. Joseph Rann, who published an edition of the works of Shakespeare with copious notes. The Church helped set up some charity schools, and after 1785 set up Sunday schools. The first in Coventry is thought to have been held in 1799 in a room in Hill Street.

The Presbyterians, descendants of the Puritans, built a church in Smithford Street in 1701 called the Great Meeting House. They held much influence over the City Council in the first half of the century but gradually became less orthodox and finally Unitarian. During the Commonwealth the Independents had worshipped in St John's Church in Fleet Street, but they also possessed a small meeting house in Bell Court in Much Park Street and were led by Samuel Basnet, who had been a lecturer in the main churches in Cromwell's time. They met here until 1724, when they opened a larger building in Vicar Lane. The congregation split in the mid-18th century and a second chapel was opened. St John's became a parish church once more in June 1734 under the Rev. Edward Jackson. The church took on a more Anglo-Catholic role at the end of the 19th century.

The Baptists were established in the city in the 17th century, and in the 18th century there were two Baptist churches in the County of Coventry, one in the city itself and one in the village of Foleshill, established around 1759. The Baptists transferred in 1724 to another building in Jordan Well. Baptisms were said to have taken place outdoors. 'The congregation used to walk out on a moonlight night through the orchards and along the path down the slope of the Park to the old Mill, near the Charterhouse, and their believers confessed their faith and were baptised in the stream.'[11] The Rev. Butterworth, the church's longest serving minster, lived in a house in Cow Lane and when it was decided to erect a new church this site was chosen. Butterworth himself is said to have 'pulled up the trees which he himself had nurtured ... for the good of the cause of Christ'.[12] Cow Lane Chapel opened in 1793 and in 1798 Francis Franklin was sent to Coventry to assist

130 *Houses in Much Park Street, drawn by Florence Weston. (Coventry City Libraries, Local Studies)*

131 *Inside St Michael's church in the late 18th century.*

the chapel's aged minister. It is said that the new chapel was in debt at this time and Franklin travelled all over the county on foot, gathering funds and finally paying off the church's debt.

In 1779 John Wesley visited the city and wrote,

> When I came to Coventry I found that notice had been given for my preaching in the park, but heavy rain prevented this. I went to the mayor, Edward Harper, desiring the use of the Town Hall [St Mary's Hall]. He refused but later the same day he gave the use of it to a Dancing Master. I then went to the Women's Market. Many soon gathered together, and listened with all seriousness. I preached there again the next morning, and again in the evening. Then I took coach for London. I was nobly attended; behind the coach were ten convicted felons, loudly blaspheming and rattling on their chains; by my side sat a man with a loaded blunderbuss, and another upon the coach.

Wesley came again in 1782 and preached in a schoolroom, and in 1786 he stated that the 'poor little flock at Coventry have at length procured a neat convenient room, only it is far too small'. This was an auction room at the rear of the Women's Market which served the small group until they took possession of the old Baptist chapel in Jordan Well. They moved to Gosford Street around 1798 and later built another chapel here. Wesleyan chapels also sprang up in Foleshill (visited by Wesley in 1779), Bell Green and Holbrooks.[13]

CRIME AND PUNISHMENT

Alderman John Hewitt J.P. was a man of unceasing energy when it came to dealing with the criminal fraternity. He stated in his journal that on taking the mayoralty in 1755 he was determined to put into force laws of the strictest severity against 'prophane swearing, cursing, drunkenness, lewdness and other immoralities'. He began to concentrate on more serious criminal acts such as murder or theft, and through his career as a thief taker he became a personal friend of the other great thief taker, Sir John Fielding in London.

One of Hewitt's early cases involved the misnamed 'Coventry Gang'. Four members of a 200-strong London-based gang with a history going back to the previous century robbed the *Castle Inn* in Broadgate on Coventry Fair Day in 1763. Hewitt had the four hanged and within two years was responsible for the destruction of the whole London gang. In 1765 his detective skills brought about the capture of the murderers of Stoneleigh farmer Thomas Edwards, who had died as a result of being clubbed with a pistol. After investigations among the military, Hewitt soon had a Coventry weaver and two soldiers under lock and key. While held in Coventry the men were model prisoners but, sent to Warwick for trial, they exhibited a sudden change of behaviour. Hewitt wrote,

> They had not only to me, but to others acknowledged the favours I had shown them and the indulgences received from the gaoler through me. They now not only deny what they said before, but have also declared that they should die in peace after having blown my brains out. Such have been the returns I have always met with from men of invidious and mean principles.[14]

The three men apologised to Hewitt for the remark as they stood on the gallows before their execution on 17 April 1765, and he accepted the apology with dignity. Hewitt's career lasted for many years and as a reward he received the mayoralty of the city three times.

132   *The Mayor's Parlour in Cross Cheaping, head-quarters of John Hewitt (19th-century engraving).*

133 *Engraving from 18th-century execution broadside.*

134 *The market square with Women's Butter Market, Watch House and stocks (19th-century engraving).*

135 *The Great Hall, St Mary's Hall.*

Coventry Gaol still stood in Gaol Lane (now Pepper Lane), and until 1773-4 consisted of the remains of the 17th-century gaol, which had been partly demolished in 1698. Because of its ruinous condition, Hewitt ordered a rebuilding, and a new gaol, including the County Court, was completed in the latter half of 1776.[15] The regime was harsh, with prisoners stripped, whipped and chained in leg-irons for hours on end. Those with money could afford a private room, one of eight supplied by the gaol; others found themselves in one of the four dungeons, probably the remains of the old gaol.

Trials took place in the new County Hall and in St Mary's Hall and sentences were harsh, with over 200 hanging offences. At the Summer Assize of 1791 William Taylor, aged 17 years, who stole two hats, was transported for seven years, John Abel, aged 17 years, on a 'violent suspicion' of taking a bed gown, a waist-coat, 15 pairs of stockings and other goods, was transported for seven years, and William Aylesbury, aged 19, who stole six silver tea-spoons, was branded. Benjamin Phillips aged 16 was condemned to death for assaulting John Vale on the king's highway and stealing four pounds of 'mixed metal'.

The condemned were visited by the clergy during their last days and accompanied to the gallows by a clergyman who would sit next to them on their coffin as it trundled through the streets on the back of a cart. The procession, controlled by a number of pikemen, would proceed to the corner of Whitley Common where the gallows was located. Here crowds of up to 30,000 would gather to watch the criminal hang. These public holidays became known locally as 'Swing'em Fair'.

LEISURE

Other forms of entertainment available locally included cock- and dog-fighting, and bull-baiting, which was still carried out in local villages. The Godiva Procession now enjoyed the participation of the Council in robes of office. In 1755 a racecourse was laid out in the Park and racing became part of the social calendar. In September 1783 the *Coventry Mercury* reported the presence of Lord and Lady Beauchamp and Lady Harriet Herbert at races which were 'prodigiously' attended. The last race on the third day was for a silver cup and was won by a local butcher. The day ended on a sad note, however, for 'one of the horses running away with his rider, made directly for the gate leading from the Park into Little Park Street, and some persons endeavouring to hinder him from going through the gate, which was open, he leapt over a turnstile by the side of it, fell upon a fine girl about seven years of age, and killed her on the spot.'[16] This tragedy caused Coventry Races to be suspended until they were held in 1834 in Stoke.

In the early part of the century gladiatorial combat was popular amongst all classes and gave rise to many heroes. Coventry supplied one of the best at the art, one John Parkes, nicknamed 'the Invincible'. Parkes was an expert with the razor-tipped two-handed sword and flail and fought 350 fights throughout Europe. Combatants were made up mainly of ex-military men who invited each other to combat in the press: 'I John Parkes from Coventry Master of the Noble Science of Defence do invite you

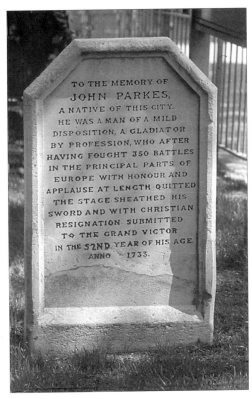

136 *The grave of John Parkes, gladiator.*
(Joseph York/DMC)

137 *Miss Sarah Siddons played St Mary's Hall on a number of occasions (1902 print).*

Thomas Hesgate, to meet me and Exercise at the following weapons, viz. back sword, sword and dagger, sword and buckler, single falchons and quarterstaff.' Parkes was described as precise and lethal, and would entertain his audience by catching coins on the end of his sword. When he died in 1733 he was mourned nationally and held in the same regard as his friend, the famed James Fig. Fig was the father of prize-fighting, another popular sport which took place around the city and on Whitley Common by the gallows, but there is little information in the press on the sport which came into its own in the 19th century.

A bowling green was set up on Barrs Hill, Radford and decorated with lighted paper lanterns. The main venue for the upper classes in the city was Drapers Hall or St Mary's Hall in Bayley Lane, where the social elite could combine the new fad of playing cards with dancing. Both buildings also supplied venues for feasts, balls, theatre and music. The most famed actress of the period, Sarah Siddons, played both buildings with companies which would perform here for up to six months. In 1797 she played Zara in *The Mourning Bride*, Isabella in the *Fatal Marriage*, Lady Randolph in *Douglas* and Jane Shore in *Jane Shore* inside one week at St Mary's Hall. During the Great Fair (Corpus Christi or Show Fair lasted eight days) of 1795 the Sadler Wells Company came with a troupe of Italian acrobats and performed the 'Harlequin Skeleton' in the Assembly Room at the *Rose and Crown* (the Courtyard) in the High Street, while the acrobats entertained in the yard.[17] The company of Messrs Watson and Hoy played no fewer than 40 dramas, comedies, pantomimes and musicals during five months at St Mary's Hall. They performed on three nights a week.

The *Rose and Crown* was also the venue for another kind of event popular in the 18th century, the exhibition of the unusual. In 1785 'a large commodious room' accommodated the 'Amazing Pig of Knowledge', which could count and tell either the time 'or any lady's or gentleman's thoughts'. The 'Queen's Ass', a zebra, was exhibited in the *Mermaid Tavern*, Broadgate in 1772, and in 1780 the Irish Giant, O'Brien, was exhibited at the *Halfmoon*, along with a baboon, the 'Ethiopian Savage' and a cassowary.

Seven

NINETEENTH-CENTURY COVENTRY

At the turn of the 19th century Coventry's population was 16,034 and there was a national shortage of wheat and other foodstuffs. This caused distress and the Corporation subscribed £40 towards a soup kitchen for the relief of the poor at St Mary's Hall, where the needy could purchase for a halfpenny each corned herring, which became known as 'poor man's beef'. Riots broke out and were quickly put down by the city's military presence. On 15 September 1800 the press stated that a recent riot was due to 'the excessive and unnecessary high price of every article of sustenance, more particularly that of the staff of life'. A large group of colliers from the Bedworth area marched to Nuneaton and drew up a statement of their grievances. They intimidated local farmers into selling their products at a fixed price and committed outrages against those who opposed them. The following day the ever-growing mob marched on Coventry armed with bludgeons and clubs and were met by the 17th Light Dragoons, who blocked their way at the top of Bishop Street. The mayor and magistrates asked them to leave and promised prices would be looked into, but the ringleaders insisted that the mayor should sign a document promising to drop prices. Negotiations began to break down and threats were made and stones thrown, so the mayor read the Riot Act. When this had no effect he deployed the Dragoons and had the mob driven from the city in what was afterwards described as a most 'humane' manner.

138 *The entrance to Coventry Barracks, dating back to 1793.*

139   *A view of Coventry in 1809. (David Morgan)*

While this was happening smaller groups got into the city through the back lanes and began to attack shops. Four of the leaders were arrested and held in the Mayor's Parlour. Soon Broadgate began to fill with sympathetic citizens, who hissed and threw stones at the soldiery. The mayor called for the Volunteer Cavalry and Infantry to assist the Dragoons and the mob was cleared without, it was claimed, a single drop of blood being spilt. Afterwards a meeting was called at St Mary's Hall to discuss how immediate relief could be given to the poor, during which it is said many took exception to the way the civil and military authorities had dealt with the mob. A body was set up called the Committee for Bettering the Condition of the Poor. It opened a provisions depot at the top of Butcher Row and sold food to the poor at below cost price.

On 9 February 1801 the committee had at its depot 10,770 corned herring for disposal in one day at a halfpenny each. During the week 16,000 herring a day would pass through, which were supplemented by the continuing supply of soup from St Mary's Hall. But there were so many poor that the soup would often run out. During this period the city fathers provided only £40 a year, leaving others to take on the burden of funding and staffing relief depots. The mayor was required by law to set the price of corn and bread, but he failed to do so, and bakers charged what they would. He was in the flour trade himself, which may explain his behaviour.

140 *Whitefriars used as a workhouse, 1865.*

A Bill was placed before Parliament enabling the city to build a workhouse, or House of Industry, for the better employment of the poor. The two existing workhouses, in Hill Street opposite Bablake, and in Well Street, were so crowded that some inmates had to sit while others slept, and up to eight children shared a bed. They were maintained by Poor Law rates from Holy Trinity and St Michael's parishes. The new Bill united the two parishes, and Guardians of the Poor, who elected 18 Directors of the Poor, governed the whole city district.[1] The new committee purchased the old Whitefriars and converted it into a large workhouse. Within three years all the poor had been transferred here and the old buildings sold. The system provided indoor relief, whereby the poor would live and work in the building, and outdoor relief, or food and money to those who lived at home, which helped to keep the number of inmates down. In 1832 there were 675 families on permanent out-relief.[2]

The New Poor Law Act of 1834 withdrew out-relief, made the workhouse less comfortable and split up married couples. The Coventry Guardians continued to provide out-relief as it was considered the only way to stop the seasonal poor becoming the permanently poor. In 1842 they conformed to the separation of couples and, under pressure, agreed to revise the inmates' diets. Despite this they were criticised in 1843 by an outside commission for being 'too comfortable' and observing 'particular cleanliness and order'.

141   *The cloisters of Whitefriars used as the workhouse dining hall.*

The Guardians did not believe the workhouse was a good place for children and had them apprenticed to tradesmen. The younger children were educated in the workhouse and from 1855 out-relief children were educated in local schools at the Guardians' expense. Things improved even more in the 1890s when all the children were sent to local schools and to live in separate houses with a 'house-mother'. The workhouse itself acquired a new hospital, including maternity and mental wards in 1889, which later became part of Gulson Hospital. Whitefriars ceased to be a workhouse in 1948.

By 1841 the population of Coventry had almost doubled to 30,781, largely on account of the industrialisation of the city. The many large gardens which can still be seen on Samuel Bradford's 1748 map had disappeared, being swallowed up and built over by the many courts which became the norm in Coventry. These consisted of a block of houses around a central court that housed toilet, water pump or well. By the 20th century these would have become slums. The city had not spread outside the boundaries created by the old city wall because of the Lammas and Michaelmas Lands, which were a barrier blocking the city's expansion. This also meant that the countryside was only a short walk away.

The first Public Health Act was passed in 1848 and the new City Council acted promptly to deal with infringements. The Act covered the water supply, burial of the dead and the condition of the Sherbourne. Following the Coventry Water Act a well was sunk at Spon End, which supplied the city with about a million gallons a day. Water mains began to be laid and service pipes to property boundaries. Not all used the water initially, believing their own free supply was purer. As for the river, a report of around 1847 stated, 'Such is the condition of this town that the quarters nearest the river suffer from the impure state of the atmosphere; and not only so but from aggravated forms of disease; the very soil being saturated with the waters of the Sherbourne, loaded with refuse at the lower parts of the town.'[3] Much of this problem was caused by three ancient mills, including the Priory mill, which impeded the natural flow of the river. Under an Act of 1844 the Council acquired these mills and had them demolished.

142   *Looking down Cross Cheaping and the Burges in the 1860s.*

The churchyards were full to overflowing and considered a danger to public health. Under the terms of the 1844 Act the Council acquired a part of Whitley Common which had at one time been a quarry. Under the direction of Joseph Paxton, Coventry M.P. and designer of the Crystal Palace, a new cemetery was laid out. In its beautiful landscaped grounds two chapels were erected, one Church of England and one nonconformist, and when Paxton died in 1865 a monument was erected to him near the cemetery gates. In 1870 the cemetery was described as being more like a 'gentleman's park' than a 'city of the dead'.

In 1849 William Ranger, Superintending Inspector of the General Board of Health, visited Coventry to make observations and to promote the setting up of a Board of Health in the city. His report stated that the city had suffered a cholera epidemic in 1832. Its labouring population was made up mainly of silk ribbon weavers and watchmakers, many of whom worked in cramped and badly

143 *Looking up Cross Cheaping and Broadgate on market day in the 1860s.*

ventilated rooms, and the biggest killers were epidemics of scarlet fever and typhus. In the years 1840-2 the death rate in Coventry was four per cent higher than the national average. Ranger considered the main problem to be overcrowding caused by the city's inability to expand over the Lammas and Michaelmas Lands.[4] He also noted that, although water mains had been laid, there was still no adequate drainage system and only 15 of the city's 98 streets had working sewers, many of which, he noted, ran directly into the Sherbourne. The new district of Hillfields had no sewers and relied like most of the city on ash or privy pits. The better houses normally had their own outdoor privy, while in some parts of the city 64 people might share just one. The residue from the pits would be collected every month at night by the 'Lavender Men', so called because of their less-than-sweet smell.

It was also noted that some of the streets were macadamised or cobbled and less than half were unmade. Filth would lie longer in the treated streets but the unmade ones, especially the new ones in Hillfields, could turn into quagmires when it rained. The result of the report was that on 30 July 1849 a Local Board of Health was established in Coventry. From 1849 to 1852 the new board supervised the construction of a sewerage system for the city and a sewage farm at Whitley, which sold its product on to farmers.

Ranger's report had recommended the opening up of the Lammas Lands, and Awards made in 1860 and 1875 finally ended the stranglehold they had had for centuries on the city. The lands were allotted freehold to private individuals and trustees. The City Freemen continued to hold the largest area and their lands were monitored by trustees elected by the freemen. Over the years these lands, almost all built upon, brought in (and still do) a revenue for the freemen which is paid out if requested to older freemen as 'seniority money'.

144 *The Coventry and Warwickshire Hospital (19th-century engraving).*

Despite the setting up of the Board of Health and the sewerage system, improvements weren't general. It was reported before 1863 that,

> Coventry is punctured with some thousands of horrible pits of privy soil and ash, and offal refuse, which are thickest in the most crowded localities. They are generally emptied at night when they get full, but are not under the control of the Board of Health until they overflow or otherwise transgress the outwards signs of decency. The sewerage at disposal of the Board is only that smaller quantity collected by sewerage from the water closets of the better classes of houses.[5]

The same report noted that, despite the introduction of sewerage, the 'cesspool system remains in triumph' and there 'is a feeble supervision of the public health'. Animals continued to be slaughtered in the street despite the city having over sixty slaughterhouses, although most of these appear vile: 'We saw in a dark slaughterhouse [in Palmer Lane], which had rooms above it, a pig in one corner feeding on the blood and offal of slain cattle.' In Butcher Row the reporter watched as 'a sheep was slaughtered in this public way. A greasy bucket was held to receive the blood, which in time overflowed and escaped down the steep gutter of the row, in company with paunch stuff and other offal.' It appears that some of this came to an end when the new market hall was opened in 1867.

145 *Broadgate in 1898.*

Coventry's first hospital, in the modern sense of the word, was opened at the bottom of Little Park Street in 1840. A large house with gardens overlooking the park, it was described at the time as being in 'a fine and airy situation'. It was soon to prove too small, however, and in 1864 work began on the erection of a new hospital on the Stoney Stanton Road to be called the Coventry and Warwickshire Hospital. On completion the building was found to be too large and for years two wards lay unused. But as the population grew so did the hospital, which was funded entirely by voluntary contributions. At the beginning of the 20th century a working men's committee raised £3,000, and later the 'Hospital Saturday Fund', paid for by workers, raised £5,000 a year. Before the birth of the Health Service, some Coventry carnivals and Godiva Processions raised vast sums for the building.

Tollgates were set up under the Street Act of 1812 to improve roads. Hertford Street replaced the narrow and congested old southern route into the city, Warwick and Greyfriars Lane, and in 1820 the north tip of Smithford Street and the west of Broadgate were demolished to widen the road and create a new area for the weekly markets. In 1843 an Act allowed the trustees of Sir Thomas White's estate to sell some of the land, which enabled the construction of Hales Street, White Street, Jesson Street, Norton Street and Ford Street.[6] The new Holyhead Road was constructed by Thomas Telford in 1827-30 and another road allowed coaches to avoid the hill on the old London Road at Whitley.

146 *Hales Street in the 1890s. (Cliff Barlow)*

On 23 March 1838 an engine pulling five carriages of officials arrived at Coventry from Rugby and by 17 September the London and Birmingham Railway had reached Birmingham. The coming of the railway meant the end of the old stagecoaches. Instead of a coach taking ten hours to get to London the train could be there in two. Dan Claridge of the *Craven Arms* tried to reinstate coach travel with 'The Good Old Days' in the late 19th century, but by then it had become a novelty.

Oil lamps illuminated parts of the city before 1821, when a gasworks was erected by private individuals in Abbots Lane at the cost of around £20,000. It was afterwards incorporated as a company and ran for many more years. In 1856 the Gas Company rebuilt its works on a larger scale by Act of Parliament and extended its supply of gas into the districts, including Foleshill, Radford, Stoke, Styvechale, Coundon and Allesley. In 1884 the Council purchased the company for around £170,000. A new gasworks was built in Foleshill in 1909. The Council also opened an Electric Light Works in 1895.[7]

Coventry politics in the early 19th century saw a continuation of 18th-century skulduggery and violence. The 1802 contest was slightly different as this time the violence involved the military; this appears to be Coventry's 'Peterloo'. A letter written at the time by Peter Moore, the unsuccessful candidate, states that,

147   *Coventry railway station in the late 1830s.*

148   *Men of the Royal Field Artillery in Coventry Barracks in the 1880s.*

Yesterday [22nd July] was the day appointed for chairing Messrs. Barlow and Jeffreys, during the whole of which the soldiers belonging to Captain Barlow's regiment (the King's Own or 1st Dragoon Guards) were extremely riotous and most unmercifully beat and [word missing] many of the inhabitants without the smallest provocation on their parts ... In the evening without the smallest appearance of riot or disturbance, the troops were let loose from the Barracks, first one by one (mounted and swords drawn) and afterwards in a body, headed by Coronets Addison and Bracegirdle, during which the most wanton cruelty ever known was practised on the peaceful inhabitants. The troops indiscriminately cut and hewn down men, women and children and forced themselves into houses, and brutally beat the persons therein. In fact it is impossible for me to described the enormities committed.[8]

The mayor, asked to explain the outrages to the Commander in Chief, the Prince Regent, stated that 16 troopers invited to join the chairing procession of Mr Jeffreys and Captain Barlow were threatened by supporters of Moore and Bird on reaching Spon Street. In the evening a group of about 1,000 gathered in Radford and had a mock chairing before marching into Coventry. The 'banditti' then attacked a soldier near Market Place, who was, according to the mayor, 'violently beaten by them, thrown down and kicked most cruelly'. As the group approached the Barracks the 'Rogues March' was played and a group of privates was attacked and beaten, as were a number of inhabitants. The troops were ordered out and the mayor reported that, 'No information has reached my ear of any one person being seriously wounded or even wounded at all.' He was a supporter of Jeffreys and Barlow, like the troopers, so his report is no doubt biased. It is also worth noting that the Prince Regent was in debt to Jeffreys to the tune of £85,028.[9]

Jeffreys and Barlow won the election by majorities of only fifteen and eight and the result was contested. Moore, Bird and others accused the mayor and council of acting as avowed agents of the men and illegally withholding payments from Thomas White's and Wheatley's charities. In fact, payments were withheld from those who voted for Moore and Bird. Several unqualified votes were allowed for Jeffreys, while qualified votes for Moore and Bird were rejected. Proceedings moved on to Parliament where Barlow was cleared, although Jeffreys was found to be unqualified to serve in Parliament.

Things had not improved by the year 1824, when well-known political writer William Cobbett contested one of the Coventry seats. Cobbett came to the city with great expectations. He had a reputation as a Radical and Coventry had its fair share of those. His opponents were the previously mentioned Peter Moore and relative newcomer Edward Ellice, both of whom would dominate the political scene for years to come. After the first day of voting Cobbett was confident of victory but Moore and Ellice brought in the heavies, and Cobbett witnessed a real Coventry election which he later described in his weekly *Political Register*: 'I, that day, saw twenty of my voters actually torn away from the polling place, and ripped up behind [with a knife] and stripped of their coats.' Cobbett noticed

Ellice leaving the booth angry and he followed a few paces behind, intending to go to the house of a Mr Grant a few yards away. He continues,

> I had to pass through the band of savages and I was scarcely amongst them when they (at Ellice's instigation) began to endeavour to press me down. They were more than a thousand in number ... several attempts were made to press me down; I got many blows in the sides; and if I had been either a short or weak man I must have been pressed under foot and inevitably killed ... with a great deal of difficulty I reached the pavement ... I had, when I left the booth, my snuff-box in my right hand. It is oblong and has very sharp corners, the savages pressed me sideways towards my left, and I had to fight with my right hand, in order to prevent them getting me down.
>
> It cut the noses and eyes of the savages at a furious rate and assisted in my safe arrival on the raised pavement ... just opposite the door of a shop ... One of the savages ... exclaimed, 'Hang him, I'll rip him up'.

Cobbett was pulled into the doorway of the shop by two young women, but not before he kicked his assailant between the eyes, sending him back into the mob. He goes on, 'For this I certainly would have been killed in a few minutes had not Mr Frank Sergeant, who seeing my danger ... happily came to my assistance ... Having got me he turned round, saying "Follow me Sir," and having beaten back three or four savages ... we arrived quickly in safety.' He made further comments in the *Register* about the voters in the city, stating, 'The will of these freemen (as they are called) is nothing, but that they are compelled, at least a majority of them, to obey the will of others. That, in fact, these poor fellows bear the name of freemen and are, all the while, real slaves as are the Negroes in Jamaica.'

The election of 1832 began with a huge mob escorting Ellice and Bulwer to the hustings. When Messrs Fyler and Thomas tried to walk from the *King's Head* to the booth they and their small band of supporters were assaulted and unable to get access until the 'specials' came to their assistance. Over the following days the men raised their own mob, made up of a number of pugilists from Birmingham and about six hundred navvies who were working on the canal at Brinklow. Well oiled with a concoction called 'gin-hot', the men armed and marched through the city at two in the morning on the Monday, occupied the polling booth, and prevented anyone from voting for the wrong side. Meanwhile the supporters of Ellice and Bulwer, numbering some two to three thousand, gathered on Greyfriars Green armed with clubs and staves. Led by local prizefighter Bob Randle, this mob marched on the booth. After an exchange of words Randle punched his opponent and at a signal mass-fighting ensued. Randle's mob won the day, many of their opponents being stripped and beaten. Many more fled back to the *King's Head*, which was said to resemble a slaughterhouse. The event became known as the 'Bloody Tenth'. The result of the election was Henry Bulwer, 1613, Edward Ellice, 1607, Thomas Fyler, 371, and Morgan Thomas, 366. At the 1833 election one thousand special constables were sworn in to preserve the peace and they did.

149   *Coventry election, 1865, Messrs Eaton and Treherne.*

In 1835 the Whig government introduced the Municipal Reform Bill, which replaced the often corrupted closed corporations in each city with a new Town Council. Members of the Coventry council were no longer elected by freemen alone, but by all rate-paying householders who had owned their property for three years. To prevent corruption, managers were appointed to act as guardians of local charities, which were taken out of council control. Provision was made for the institution of a police force. The Coventry Corporation lobbied against the Bill but was unsuccessful and the inevitable change came. The new Council met for the first time in early January 1836 and in July of that year sold all the paraphernalia of the old Corporation at a sale in St Mary's Hall, including the 'Original Cap and Side-saddle, Whip and Bridle of Lady Godiva.'[10]

The Municipal Reform Act had other major effects on the city, which was divided into six wards, the sixth being the villages which made up the ancient County of Coventry. This meant that those who lived in the villages were expected to pay the same rates as those who lived in Coventry itself, without the benefits. Not surprisingly, many refused to pay and legal disputes flourished. In some villages, such as Walsgrave-on-Sowe, only part of the village lay within the county. The disputes worsened and in 1842 Parliament passed the Coventry Boundary Act. This decreed that all that part of Coventry known as the County of Coventry should return to Warwickshire. Thus the county created in 1451 by King Henry VI came to an end. By 1888, however, Coventry was said to have a population of 50,000 and therefore constituted a County Borough.[11]

Industry

Ribbon Weaving

The cloth trade and weaving had been a staple industry in Coventry for a number of centuries. In the 19th century ribbon weaving still brought prosperity to the city, and the introduction of the French Jaquard loom to the city in 1820 led to great improvements in decorative ribbon manufacture. Many weavers worked from their homes, and weaving districts grew in Foleshill and Hillfields, but factories were also created. Workers didn't always see eye to eye with employers, and one government report states that 'a Mr. Horsfall [aged 70], a ribbon manufacturer, a man of considerable property, having given offence to the men, the latter, in order to revenge themselves, had recourse to what in Coventry is called "donkeying"; that is, they seized him, and setting him on a donkey, paraded him through the streets of Coventry.'

The incident lasted two hours, which was brief compared with that which overtook Josiah Beck, whose 'factory' lay at the end of Beck's Court, off New Buildings. Beck had created large steam-powered looms which he paid young women to mind. On 7 November 1831 seven hundred weavers gathered by the Mill Dam and speeches were made about the state of the industry, reduced prices and growing unemployment, and the threat the steam-powered loom posed to the artisan weaver. Beck's name came up and a mob of 500 headed to his factory. The mob banged on the door, demanding to see the steam looms, and Beck agreed to let Joseph Day, one of the ring-leaders, in; but as he stepped aside the mob charged. Beck was forced out, stoned with bricks and coal and suffered a beating before he managed to escape over a wall. He was caught again in the street and John Deeming and others dragged him back to the factory and forced him to open the engine room. Thomas Burbury encouraged the mob to torch the looms and Benjamin Sparkes led the attack on the steam engine, smashing it with a sledgehammer. Then the mob began to destroy the building and its contents, throwing pieces of loom through the windows as the factory burned. Beck escaped again but was recaptured and dragged to the Mill Dam. Threats were made on his life and, as he begged for mercy, he was punched. At this point Thomas Burbury appeared to talk the mob out of their final act of violence.

The riot was brought to an end when the Riot Act was read and the 14th Light Dragoons and the 7th Hussars from the Barracks dispersed the crowd with charges. By the time the streets were cleared Beck's factory had burned to the ground. A group of men were arrested and later put on trial. Benjamin Sparkes, aged 20, and Thomas Burbury, aged 29, were sentenced to death, and Alfred Toogood, aged 17, was sentenced to transportation. Others later tried were Joseph Day, William Westwick and John Deeming, who were imprisoned with hard labour. Later Sparkes and Burbury had their sentences commuted to transportation for life. Years later Toogood returned to Coventry a rich man, but Josiah Beck never prospered again and died a poor inmate at Bond's Hospital.[12] It would be another five years before anyone risked building another steam-powered factory in the city, but by 1857 Coventry and its districts employed 25,000[13] weavers and by 1860 there were 2,500 steam looms in the city.[14]

Duties paid on the import of French ribbons lessened the problem such competition might have brought, but in 1859 there was disruption when factory weavers demanded to be paid by piecework and not by the fixed weekly wage system. A lockout began which lasted for eight weeks. The Council, fearing the effect on the city's prosperity, intervened; some mill owners capitulated and the weavers returned to work, but one owner held out and employed blacklegs. This resulted in a mob of 1,000 attacking the factory. When James Hart, who owned a factory in West Orchard, decided

CITY of COVENTRY.

Whereas,

TUMULTUOUS

ASSEMBLIES

OF PERSONS

HAVE THIS DAY TAKEN PLACE IN THIS CITY,

AND

Tumult & Riot are Apprehended,

The Mayor & Magistrates

Of this City hereby Order and Direct every Licensed Victualler, and every Person Licensed to Sell Beer by Retail, within the said City and Suburbs, to

Close their respective Houses,

At the Hour of   in the   of this Day, pursuant to the Statutes in such Case made and provided.---Dated the   day of   183

GEORGE ELD,

MAYOR.

Police Office,

HENRY MERRIDEW, PRINTER, SMITHFORD-STREET, COVENTRY.

150 *Order to close licensed premises after riots, 1830s.*

to return to paying fixed weekly wages his workforce went on strike, and he too hired blacklegs. A crowd of nearly 3,000 weavers attacked both the blacklegs and the police who guarded them. Fifteen months late Hart gave in and the workers returned on piecework.

All Coventry weavers were now on piecework and things were looking up, but in 1860 a new Free Trade Act or Commercial Treaty was agreed which allowed French ribbons into the country without duty and the market was flooded. The following year America put a massive import duty upon English ribbons and, to make matters worse, the ribbon became unfashionable. The silk ribbon weaving trade in Coventry declined rapidly. Employers attempted to reduce wages and the weavers went on strike. Nearly eight weeks into the strike Charles Bray, owner of the *Coventry Herald* and ribbon manufacturer, wrote, 'It is a severe lesson that our operatives have to learn, but learn it they must, or every inhabitant of the

151   *Weavers' soup kitchen in St Mary's Hall, 1861.*

district will forever suffer the consequences. If they have really made up their minds to die of starvation rather than earn a comfortable living under the only conditions possible at the present time, they must take the consequences.'[15] The strike money held by the unions was inadequate, and when the Directors of the Poor were told they could offer work for weekly wages, all poor relief was withheld.

After selling all their belongings the weavers and their families were on the brink of starvation. One weaver was reported to have sold all his goods but asked for nothing, his pride preventing him from taking charity, and he died of starvation. An eyewitness stated, 'Such a general state of extreme poverty was never known in Coventry before. Weavers with large families were compelled to make raids upon the field crops of turnips and potatoes to save their children from utter starvation.'[16] In November 1860 Lord Leigh opened an appeal fund and money for food was given in the form of vouchers. Soup kitchens were opened in St Mary's Hall and Browett's factory in Raglan Street, funded by private individuals and the Church. By February 1862, 14,000 were dependent on the fund and it was soon exhausted.[17] A national appeal raised £40,000 which was used to create work such as levelling Whitley Common.

Soon after the beginning of the strike weavers began to move from the city into other weaving districts of England. In February 1862 there was a lecture on overseas emigration in St Mary's Hall, to which thousands came. It is said that over 4,000 left the city, many to America, Australia and New Zealand, their journey funded by Leigh's relief fund. What began as a strike became a slump and the ribbon weaving trade spiralled into decline. Many who would have returned to work couldn't because the work no longer existed. The trade in Coventry never again reached the heights it had previously, when it was one of the most important centres in the world. A surviving firm was that of Thomas Stevens, which in 1862 changed direction and began weaving silk bookmarks, decorative medal ribbons and silk pictures depicting famous people and places known as Stevengraphs. These became highly collectable and still are today. Another was J. and J. Cash, which set up the model Kingfield Cottage factory in the 1850s.

By the mid-1860s the worst of the slump was over and new trades such as worsted weaving and cotton spinning were developed. Looms were adapted to weave elastic web, coach lace and muslin frilling, but

152 *A medal of 1880 with a Thomas Stevens decorative ribbon.*

none of the industries employed many men and there was a permanent group of unemployed weavers in the city. Apart from a short revival in 1870, weaving continued to decline. In 1890 ribbons again fell from style and prices halved, leaving hundreds destitute and the trade on its knees. It continued in a small way into the 20th century with firms such as Cash's, Stevens and Courtaulds. It was reported in the *Coventry Standard* in 1927 that five handlooms were still being used in the Foleshill area.

Watchmaking

The third major trade of the 19th century was watchmaking, Coventry being one of the most important centres in England for the production of high quality hand-made gold and silver pocket watches. The census of 1841 informs us there were 474 men and 130 apprentices in the local trade. By 1860 there were 90 manufacturers in Coventry, 1,340 journeymen, 667 apprentices and 30 women bringing the total in the trade to 2,100. A great deal of the work was done outside the factory system by individual small watchmakers, case-makers and others based in Spon End, Chapelfields and Earlsdon. These areas had been built up almost exclusively to house the watch trade. Some firms employed a small workforce and outworkers. These included Mercer & Sons, Bradshaw & Riley, Waterfall, Player, Flint, Hill and Wooton, to name but a few. Most of them produced a single part of the watch – balances, dials, hands, cases, etc. – the complete watch almost always containing a semi-finished movement from Prescot in Lancashire. Among the bigger firms producing the complete watch were Errington's and Rotherham's, one of the city's oldest companies, which was based in Spon Street until 1973.

153 *Late 19th-century Coventry watches made by A.H. Read, Hill Street.*

154 *Assembling and Timing Room at Rotherham's in Spon Street.*

Coventry watchmakers who worked outside the factory system prided themselves on their craftsmanship and were the high earners of the day. Many lived in the better villa areas of Earlsdon, kept their wives at home, sent their children to school and belonged to societies which promoted the artisan's life. Coventry watches in the main remained hand-made, although factories such as Rotherham's were at least partly mechanised by 1888, when watch cases were made by machine and 'outers' were stamped by presses. At the time the firm employed 400, and by 1903 this number was 556.[18] Those in the factories were expected to work from 6 a.m. to 8 p.m. Monday to Friday and 6 a.m. to 6 p.m. on Saturday.

The watch trade suffered from the same Acts that caused distress amongst the weavers. Kevitt Rotherham, the watch manufacturer, said of the time,

There is no doubt that both the weaving and the watch making were very badly hit by the Free Trade Acts of 1860. Before this date a large number of watches were exported to America, but as soon as America began to manufacture she placed a tariff on English watches which became quite prohibitive … Later on, when America's production had become really strong and she had to find markets for her watches, these were dumped upon our market in England, at such a price that it paid people … to buy these American watches.[19]

155 *Thomas Chapman working as a watchmaker at 4, Priory Row. (Peter & Margaret Porter, U.S.A.)*

American watches were so cheap they were bought in England and resold in America at a profit. The major movement works at Prescot, which supplied Coventry, tried to fight against the imports, but that ended with mass redundancy. Soon machine-made Swiss watches also began to sell here. In 1860 there were 99,000 watches imported into England but by the following year this had risen to 160,000. Although the watch trade had a brief resurgence in the 1870s and '80s, when it employed 3,410 people, it never recovered its former position. In 1911 the trade employed 1,429.

Cycles

In 1923 Kevitt Rotherham of the famous watch firm gave an after dinner speech in which he said,

> When the slump in the ribbon and watch trade overtook Coventry, and the Coventry Machinist Company and the original J.K. Starley started to make bicycles, there is no doubt that many of the watchmakers of Coventry, who were driven through want of work to take up with this new trade, were one of the greatest assets that it possessed, for they were skilled men, used to working to very close measurements … These men certainly had a great part in securing the high quality for which the Coventry bicycle has always been renowned.

In the summer of 1861, when James Starley arrived in Coventry, he knew the city already had a skilled workforce of unemployed watchmakers. With Josiah Turner and others he set up the Coventry Sewing Machine Company in King Street. Sussex-born Starley was an inventive genius and his improvements soon led to the company's successfully selling machines across the world.

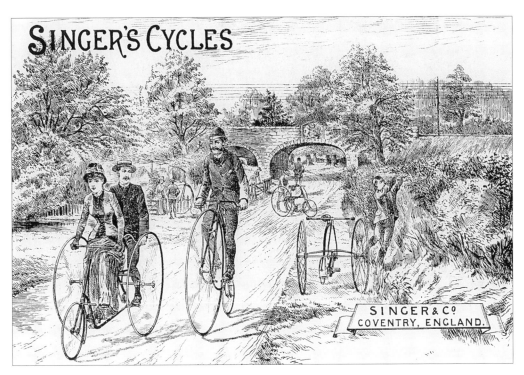

156   *Singer cycle advert from 1886 in Coat of Arms Bridge Road.*

In 1866 Turner's nephew, Rowley Turner, the company's agent, was sent to France. While there he noted the 'boneshakers' which were taking the continent by storm. Two years later he rode one of the machines, a Michaux cycle, from Coventry station to the factory and caused quite a stir. There are two versions of what happened next. One says he convinced the company to produce the cycle; the second states he had an order to produce 400 boneshakers for a French company. Whichever is true, within the year the company had produced for home and overseas markets a cycle called the 'Coventry Model', a solid-wheeled vehicle with pedals on the front wheel, alongside its sewing machines. Around this time it changed its name to the Coventry Machinist Company and opened a new factory in Cheylesmore. The company would later produce the popular 'Swift' cycle and rename itself the Swift Cycle Company. Later still it would produce motor cars. Starley and William Hillman split from the company in 1870 and began to produce cycles of their own design, the first of which was the 'Ariel', the first all-metal-framed geared penny-farthing. The cycle became so common it acquired the name the 'Ordinary'.

As the 'Ordinary' was unsuitable for some, Starley also produced the 'Wonder', and, after falling off it into nettles on Knightlow Hill, he invented the differential gear, which is found on all modern motor vehicles. In June 1881 he was commanded to attend the Queen with two of his 'Salvo Quad' tricycles and was

157   *Advert for J.K. Starley's 'Rover' safety cycle dated 1896.*

presented with an engraved watch and permission to rename his design the 'Royal Salvo'. Later that summer Starley died at his home in Upper Well Street. He was considered by many as the city's saviour for, thanks to him, Coventry had gone from slump to the centre of world cycle production.

When, in 1876, the Ordinary was at the height of its popularity, Harry Lawson designed a chain-driven 'safety' cycle. In 1878 George Singer brought out the 'Xtraordinary', which was another penny-farthing with improved pedals, but gradually all manufacturers copied Lawson's design, making their front wheels smaller and smaller until they were the same size as the back. In 1885 John Kemp Starley, James Starley's nephew, produced his 'Rover' safety cycle, with a diamond-shaped frame and newly invented (by Dunlop) pneumatic tyres, which was more sturdy than Lawson's cycle and is the truly modern cycle.[20] During the late 19th century two volatile camps in the city actively supported whoever they regarded as the inventor of the safety cycle, Lawson or Starley. In an article for the *Temple Magazine* in the 1890s, Starley says, 'The machines which have contributed to the evolution of the cycle are the Ordinary, the Xtraordinary, the Facile, the Salvo, the Humber, the Kangaroo, the Cripper and the Rover,' and fails to mention his rival Lawson. But it would be fair to say that Lawson produced the forerunner of Starley's first modern safety cycle.

A Mr. J. Newark claims to have built the first pedal cycle in Bayley Lane in 1865, using plans made by Edward Fardon of Stoneleigh, a smith. Fardon said he started building the first all-metal wire-spoked-wheel cycle, with Indian rubber tyres, in 1868 and rode around Coventry on it for six months before selling it to a Parisian chef. By the 1890s over 40,000 people worked in Coventry's cycle trade and between the 1860s and 1930s the city was home to 248 cycle manufacturers.[21] The firm Hillman, Herbert & Cooper, makers of the Premier Cycle, advertised themselves as the world's largest cycle manufacturer, producing 21,000 in 1895 and 40,000 in 1897.[22] By 1954 only one cycle maker remained in the city, the Coventry Eagle Company, founded in 1890.

Motor Cars

As the decline in the watch and weaving trades assisted the cycle trade, so the decline in bicycles led to the birth of the motor car industry. The foundation of the British motor industry took place in London on 17 April 1896, when Harry Lawson, cycle inventor and entrepreneur, held the first extraordinary meeting of the British Motor Syndicate. Lawson had acquired millions of pounds from numerous investors in the motor car, which was already taking over the continent. He used the money to buy up all the patents he could so that he could personally control the industry. Knowing there was a pool of experience in Coventry, he came to the city to find a site to start the industry. An old cotton mill in Drapers Field, Radford, suited his purpose.

In May 1896 he launched the Great Horseless Carriage Company, having purchased the main four-storeyed block of Motor Mills for £20,000 from Daimler, who retained the outside workshops, ten acres of land and a profit of £12,000. The company occupied 100,000 square feet in the main building and rented out floor space to Humber and the other motor companies.

In May 1896 Lawson and other members of the syndicate, Henry Sturmey and B. Van Praagh, brought Frenchman Arnould Bollée to Coventry to demonstrate his petroleum-driven tri-car. It had caused a sensation in France and orders for 350 machines arrived in a fortnight. The syndicate acquired the British rights for £20,000, which were given to the Great Horseless Carriage Company, who shared Motor Mills with American E. J. Pennington as well as Daimler. Pennington had a £100,000 deal with the syndicate to the rights for his vehicles, but he was a dubious character who claimed many things for his designs, none of which were ever built. He later fled to America owing money and accused of fraud.

Autocar reported on 9 May 1896 that, 'The venerable Mayor of Coventry (Alderman J.B. Loudon) himself became publicly engaged with the assistance of six policemen, in breaking the law, in other words, in riding through the streets upon Mr. Bollée's petroleum tricycle.' At this time the Red Flag Act was still in

158   *Great Horseless Carriage Company vehicles photographed in June/July 1897. In the left vehicle sits Francis Baron at the tiller, works manager, J.H. Barrows, chief cashier and, behind, a London friend. The next vehicle has at the tiller W. McNeil, wages clerk, and Baron's assistant, Davies. Behind (left) is Pilkington the cashier's assistant and an unknown.*

force and meant that any vehicle moving over four miles per hour had to be preceded by a man holding a red flag, which effectively kept motor cars off British roads.

As Motor Mills was not yet ready, Bollée's vehicle was taken to the Humber cycle factory in Lower Ford Street. The workers were dismayed to find that Bollée had supplied metric plans, so new ones had to be made. They had just been finished in July when Lawson, in London, received a telegraph: 'Works burnt down. Bollée machine and drawings lost.' Lawson caught the first train up and personally searched the smouldering building, but all that remained were a few gears, nuts and bits of car which had plummeted through the burning floors. He sent to Bollée for replacement plans and the Humber works was temporarily based at Motor Mills.

The first British-built Bollée was constructed in the 'Motette' Works behind Spon Street.[23] Boulée himself came to Coventry to drive the vehicle from the factory, only to find it wouldn't start. It was suggested that his special petrol may be at fault and benzene was tried. The engine burst into life and the party drove the machine to Leamington.

After the abolition of the Red Flag Act in 1896 production work began on the first motor vehicles legally allowed on Britain's highways. History is generally vague about the origins of the industry but in the summer of 1897 Major General Montgomery of Winchester ordered a Daimler car and is therefore said to be the first owner of a British-built motor car. Montgomery's car was used by Henry Sturmey in a proving run from Land's End to John O'Groats. That car wasn't finished till late summer and the run finally took place in October 1897. But the Great Horseless Carriage Company had built many vehicles before Daimler's first car left the factory. Francis Baron, the works manager, wrote of his experiences with early traction engines and motor cars in 1944: 'Those experiences were of the greatest value to me in designing and building the first Light Locomotives called Motor Cars.' Baron says he was involved in the production of Bollée tri-cars, which were leaving the factory in 1896, around the same time that Daimler were building their first engines.

The obituary of W.J. Maude in 1926 noted that, 'Mr. Maude was most probably the first private owner of a motor vehicle in Coventry, and amongst the half dozen in Warwickshire, having purchased a Bollée from the Great Horseless Carriage Company in 1896.'[24] In a letter in the *Midland Daily Telegraph* dated 8 February 1946, W.S. Taylor of Coventry wrote, 'I know that the Great Horseless Carriage Company got off the mark before the Daimler and I well remember seeing Mr. George Iden, the manager, trying out their first car in the drive in front of the main building.' And in 1928 Francis Baron wrote,

> In 1897 at the Motor Mills, Coventry, I built the first 'petrol' motor cars in England for the Great Horseless Carriage Company Limited. I supplied one to Lord Iveagh for the use of King George (then the Duke of York). In that year, Mr Oliver Stanton, then cycle instructor to the Prince of Wales (later Edward VII), was sent from Sandringham to Coventry to investigate the use of cars by other members of the Royal Family.[25]

Baron says that the vehicle supplied to the Duke of York was completed in May to June 1897 and was photographed with him at its tiller in July before delivery, at least a month or two before the completion of the first Daimler motor car. The vehicle was later renamed 'Iveagh Phaeton' and Baron said that 'several hundred cars were made from that car'. Baron wrote in *Autocar* in 1935 that the car 'was one of the first dozen built by me, as works manager... . I contend that the car I have mentioned, which worked continuously without the slightest hitch, being the first petrol car built in England, contributed as much to the present motor industry as George Stephenson's first locomotive to railway development.'

The G.H.C.C. became the Motor Manufacturing Company in the spring of 1898 and continued producing cars, as did Daimler. Francis Baron died in 1947 and was remembered as 'a charming host, a grand man, with individual ideas and a wonderfully accurate memory'. The M.M.C. moved to Parkside in 1905 and Daimler took over the whole Motor Mills site. From these early beginnings the British motor industry was born, although of the original companies only

Daimler's name survives. Harry Lawson over-reached himself and squandered hundreds of thousands in his financial dealings. As English engineers refused to copy foreign designs, his many patents were useless and lawsuits were taken out against him. In 1904 he was found guilty of fraud and sentenced to one year's hard labour. He died in 1925 with less than £10 to his name. The motor industry went from strength to strength as the city's many cycle firms, such as Humber, Swift and Singer, converted to car production.

EDUCATION

Despite charity and private schools, much of the population at large remained illiterate in the early 19th century. The Grammar School in Bishop Street remained in the old Hospital of St John until 1885, when it moved to Warwick Road. Bablake became a higher elementary school in 1887 and moved to larger premises at Coundon in 1900. For most of the 19th century the charity schools continued as before. The Blue Coat School for Girls was rebuilt on its original site in 1856, unearthing the west entrance of Coventry's great medieval cathedral. The girls received a three-year education, one year of which was spent boarding at the school, and learnt the '3 Rs' and the fine art of housekeeping.

The first Sunday School was set up in 1799 in a timbered house in Hill Street. Then, in 1811, the National Society was founded, which promoted the education of the poor in the elements of the established church and the '3 Rs'. It opened its first National School for Boys and Girls in Little Park Street in 1813.[26] Within a few years this had become overcrowded and a new school, the Central National School, was opened in Greyfriars churchyard in 1826. It held 480 boys and girls and was built like an old market house, the classrooms standing on arches above the playground. The British and Foreign Schools Society was officially started in 1814, although it had already established a school in St John's Bridges (Burges) in 1811. These schools were non-denominational and were known as British or Lancastrian schools. They relied on grants, subscriptions and fees.

The early 19th century was the heyday of the church schools, run on grants from the National Society and often founded by local vicars and squires; most of the villages that now make up the district of Coventry acquired a village school at this time. Walsgrave Church of England School in Schoolhouse Lane opened for the education of village children in 1837 at the instigation of local vicar the Rev. Frederick Perkins, the Earl of Craven of Coombe Abbey, William Wale Brown of Walsgrave Hall and Lord Willoughby de Broke, lord of the manor. The school was supported by grants from the National Society, voluntary contributions and payments from parents according to their means. Another school opened in Allesley in 1705 is claimed to be the earliest church school in the city, and its founder Martha Flint stipulated that it should teach poor children the doctrine of the Church of England, including the Catechism and the principles of Christianity.

159   *The schoolyard of Bablake with Bonds Hospital (left).*

Thomas Street Infant School was built in the garden of industrialist Joseph Cash, who would later create an infants school in his Kingfield factory. There were also 75 dame or private schools in the city, one of which was attended by Mary Ann Evans, who would later become novelist George Eliot. She was one of a number of girls who attended the private school of the Franklin sisters based at different periods in Warwick Row and in Little Park Street. In 1847 it was said there were still 4,000 children in Coventry receiving no education at all, while those who did attended only sporadically, and the 'Ragged School' movement to educate the very poorest was established. The first such school was opened in 1847, and by 1875 three more had opened in St Nicholas Place, Spon End and the old ribbon factory in New Buildings. The teachers were volunteers and classes were originally held on Sunday evenings and, later, on weekdays.

In 1833 the government made its first grant towards educational provision, which encouraged the building of St John's School (1839), St Peter's School (1844), St Michael's School (1853) and Holy Trinity School (1854), later regarded as the largest parish school in the county. Built at the junction of Ford and Hales Streets with grants from the state and the National Society, it accommodated 863 children.[27] In 1855 a new school built in Early English style was opened in Much Park Street.

160   *Band of the Bayley's Blue Gift Charity School with W.G. Fretton, master, on right.*

Following the Education Act of 1870, school boards were set up in the city. Their first schools were in the Ragged School's premises in St Nicholas Place, Spon End and Bishop Street. Spon School, accommodating 766 children, was opened in 1873, and South Street School in 1874.[28] In 1880 elementary education became compulsory and by 1891 it was free. A showcase board school opened in Wheatley Street in 1893 and Red Lane in 1895. Edgewick School opened in 1876 and Foxford in 1877.

It is said that when William George Fretton, last master of Katherine Bayley's Charity, suggested that his children should also be taught history and geography, the chairman of the trustees said, 'Gentlemen, You cannot do it. The will expressly states that these children are to be taught reading, writing, ciphering, the Church catechism, together with sound moral and religious conduct, and no damned nonsense besides.'[29] It wasn't until the last quarter of the century that church schools dared deviate from the basic doctrines of the National Society.

ENTERTAINMENT

The Godiva Procession had grown in importance since its inception in the 17th century. The event was attached to Coventry Fair, which lasted eight days and attracted visitors from miles around. In 1824 it was described thus:

> At eleven o'clock, the Mayor, Magistrates, and Charter Officers, attended divine service … At half past 12, the Procession moved forward, and having passed through all the principal streets, terminated at 4 o'clock … The fair Godiva was never personified by a female who looked more lovely … St. George, in black, and a Knight in polished steel armour, added dignity to the scene … The Cavalcade was of unusual extent, owing to the increased number of followers introduced by the Societies, there were upwards of 70 children … We are sorry to learn that the diving fraternity [pick-pockets] were too successful in their depredations.[30]

The original procession had the mayor and entire corporation following Godiva in full civic regalia, but this ceased with the Municipal Act of 1835. The new council's efforts to dissociate themselves from the corrupt practices of the corporation even extended to changing the day for proclaiming the fair from Friday to Monday. The council's place was taken by historical characters associated with the city, plus others such as Robin Hood and Little John. It also included fraternities and societies and a shepherd and shepherdess in a magnificent carriage always described as a 'Sylvan Car'.

A description of Fair Day from 1839 includes, 'The Railway trains, one after another, poured in company by thousands; while from the surrounding bye-roads, vehicles of every description, from the very first rate equipages, down to the dog-cart and donkey, contributed their respective loads to swell the multitude.'[31] The procession of 1842 was probably the first which encouraged the notion that Godiva would ride naked. She actually wore a body stocking, but caused such a sensation that fights broke out amongst those trying to get a better view. In 1844 thousands packed the city after hearing of the previous procession.

By 1845 many had turned against the procession. At a meeting in St Mary's Hall the mayor, William Clark, promised to put down the event, 'which has for too long disgraced our city'. He read out various memorials, one of which was signed by all the main church leaders in the city and stated,

> Sir, We the undersigned Clergy of the City of Coventry, have heard with much regret that it is proposed, during the approaching Fair, to get up a procession similar in character to those by which the streets of this City were disgraced in 1842 and 1844.
> It is not necessary for us to refer particularly to the circumstances which make such an exhibition a disgrace to the moral character of the City, and a direct insult to the Christian feelings of a large portion of the community … we respectfully request you, as the Chief Magistrate, to interpose your authority in the matter.[32]

The bishop of the diocese was even more blunt:

> My attention has been called to a custom which I am told prevails at Coventry every third year, and which is so offensive to every right feeling, that I could not have believed it to have been permitted in a civilised and Christian country … It is stated to me, that every third year a common prostitute is hired at Birmingham, for the purpose of being paraded through the streets of Coventry, as a representative of Queen Godiva; that the said prostitute is dressed in a tight fitting dress of flesh colour, so as to give her the appearance of being naked, and is of course followed by a mob of the lowest rabble in Coventry.[33]

He goes on to say that, if this is the case, the magistrates of Coventry should put an end to the procession. William Clark replies, 'I quite agree with your Lordship, that the Procession tends to promote great immorality, and should be prevented if possible.'

Yet, despite the mayor and Church, the procession of 1845 did go ahead. Godiva dressed in Mr Bird's in Earl Street and wore over her flesh-coloured dress 'a tunic of white satin' and a 'girdle of the same kind', scarves thrown over her shoulders, sleeves, a mantle, and an ostrich-feather-plumed headdress. It is said that as she entered St Mary's Hall and was checked by a clergyman, the lady, a music hall artist from London, said amid laughter, 'Why, bless you man, I've never had so many clothes on in my life.'[34] From 1862 onwards the procession took place less often, never again reaching its riotous peak of the early 1840s.

The re-introduction of Coventry Races at Stoke took place in 1834. By March it was reported that, 'Stoke Races may now be considered fairly established as a festival of the sporting calendar … During the morning visitors of all classes were arriving in great numbers … supposed to amount to 10,000 including many distinguished personages and gentry of the county and sporting characters of celebrity.'[35] The one-mile circuit was slightly shorter than the old course in the Park but it did attract some quality horses, and one of the races, the Craven Trial Stakes, was a qualifying race for the Derby. In 1849 the races moved again to Radford around the Conduit Meadow/Crampers Field area. They consisted entirely of steeplechases until a new one-mile circuit, considered one of the best in the land, was completed on 4 March 1852. The races were discontinued for a time and then revived in October 1874 despite protests from those who regarded them as a social problem. But supporters among the local gentry included Lord Craven, the Earl of Aylesford and Lord Maidstone. The races included the Godiva Plate and the Craven Stakes. Fred Archer, who rode to victory on 'Anina' in the Packington Nursery Plate and on the following day rode three winners, was one of the greatest jockeys of all time. Racing was ended at Radford in the 1880s after a clampdown by the Jockey Club on smaller courses.

Another sport which attracted race-goers was prize-fighting, or 'Fistiana', which had been popular since the late 18th century. In the 1820s a fight between

161 *Horse-racing in 1845.* (Illustrated London News)

Townsend and Browning at Coundon was watched by 8,000, including 500 horsemen. The fight lasted for three hours and 57 minutes and was declared a draw. Among the most notable prize-fighters in the city were Bob Randle, who kept the *Woolpack Inn*, John 'Fatty' Adrian, another innkeeper, 'Game'un' Shilton, 'Ginger' Berry and William Heap, all ribbon weavers, and others such as 'Whopper' Flint and the 'Chicken Killer'. Coventry's most famed fighter was William 'Paddy' Gill. Gill fought and won his first match on Radford Common in 1838. He consistently won his local fights before being matched with national competition. On 22 June 1845 he fought Londoner Young Reed the 'Invincible' for £100 aside. After 59 rounds Gill was returned the victor. His stamina was extraordinary. Once he walked over twenty miles then fought for over three hours and won.

Gill had a second encounter with a fighter called Norley in 1846, for a huge purse of £500, and after a battle which lasted over four hours he was again victorious. He then beat Tom Maley of London for £400. The *Coventry Standard* of 1851, however, noted that, 'William Gill of Coventry, alias "Paddy Gill", was tried at these assizes a few days since, charged with the manslaughter of Thomas Griffiths, in a prize-fight, at Frimley Green, of the 23rd of last July. The witnesses were unable to identify the prisoner, and the jury returned a verdict of not guilty.'[36] It is likely that no one present would testify against Gill, Coventry's nationally acclaimed fighter, but the pugilist appears to have been affected by this fatality and probably lost his spirit. His next fight was against McNulty at Woolwich, and he lost. He withdrew from the ring, settled into family life, and used some of his earnings to buy the *Lamp Tavern* in Market Street. A few years later he was declared insane and placed in Hatton Asylum, where he died aged 50 in 1889.

Theatrical entertainment was on offer in venues ranging from a dilapidated tithe barn on Gosford Green, home to plays such as *Maria Martin, or Murder in the Red Barn*, to St Mary's Hall and the Drapers Hall, both in Bayley Lane. In 1818 a theatre was opened by Sir Skears Rew in Smithford Street. St Mary's had multiple uses at this time, as a courtroom, lecture theatre, public meeting place, concert, exhibition and dance hall. In 1814 it is recorded that Elliston's Company, which played the hall for six months, adapted the building, painting the boxes with beautiful decorations and hanging glass chandeliers.

> Every attention has been paid to the comfort of the audience by the application of covers to the seats and cushions around the boxes decorated with brass nails, and the *tout ensemble* certainly furnishes as elegant an appearance as any theatre, temporary or otherwise, can boast in the kingdom. The scenery, dresses, and decorations on the stage are all new and complete of their kind.[37]

Elliston's Company performed a variety of shows including the tragedy *Jane Shore*, the musical farce *Turn Out*, the comedy *The Students of Salamanca* and, at Christmas, *Cinderella*. The Opera House was built in Hales Street in 1889. Smaller venues combined drinking with entertainments such as Britannia Music Hall and the Sydenham Palace. The latter was occupied for one week by the 'Tichborne Claimant', Arthur Orton, who talked to packed audiences about his claim to be Sir Roger Tichborne, heir to the Tichborne estate. The real Sir Roger's predecessor had attended the Roman Catholic school in Radford (the *Radford Hotel*) and married Miss Petre of Whitley Abbey at St Osburg's Church. The case enthralled the nation until Orton finally admitted that he was an impostor and was imprisoned.

Another favourite of the later 19th century was the public lecture, which was held mainly in St Mary's Hall and the Corn Exchange in Hertford Street. Charles Dickens read his *Christmas Carol* in the Exchange on 15 December 1857 to raise funds for the Coventry Institute. One of many who lectured at St Mary's was William Makepeace Thackeray, who gave a talk on the 'English Humorist'. The 'Life of George Eliot' by George William Cross records that Mary Ann Evans attended the first lecture of the Temperance League in the Hall and had to be talked out of signing the pledge. The Hall itself found its way into Eliot's *Adam Bede*, where it became the venue of the trail of Hetty Sorrel. Coventry was the novelist's home for a number of years and the place where she was encouraged to become a writer, and she immortalised the city in *Middlemarch*.

162 *Mary Ann Evans,* alias *George Eliot, in 1864.*

'Wombwell's Menagerie' often came to the city in the week of the Great Fair. It was the greatest menagerie in the land, with many exotics including elephant, hippo, giraffe and the now extinct Quagga. Amongst the lions was the famous Nero, the 'Great Lion which is matched to fight six bull or mastiff dogs for the sum of five thousand sovereigns'.[38] When the keeper of the menagerie retired he became landlord of the liquor vaults in Earl Street. William Wombwell, the owner's nephew, was buried in Coventry's London Road cemetery after he was accidentally crushed and killed by an elephant during one visit.

CRIME AND PUNISHMENT

In 1800 Coventry Gaol was visited by a Mr Nield, who described it thus:

The city gaol accommodated both debtors and felons, and the gaoler was paid £120 a year, but he received much less as a matter of fact, as he had to defray the cost of the removal of convicts! The city provided straw for poor debtors (changed every three weeks), a blanket and a rug, for which the unfortunate people had to pay 6d. a week. Felons were in a way better off, as they had, besides straw, two blankets and two rugs each. On the other hand, they had to sleep in noisome dungeons twelve steps below ground, lighted by a window 11 in. by 7 in., and so foul that every other day torches with kettles of pitch and tar were burnt; while the sleeping places of the debtors were fumigated with vinegar. Well might the visitor declare the dungeons were a disgrace to this large manufacturing city.[39]

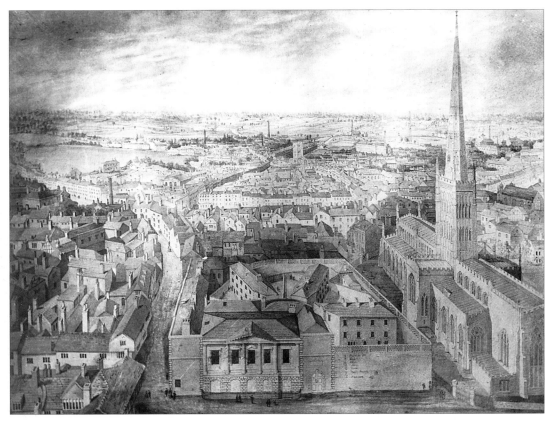

163   *View of Coventry looking north-west, c.1838. In the foreground stands the gaol.*

But this could have been said of almost every prison in the country.

The *Coventry Herald* reported in 1829 that, 'On Saturday last a jury was empanelled at the Grand Jury Room, County Hall to assess the compensation to be paid to the Trustees of the Bablake Boy's Charity in this city for their interest as proprietors of the house and premises occupied by Mrs Baker, adjoining the County Hall, which is required for the purpose of enlarging the gaol.'[40] Only the month before 13 inmates had tried to escape by making a hole in the wall of their cell, then using iron bars to hammer a way through the exterior gaol wall. The new prison, completed in 1831, took in Pepper Lane (the old Gaol Lane), Cuckoo, Derby Lane and the side of Trinity and was surrounded by a huge spiked wall. It consisted of 86 tiny cells, nine exercise yards and eight day rooms. The treadmill could be walked by up to 12 male prisoners and adapted to grind barley and beans, and when worked by five prisoners it produced six bushels a day. The men worked twenty minutes on and ten minutes off and the labour was considered most beneficial. The new prison also took on the role of the old Bridewell, a long and narrow prison for petty offenders which had stood behind St John's Church since 1571.

Overseeing it was the Prison Governor, whose house formed the corner of the gaol, with two turnkeys, a matron, a chaplain, who had his own chapel within the gaol, a surgeon and a number of guards. In 1848 another escape attempt was made when prisoners acquired a saw, two files and three skeleton keys, which had been thrown from the churchyard of Holy Trinity into number two yard. A massive overhanging curved iron railing was built to prevent a repetition and bells were installed throughout the prison to raise the alarm.

As for food and sleeping arrangements, convicted criminal George Parker from London complained to the Secretary of State, saying, 'The gruel we have at night and at morning is just like water and not thicker, and besides it is quite musty … The scale of the diet at Warwick is the model diet as certified to be enforced by the late Secretary of State, and it is not the same at Coventry.' He also complained about the bedding, saying it 'was very different to the kind given to the prisoners in London'.[41] The Secretary of State ordered an investigation and a visiting magistrate reported that, 'Thomas Saunders, one of the prisoners, makes the gruel under the superintendence of George Mann, the principal turnkey, and twice a day puts seven pounds of oatmeal to nine gallons of water, which after being boiled for half an hour, fills three buckets, which serves 75 prisoners, at two pints each per day.' Parker complained that there was not enough meat in the stew, but the magistrate said it was 'not only too good, it was too rich'.

The last inspection of Coventry Gaol took place in 1858 when 43 men and eight women were interned. When Coventry lost its county status the main prisoners began to be transferred to Warwick, and when Warwick's new gaol opened in July 1860 all the remaining inmates went there. Coventry Gaol lay empty for some time, before it was put up for sale and finally demolished in May 1872.

Coventry's last public execution took place not on Whitley Common, as was usual, but in front of the gaol wall. Nuneaton housewife Mary Ball was hanged on 9 August 1849 for poisoning her husband. An eyewitness described the execution:

> The space in front of the gaol was packed so closely with people that you could have walked on their heads and every vantage point was occupied: the windows of all the houses, some roofs, the churchyard wall, even the windows of St. Michael's tower, the church roof and battlements. The crowd partially filled the churchyard and extended towards St. Mary's Hall, down the Avenue, Priory Row and along Hay Lane. Many stood in Bayley Lane and others along by the side of Holy Trinity Church, where they could not possibly see the execution, but where they were in touch with the crowd.[42]

Mary Ball had her elbows tied in the governor's office before she left through the Lodge Gate, then walked about 15 feet to the gallows, which stood against the gaol wall. She stood straight and silent as the hangman placed the noose around her neck and covered her head with a black hood. He descended the steps and, as St Michael's bell struck eleven, the trapdoor dropped and Mary fell, instantly breaking her neck. A local reporter wrote, 'a subdued thrill of horror

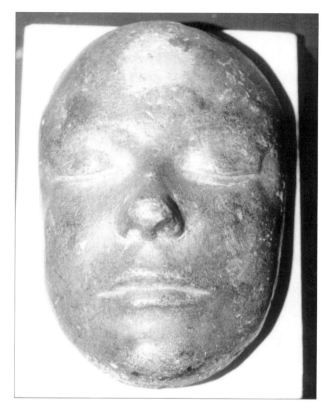

164   *The death mask of Mary Ball, the last person to be hanged in Coventry.*

appeared to pass over the multitude of sightseers'. An hour later the body was taken down and a plaster death mask made before it was buried ten feet below the treadmill yard, near the present replica of Coventry Cross. Executions would thereafter take place at Warwick.

Before 1836 the policing of the city was undertaken by paid watchmen, who for a small remuneration would patrol the city at night. These men were administered by the Street Commissioners under one styled 'Chief Constable'. Under the powers of the Corporation Act of 1835, a new 'Watch Committee' carried out a survey on policing at the time. It reported:

> several persons engaged in the Police and Watch under the late Corporation and the Street Commissioners and finds the Chief Constable the only person in the police responsible to give assistance in the apprehension of felons ... there being no paid constables ... They also find the establishment under the Street Commissioners to consist of eight watchmen receiving 12 shillings per week, a watch-house keeper receiving 20 shillings per week, an Inspector receiving 18 shillings and a superintendent receiving £40 per annum.[43]

The watchmen were on duty from Michaelmas to Lady Day, 10 p.m to 4 a.m., and through the rest of the year 11 p.m. to 3 a.m. The committee's report also mentioned the Watch House in the Market Square, known locally since the 18th century as the 'bog-house prison', because the stench in the building was so

165   *Youngsters pose in the stocks before the Watch House in the Market Square for Joseph Wingrave in the 1860s.*

great that few of the watchmen could bear to stay there. Despite this there were often up to twenty prisoners in the building.

Under the Act a revised police force came into being led by a Superintendent, with an Inspector in the refurbished Watch House, a sergeant, whose duty was to patrol and supervise during the whole of the night, and a number of watchmen working constantly in ten-hour shifts. The first Superintendent was ex-Bow Street Runner Thomas Henry Prosser. His men were ill-educated and between the ages of 22 and 35, and in the early days Prosser came across watchmen drunk on the beat or asleep. On 25 June 1836 he recorded one watchman's 'Improper conduct by violently springing his rattle at 11 o'clock last night without occasion and creating a disturbance in Broadgate'.

In March 1858 the first detective from the Liverpool force joined Coventry police and a letter was sent to the press asking,

> Can you enable a few anxious enquirers to detect whether the thieves who robbed several houses in this city last week and got away in broad daylight undetected have since been detected by the detectiveness of the Liverpool detective, who was thought to be so detectiveable as to be worth £91 a year ... Believing that some of our old officers at £1 a week, have shown greater detectivity, I think in justice to them and to the ratepayers, we ought not be saddled with an imported servant at 35s. per week.[44]

By 1899 Coventry Police had 68 officers.

Religion

In 1837 Coventry's ancient connection with the see of Lichfield came to an end. On 22 December 1836 the archdeaconry of Coventry, which comprised much of Warwickshire including Birmingham, became part of the diocese of Worcester.[45] Re-establishment of the original diocese was pursued from 1852, although it wasn't until the 1880s that anything happened. But the creation of a suffragan bishopric for the Rector of St Philip's in Birmingham, who took his title from Coventry, was to prove unsatisfactory to all. In 1902 Charles Gore became the Bishop of Worcester and allowed the post of suffragan bishop to lapse. Gore was followed by Bishop H.W. Yeatman-Biggs, who supported the return to a separate diocese for Coventry. In 1908 St Michael's was constituted a collegiate church and in 1918 Yeatman-Biggs was enthroned in what had become a cathedral.

The restoration of the church of St John the Baptist in Fleet Street was carried out between 1858 and 1861 by George Gilbert Scott, who refaced many of the light sandstone walls with local red sandstone. Scott carried out a second course of more extensive work between 1875 and 1877, when it is believed his usual excessively heavy restoration work was checked by the presence of historian William Fretton. Another church to receive attention was St Michael's, which underwent a major restoration between 1883 and 1890 that included the complete refacing of the tower, badly eroded and bearing the semblance of a cliff face.

The 19th century also saw the building of a number of new churches. The ancient tower of the old church of the Greyfriars had a new church added to it between 1830 and '32, and re-opened as a chapel of ease for St Michael called Christchurch. In 1841, as the population increased, St Paul's was built on the Foleshill Road and St Peter's in Canterbury Street. In 1849 St Thomas's was built in Albany Road to serve the growing watchmaking district between

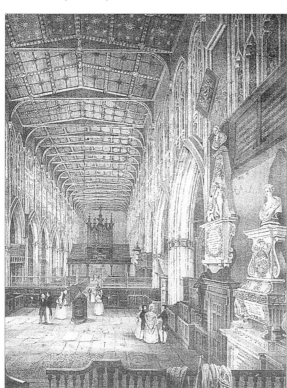

166 *Interior of St Michael's in 1841.*

167 *The choir and apse of St Michael with its Francis Skidmore lights and pulpit photographed in the 1860s.*

168 *Greyfriars was rebuilt as Christchurch in the 1830s (19th-century engraving).*

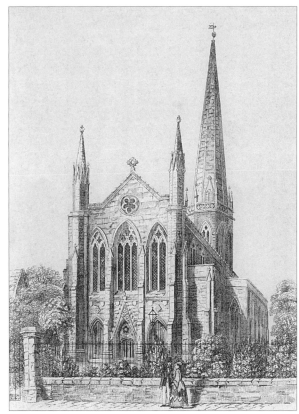

Spon Street and the Butts. The year 1869 saw the consecration of All Saints in Far Gosford Street and St Mark's in Bird Street. In 1874 St Nicholas's Church on the Radford Road was consecrated as a chapel of ease to Holy Trinity.[46] Out in the village of Keresley, St Thomas's was consecrated in 1847 to serve the industrial families of the larger houses in that area, such as the Cashes, Rotherhams, Waters and Singers. Another wealthy family, the Gregorys, demolished the medieval church of St James at Styvechale and built themselves a new one within the grounds of their estate. It was built by one mason and one labourer only and was completed in 1817. From the 1860s mission chapels were first set up by St Michael's: St Mark's in Red Lane, for example, was set up in 1894.

From the beginning of the 19th century the Catholic faith in the city was served by Franciscan father James Vincent Sharp. In 1803 the Benedictines re-established themselves in the city under Father John Dawber, and worshipped in a house in Little Park Street owned by a Miss Latham and known until its destruction in the war as the Mass House. Following Miss Latham's death Father Dawber opened a new red-brick chapel at the cost of £155 in Hill Street in December 1807. In 1843, under the guidance of Bernard (later Bishop) Ullathorne, the medieval-style Church of the Most Holy Sacrament and St Osburg was built in Hill Street. It was funded by monies raised by Ullathorne in Belgium and Germany. St Osburg's was consecrated on 21 June 1846[47] and quickly became one of the best attended Catholic churches in the county, with a congregation up to 1,000 in 1851.[48]

In 1808 the Wesleyans or Methodists built their first chapel at the bottom of Gosford Street. The first Coventry Circuit was formed in 1811 under Simon Day, and in 1835 the group, led by the Rev. Thomas Collins, purchased part of the old Whitefriars burial ground for £200. Money to build a new chapel was raised by the Rev. Thomas Stephenson who travelled by coach throughout the Midlands in his quest for funds. While it was under construction, the Wesleyans were allowed to conduct their services in St Mary's Hall, an arrangement made by the mayor, George Eld, in atonement for the civic insult offered the founder of the religion in 1779. On 11 August 1835 the Rev. Stephenson laid the foundation stone and on the opening day William Dawson preached to an 'overflowing congregation'. The building cost over £2,000 and left the congregation in debt for a number of years. The chapel was restored in 1899 under the Rev. Bell, and a school was built adjoining it, and from these beginnings Methodism spread throughout the city.

As mentioned in the previous chapter, the 'Particular' Baptists had built their chapel in Cow Lane in 1793. In 1798 the Rev. Francis Franklin arrived to assist the ageing Rev. Butterworth. Franklin walked from town to town and village to village to raise the money with which he finally paid off the debt of construction. Apart from his fame as a good minister, Franklin was immortalised by his daughter's pupil, George Eliot, as Rufus Lyon in the novel *Felix Holt*. After many years of service the Rev. Francis Franklin died in 1852 and was laid to rest in

169 *St Osburg's Catholic Church in Hill Street.*

London Road cemetery before a huge crowd. His death caused a split in the congregation, and in 1856 cottages on the corner of Hay and Bayley Lane were purchased and demolished and in February 1858 the new St Michael's Baptist Church was opened on the site. The church suffered in the early years because the costs of building were not cleared for many years, but Cow Lane prospered and in the summer of 1882 began to build a new church on the Bull Fields. The dedication of Queen's Road Baptist Church took place on 1 May 1884 and the old chapel was converted to a lecture hall and classrooms which became known as Cow Lane School.

The Barton Society introduced the Salem Baptists' church into the Exhall district before 1760. Despite opposition, they later established a chapel in Longford called the Salem General Baptist Chapel. In 1835 the Rev. Jabez Tunicliffe became minister of the church and about two years later two more churches were opened in Walsgrave and Bedworth. When Tunicliffe first preached in Walsgrave a 'ruffian' was hired to throw him down a well but, being too drunk he failed to fulfil his contract. The baptisms themselves took place in the nearby canal, often in the face of ridicule and violence. It wasn't until 1865 that a baptistery was built in the chapel yard at the Salem Chapel.

The Presbyterians and Unitarians originally met at the Leather Hall in the 17th century, but in 1701 they opened a new meeting house called the Great Meeting in Smithford Street. The first split occurred in 1724 and those who left joined the Independent Vicar Lane chapel. The church suffered constantly from lack of finance but when its most noted minister, George Heavyside, proposed to drop collections and charge pew rent he was overruled and his salary was reduced.[49]

The Congregationalists occupied a new meeting house in Vicar Lane in 1724. Its later proximity to the Barracks would lead to complaints, especially if the military band struck up during worship. There appears to have been some co-operation with the Great Meeting House, but when the latter began to acquire Unitarian beliefs a split occurred, following which some Meeting House worshippers transferred to Vicar Lane. The 1776 schism led to the founding of another church in West Orchard and a decline in the Vicar Lane congregation, which was halted with the arrival of John Eagleton in 1812, who brought with him views and followers of the Calvinistic persuasion. Eagleton was succeeded by the church's most famous pastor, John Sibree, who became one of Coventry's most notable characters of the century. The West Orchard Congregational Church was led until 1803 by George Burder, who was behind the foundation of Coventry's Sunday Schools. Both Sibree and Burder were known for their missionary work around the county. Burder's successor was John Jerard, who led the church for 48 years.[50] During his ministry a new church was opened in West Orchard in 1820 which accommodated nearly 1,200 souls. After restoration in 1855 the chapel was considered the best nonconformist house in the city and it stood till its destruction in the war. In 1891 the new Congregational church was opened in Warwick Road, replacing the chapel in Vicar Lane.

There is practically no record of where Jewish worship was carried on and in the 19th century a synagogue was recorded in the rear of a house belonging to a Mr Cohen in Butcher Row. After this the synagogue moved a short distance to the Trinity churchyard/Derby Lane area, before moving first to Fleet Street and then to an upper room in Court 16, Spon Street. Some of the congregation didn't move from here until the erection of a synagogue in Barras Lane in 1870.[51] The first minute book kept by the Coventry Hebrew Congregation records, 'At a meeting held on the 20th day of September, 1868, Mr. P Cohen was in the Chair. He also contributed £50 towards the Burial Ground, which had become a matter of urgent necessity owing to the considerable inconvenience and expense involved in burying their dead in Birmingham.'[52]

The Spiritualists began to hold séances in the city from 1849.[53] In 1880 the church was said to be established in Foleshill and in 1907 the Foleshill Spiritualist Church opened in Broad Street.

Eight

Coventry in the Twentieth Century

Housing, Health and Public Services

When Dan Claridge, owner of the *Craven Arms* and last man to drive a coach from Coventry to London, was interviewed in around 1916, he told the reporter that ten or fifteen years earlier he could not walk the street without being greeted with smiles and cries of, 'Good morning Mr Claridge.' But today, he said, 'It's a matter of surprise if I meet one person who knows me.' He continued, 'It's gone sir, the old Coventry spirit; its dead; it don't exist anymore; the day when we all knew each other, like a happy family, that day is past; and today, why sir, Coventry is a city of foreigners. It's the influx that did it, sir. Fifteen years ago the influx began, and its been keeping on ever since — Scotch, Irish, Welsh, and God knows what else — all foreigners. I think it's a pity.'[1]

170 *The opening of Coventry Fire Station in 1902.*

Claridge was right. The influx of 'foreigners' from all parts of Britain, including my own great-grandfather, was changing the old city. Coventry's burgeoning industries drew people from all around. When Claridge had set off on the last coach for London in 1874 the population was around 40,000. In 1901 it was 69,978, and it had risen by 1911 to 106,377. By 1935 the figure reached 184,900, and continued to grow apace.[2] In 1966 the population peaked at 335,238 but by 1971 this had dropped with the decline of the motor industry to 310,216. By 1991 the population had fallen to 294,387, but with the present increase in employment opportunities it has grown again to around 302,000.

It is believed that the first West Indian to move to Coventry was Charles Hall, who came from Newcastle to work at the Daimler factory in 1905.[3] His sons run a very successful building business and are also major landowners in the growing Walsgrave district. During the Second World War 1,000 Indians came as war workers and some remained, but the largest overseas immigration was during the 1960s and '70s, when many more from India, Pakistan and Bangladesh settled in the city, initially basing themselves in the Foleshill area. In recent years the city has also become home to a number of international refugees.

Between 1900 and 1908 nearly six thousand houses were built in Coventry by private builders. The council felt no responsibility to provide housing, but reports of four-roomed houses containing twenty people were not uncommon and a housing committee was set up in 1907. In the following year the council began to construct their first houses in Narrow Lane (later called Kingfield Road) and flats in Short Street.[4] These houses, described at the time as being six-roomed, comprised a large sitting room, kitchen, scullery and three bedrooms. They were built at a cost of £200 and rented at 5s. 6d. a week. The Kingfield Road estate consisted of 184 houses with four shops and was completed in 1914. In 1914 and 1915 houses were constructed in Hastings Road, Goring Road, St George's Road and Severn Road.

In 1916 the Ministry of Munitions built more than 800 houses on the Stoke Heath estate. The houses were purchased by the council with government help since they were intended to house war workers based mainly at the Red Lane factory, which produced naval guns and other ordnance. During the war temporary accommodation for war workers was built by private firms, such as Munition Cottages in Holbrook Lane. Most of these were later acquired by the council and were still occupied in the 1930s.

The next major municipal building phase occurred in 1925 with the creation of the Radford Housing Estate on what had previously been Lammas and Michaelmas lands.[5] These had been purchased for £45,000 and the council sold some parts to private builders, bringing in £86,000.[6] By May 1930, 1,664 houses had been built on the estate. In 1926 the council purchased part of the Stoneleigh estate from Lord Leigh, which included the spinneys that line the beautiful Kenilworth Road and a cottage in Canley, the birthplace of Sir Henry Parkes,

Premier of New South Wales and pioneer of the Australian Federation. The estate began to be built upon in 1928, but the character of Styvechale hamlet itself was retained. The Styvechale Hall estate would later come into council hands and be entirely built upon, as would a large part of semi-rural Coventry.

In 1928 the city boundary was extended from 4,147 to 12,878 acres, and in 1932 increased to 19,167 acres. In that same year the Hen Lane Housing Estate reached completion, followed by the Cheylesmore Housing Estate and the Hill Farm estate in Radford. In 1935 houses began to be built on the Coundon and Henley Road estates and a number of better quality houses were erected without government subsidy on the Radford Aerodrome estate. In 1937 work began on the Barras Heath estate. By 1945 nearly 20,000 houses had been built mainly around the city districts, including Tile Hill and Bell Green.

House building stopped during the Second World War, when a large percentage of the city's housing stock was destroyed. Houses were either demolished or patched up using salvaged material. To deal with the homelessness caused by the bombing in 1944, Coventry's architect Donald Gibson worked on various ideas for experimental pre-fabricated houses and the 'Coventry Experimental House' was the result, a steel-framed building to which pre-cast blocks could be fitted that was erected in a day.[7] Examples were built after the war in Tile Hill and Canley and most still stand. Other houses of this period are the single-storeyed pre-fabs in Coundon, which are now listed buildings.

Municipal building work continued in the city during the 1950s, '60s and '70s, much of the recent work consisting wholly of private housing, the latest being the huge Daimler Green estate on the site of the old Daimler factory in Radford.

In the *Coventry Guide* of 1937, a 'provincial newspaper' is quoted as saying, 'By common consent, Birmingham had yesterday one of the most beautiful days of the early part of the years within living memory. But in Coventry the dust free atmosphere, for which the city of spires is justly famed, gave the day the tone of a Southern clime in early summer.' The city was justly proud of the fact that its air was unpolluted, most of the factories working on gas or electricity.

Around the turn of the century, as the use of privies decreased and the number of water closets increased, Baginton Sewage Farm was constructed. By 1915 the farm was failing to cope and a new scheme using the Bacteria Bed System was adopted which was capable of treating two million gallons of sewage a day. In 1925 an Activated Sludge Plant dealing with a million gallons a day was added. The Finham Sewage Works was opened in 1932. The Victorian Whitley works and those created at this time still serve the city in 2003.

In 1909 it was noted that because of 'satisfactory sanitation … Coventry now is one of the healthiest of British cities'. The death rate in 1884 was 18.5 per 1,000, but in 1907 it had dropped to 14.8 per 1,000 compared with an average of 15.4 in 76 other towns. By 1933 it had dropped again to 9.9. Infant mortality in 1907 was also low for the time, 104 out of every 1,000 compared with 127 per 1,000 elsewhere.[8] To control the spread of smallpox and scarlet fever, isolation hospitals were opened first by the Coventry and Warwickshire Hospital and later at Pinley and Whitley. Whitley opened in 1934 at a cost of £113,500 and contained 148 beds. Seventy-five people had died from scarlet fever in 1874 but with the introduction of isolation hospitals this number dropped to zero. In 1930 the council acquired the old workhouse infirmary at Gulson Road, which was expanded in 1937. At the same time Allesley Hall was acquired as a convalescent home, joining Keresley Hall which had opened the previous year. At a Public Health Committee meeting held in 1938 Lee Gordon informed those present, 'Coventry is the healthiest place in the world'. Among the city's estimated population of 226,000 there was very little sickness, few maternal deaths and deaths of children under one, and an increase in lifespan. He also noted that the isolation hospital at Whitley was more often than not two-thirds empty.[9]

The war was to change things in various ways. The main hospitals suffered bomb damage and casualties amongst the staff. There was a sharp rise in tuberculosis and other diseases for which mass vaccination had to take place. It is said people ate more healthily, but after the war the increased eating out, in British Restaurants and in factory and school canteens, led to a dramatic rise in food poisoning. This was dealt with by providing hygiene courses and the use of more food inspectors.

The early post-war years were a strain on the hospital system, with damaged buildings, staff and bed shortages, and a massive increase in the birth rate as men returned home. The National Health Service Act was passed in 1946 and came into effect in 1948, offering free medical, dental and hospital services. It resulted in the birth in Coventry of a single integrated service in 1953. In the years that followed hospitals and convalescent homes have come and gone. In 1953 talks were held on building a hospital in the grounds of Walsgrave Hall, which had recently left the hands of the Wakefield family. In 1955, 47 acres were allocated for the building but work did not begin until 1963. Walsgrave is now set to become a 'super-hospital' and the future of the old Coventry and Warwickshire Hospital is uncertain.

The expanding population meant that Coventry's schools were sometimes overcrowded, including the ancient foundations of Bablake and King Henry VIII. This was remedied by the expansion of existing schools and the creation of new ones, although some of the Victorian schools closed, including Trinity Schools, St Peters and St Michaels, and expenditure per child was recorded as being below the national average. In 1931 the new Barker Butts and Radford Schools were reported to be overcrowded. In 1908 Barrs Hill Girls Secondary School was opened in the former residence of cycle inventor and manufacturer, John Kemp Starley. In 1919 some of the school's pupils moved to the new secondary school

171   *Girls on the lawn of Barrs Hill Girls School around 1905.*

in a Victorian mansion in Harefield Road, Stoke. The original house was superseded by a new building in the late 1940s. Barrs Hill also trained girls to become teachers. Entry was by oral and written examination or for a fee of £5 a year. Thirteen-year-old girls gained admission by passing an oral exam. They were placed in the Lower Fourth and trained as teachers, so when they reached the fifth form they were spending only one day a week at Barrs Hill and the other four days teaching in city schools.[10] Barrs Hill Secondary School became Barrs Hill Comprehensive and Community College in 1975, and for the first time boys and girls were admitted because they lived in the school's catchment area and not because of academic achievement. Another girls school, Coundon Court, set up in the home of industrialist George Singer, followed the same path as Barrs Hill. More comprehensive schools were built, including Woodlands, Woodway Park and President Kennedy.

The School of Art, established in 1844, was in Ford Street and the Technical College in Earl Street. Other training establishments that opened around the city included Henley, Bell Green and Tile Hill colleges. In the city centre the Lanchester College of Technology opened in 1960. It expanded in the 1960s to include the College of Art. It was renamed the Coventry Polytechnic in 1970

172   *Looking up Broadgate in 1929.*

and, more recently, Coventry University. The oddly named Warwick University in Coventry's Canley/Westwood Heath area, which was opened in 1965 and presently holds nearly 16,000 students, has grown to become one of the top universities in the land.

Public transport in Coventry began in 1884 with the introduction of steam-powered trams, which ran from Foleshill Depot to the city centre. The system was taken over by Coventry Electric Tramways Limited, electrified and reopened on 5 December 1895, running from the railway station to Foleshill. A week after its opening the line was extended to Bedworth. In the following years the trackway was extended into all districts of the city, and in 1912 the corporation acquired the system. In 1914 the corporation introduced six Maudsley open-topped buses onto the city streets, which were followed in 1923 with the first double-decker bus. The intention was to replace the entire tram system with buses, and in 1932 the Broadgate to Allesley Road tram was the first to go. More and more tram routes were taken over by buses in their maroon and cream livery. But it was the bombing of 14 November 1940 which brought a premature halt to Coventry's tram system, which was so badly damaged in one night that it was decided to abandon it altogether. Three surviving routes were formally abandoned in February 1941.[11]

INDUSTRY

Coventry's 19th-century industries survived in the main into the 20th century, although weaving only continued on a smaller scale at places like Stevens in Priory Street, Leigh Mills in Hill Street and Cash's, who began to supply the world with nametags. Courtaulds developed and produced the first man-made fibres, such as Rayon, which became one of the most common fibres of the 20th century. These industries employed some 10,000 people in 1936.

Famous names such as Swift, Rover, Singer and Rudge continued production of cycles into the 20th century alongside cars. The Coventry Cross Cycle Co. in West Orchard and the Foleshill Road was one of the last to disappear. The Premier Cycle Company, which sold over 20,000 cycles a year, was so successful it opened a second factory in Nuremberg to handle its continental business.[12] The Triumph Cycle Company, originally based in Little Park Street, expanded and opened a new works in Priory Street. Throughout its time as a cycle manufacturer, Coventry was home to a remarkable 269 different companies. The last of these was the Coventry Eagle Cycle Company, which after limited revivals finally ceased to exist at the end of the 20th century.

173 *Broadgate and High Street, rush hour 1926.*

In 1936 the main motor car producers in the city were Alvis, Armstrong-Siddeley, B.S.A., Daimler, Hillman, Humber, Lancaster, Riley, Rover, Singer, Standard and Triumph. All except Alvis and Daimler began life as cycle manufacturers. It is said that within a decade of the birth of the motor car in Coventry, 10,000 people were employed in the industry; by 1938 this had risen to 38,000 and by 1972 to over 60,000.[13] In 1928 the Rootes brothers acquired Humber and Hillman and built an economy car at their Stoke plant called the Minx, which went on sale in 1931 at £155. Rootes also built the famous Humber Snipe used by Field Marshal Montgomery in the Second World War. By 1962 the Rootes group had a worldwide reputation and had swallowed up other companies such as Sunbeam and Singer. They produced in that year such notable vehicles as the Humber Super Snipe for £1,050, the Humber Hawk, Hillman Super Minx, Sunbeam Rapier, the sporty Sunbeam Alpine for £695 and their cheapest, the Singer Gazelle for £585.[14] The American company Chrysler acquired shares in the company in the mid-1960s, which eventually led to a takeover. Chrysler had its own troubles and in 1978 was bought by Peugeot-Citroen for one dollar. The company still produces cars at its Ryton Plant.

174　*A 1936 advert for the Humber Snipe and Hillman Minx Magnificent.*

The Standard began in a small factory in Much Park Street in 1903; by 1916 the company had grown large enough to move to a specially constructed factory in Canley, where they also produced aeroplanes. In 1929 Captain Black joined the company and reorganised the Canley works for mass-produced cars, and within seven years the famous 'Flying Standard' range was introduced. During the Second World War the Standard built two other factories, one at Fletchamstead Highway and a shadow factory in Banner Lane, next to their old works. This plant later became the home of the world famous Massey-Fergusson tractors. The company turned out the 'Vanguard' from 1947 and the 'Ensign' from 1954. The last vehicle left the production line in 1963, when Standard was owned by Leyland. The Canley and Fletchamstead plants were switched to Triumph cars, which had been made in the city from 1923, until 1981 when the last Triumph left the factory.

Jaguar came from Blackpool in 1928 to set up in part of the old White and Poppe munitions factory in Holbrook Lane, under the name of the Swallow Sidecar and Coach Building Company. In 1931 company director William Lyons introduced the first Swallow Sidecar called the SS. Just before the war the company developed the SS 100, one of the greatest motor cars ever made. During the war the letters 'SS' acquired other implications and the company gradually changed its name to Jaguar Cars. During the 1950s Jaguars sold well, prompted by their major successes on the race tracks of the world. The famous 'C' Type and 'D' Type were introduced, including the highly cherished Mark II, followed by the 'E' Type in the 1960s. Unable to expand his works, Lord Lyons moved to Browns Lane, the old Daimler shadow factory, in 1952 and production of the Ford-owned Jaguar continues there today. Jaguar purchased the Daimler in 1960 and the old Daimler plant in Radford produced Jaguar engines. Demolished in 2000, this is now a housing estate called Daimler Green. Most of the sites of the city's major car manufacturers are now occupied by houses, industrial units or shops, the latter being the fate of the Alvis car plant on the Holyhead Road.

Car production began to suffer in the mid-1970s, when most cars sold in England were made in Germany, France or Japan. The government were asked to save Chrysler and British Leyland, but they didn't and now car production in Coventry only employs a tiny part of the city's workforce. The city's name is still borne throughout the world by Jaguar Cars, who have had something of a revival in recent years. There have been 110 different car manufacturers in Coventry since 1896.[15]

It is generally forgotten that Coventry was also home to the aircraft industry, but many car firms also produced aircraft. Daimler built engines and BE12 fighters, Standard built Sopwith Pups, RE8s, Bristol fighters, Buzzards, Oxford trainers, Gypsy Moths, Mosquitos, Beaufighters and Hercules aero-engines. Humber built early monoplanes and biplanes such as the Lovelace, Le Blon and the Bleriot. The largest manufacturer was the Armstrong Whitworth Aircraft

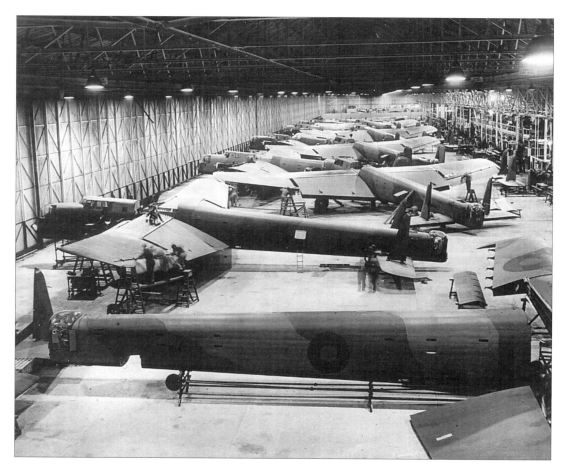

175   *Production of Whitley bombers by Armstrong Whitworth at Baginton. (Midland Air Museum)*

Company, formed in 1920 at Whitley Abbey aerodrome. The Siskin fighter was the first plane produced at Whitley and it became the standard fighter for the RAF. It was followed in 1927 by the Atlas biplane, and in 1929 by the Argosy Mark II, the company's first passenger airliner, which served the Imperial Airways London to Paris route until 1933.[16] In March 1936 the first Whitley bomber took off from Whitley Aerodrome and two months later the company began production of the bomber for the Air Ministry at their new Baginton Works. By the outbreak of war the Whitley Mark V had been perfected and it became the workhorse of the RAF. By June 1943 Bomber Command had received 1,466 Whitley bombers; the works produced a total of 1,812 planes, none of which has survived.

Throughout the rest of the war, and after, AWA continued with production of Lancaster, Albemarle, Wellington, Manchester and Lincoln bombers. One of the firm's most notable aircraft, fifty years ahead of its time, was the AW52 Flying

Wing. As a result of wartime tests, a glider version was flown in 1946. The following year the 100-foot-wide flying wing, covered in a metal skin called 'Alclad' (later used on Concorde) and powered by two Rolls-Royce Nene engines, took off from the Baginton Works. The plane reached speeds of up to 350 miles per hour and would have had a bright future had the government not pulled out of aircraft development. Sir Frank Whittle, inventor of the jet engine, was born in Newcombe Road, Earlsdon in 1907. He conceived the jet engine in 1928 and ran the first in 1937; the first test flight was in 1941. He later said that if the government had shown more interest we would have had jet-powered flight by 1942. AWA continued to produce aircraft such as the NF14 fighter from 1950 and the Argosy right up until the factory's closure in 1965.

GEC Telecommunication, founded in 1920 to produce telecommunications equipment, was once the city's largest employer. The company's factory in Spon Street was demolished in recent years and is now the site of an entertainment complex, which includes the Skydome Arena. But the company still employs a much-reduced workforce in their Stoke Plant. Another world-famous employer was the machine tool company Alfred Herbert Ltd. 'Herbert's', as it came to be known, was set up by the son of a Leicestershire farmer. Alfred Herbert completed his apprenticeship and took charge of a firm in the Butts, which by 1894 was called Alfred Herbert Ltd.[17] The firm moved to larger premises in Edgewick in 1928 and became the largest machine-tool manufacturing company in the world. Sir Alfred died aged 90 in 1957 and left behind a legacy of great benefactions to the city, such as Lady Herbert's Garden and £200,000 to build the Herbert Art Gallery and Museum. He also gave £10,000 to the city's hospital, £25,000 for the rebuilding of the cathedral and, on his 90th birthday, £25,000 to his employees to celebrate.[18]

Other notable engineering firms in the city included Dunlop in Holbrooks and Coventry Gauge & Tool. Firms such as Wickman's, Brico, Renold Chain and Matrix-Churchill have disappeared. In 1972 it was noted that 200,000 people worked in Coventry, 68,000 in motor car production, 45,000 in electrical and general engineering work, 15,000 in professional posts including scientific work, 13,000 in distribution, 7,000 in administration, 7,000 in construction and 6,000 in textiles.[19] But the city suffered from the national depression in the 1970s and many long-established firms went to the wall. As we passed into the '80s even the world-dominating Alfred Herbert Ltd could not save itself. Much of the city's car and engineering trade collapsed, the survivors being companies like Jaguar, LTI, the black cab makers, Peugeot and Lee-Beesley. More recent years have seen yet another revival in the city's fortunes. Major firms such as Marconi Communications, Parcel Force, Wireless & Telegraph, National Grid and Powergen have moved in. Only a quarter of the present population now works in engineering and most people work in the many service industries based in business and science parks around the city.

The Two World Wars

On the evening of 14 July 1914 notices were served on all servicemen on leave in Coventry to return to their barracks the following morning. The 7th Battalion of the Warwickshire Territorials had left Coventry Barracks for their annual camp at Rhyl. Over the following days they returned home and Colonel William Wyley of the Charterhouse called for volunteers to raise a second battalion. Men responded to the call and a recruiting office was set up in the Masonic Hall, where it is said young men lined up in their thousands. England was at war with Germany.

As men left for the front, refugees from Belgium arrived in their hundreds and were housed initially at Whitley Abbey. Large naval guns were already produced at the Red Lane Ordnance Works, and during the war years the city produced 'ordnance, quick-firing guns, aeroplanes and parts, machine tools, shells, small arms, ammunition, motor vehicles of all kinds, cycles, tanks, ambulance trailers, aircraft engines, magnetos, gun and submarine parts, bombs, incendiary bullets, drop forgings'.[20]

176 *Making naval guns at the Ordnance Works in Red Lane.*

Between the present Holbrook Lane and Beake Avenue, White and Poppe's National Filling Factory was set up to provide munitions. The labour force consisted mainly of women whose hands were stained yellow and who thereafter bore the name 'Canary Girls'. Munitions from the factory were stored in underground dumps and transported from the site via a partially sunken rail link. The first order of the war was for 100,000 18-pounder shells. It is recorded that during the war years the factory also produced 19,940,000 fuses, 9,880,000 grenades and 31,060,000 detonators. One successful Coventry invention was the incendiary bullet: 26 million were made here and at the Ordnance Works, and they are believed, with one exception, to have been responsible for all the Zeppelins shot down over English soil. Five hundred temporary wooden buildings were erected by the factory to house its workers. A letter dated 30 March 1917 states,

> There has been a dreadful lot of accidents at White and Poppe lately. Only this morning the magazine caught fire and we all sat here in the office waiting to be blown up. The girls were running down the lane for dear life in their overalls ... On Wednesday a girl got her arm and half her face blown off. She died yesterday.[21]

The Ordnance Works in Red Lane ran a fuse-filling section as well as producing 15- and 18-inch naval guns, the largest available to the Royal Navy. During the war 30,000 workers were drafted into the city to keep the factories running day and night, and by the end of the conflict the War Department had spent over £40.5 million in Coventry.

The production of aircraft first began in Coventry in 1910 and war production included the famous Sopwith Pup, built by the Standard Motor Company, and BE12s at the Daimler Works, which were flown from the Radford Aerodrome built hard by. The letter writer quoted above noted in 1917, 'Yesterday another aeroplane came down bang and the lieutenant killed. That makes six poor fellows who have been burnt to death around here in the last three weeks.' During this period the Daimler also built forty 35-ton tanks a week.[22]

No damage occurred from air raids in the First World War, although the city suffered two attacks. On 31 January 1917 a Zeppelin skirted the city and passed into Staffordshire. On 12 April 1918 raiders dropped bombs in the grounds of Whitley Abbey and on the Baginton Sewage Farm. They were tracked by powerful searchlights and guns were used against them in Keresley and Wyken Grange; BE12s took off from Radford Aerodrome but could not find their target. Fear of further raids meant the city's ancient valuables, such as the Coventry Tapestry, windows and muniments, were moved from St Mary's Hall to safety.

As the war progressed and manpower became short, women took over the jobs of policemen, postmen and tram conductors. Schools and shops were staffed almost entirely by women and women acted as porters, farm workers and in other normally male-dominated trades. It would not be until the next war that women would return to such work. It is estimated that 35,000 Coventry men joined the forces and at least 2,587 never returned. A memorial was raised to the dead in the War Memorial Park and unveiled by Field Marshal Earl Haig before fifty thousand people on 8 October 1927.

The Great War ended on 11 November 1918, when nearly ten million lay dead, and gradually men started to return home. It was difficult to find work and riots broke out across the country. In 1919, following the Godiva 'Peace' Procession, there were riots in Coventry. There were rumours that some of the shops attacked in Broadgate were German-owned, but the real cause was a combination of the shock of returning to civilian life and the problems caused by lack of work.

At the outbreak of the Second World War no one could have foreseen that this would be a turning point in the city's long and illustrious history. Air-raid shelters were dug in the city's parks and shopping centres in September 1938, a full year before the beginning of hostilities. Gas masks were issued and were carried by all but nothing happened throughout the period known as the 'Phoney War'. Blackout regulations came into force and on 30 September the first test blackout took place with nearly 1,400 air-raid wardens on duty until 1 a.m. One unforeseen risk of the blackout was the rise in numbers of people run down by cars and buses. No one could see the point in evacuating children since Coventry, so far inland, could never be under serious threat; the initial response was limited and only 4,000 children were evacuated, leaving 10,000 at risk.[23]

Coventry's industries again went into overdrive and shadow factories were built outside the city. Armstrong Whitworth Aircraft began producing the Whitley bomber for the RAF and a Coventry Whitley was the first plane to penetrate German airspace. Humber produced scout cars, troop transporters and staff cars, one of which was used by Montgomery himself, and Rommel also favoured a captured Humber scout car. The Standard Motor Company at its shadow works in Banner Lane produced 1,066 Mosquito fighter-bombers. Dunlop in Holbrooks produced disk brakes for aircraft and firing mechanisms for Spitfires, and Cash's produced parachute equipment. This was just a small part of Coventry's massive war effort.

Workers had to be brought in by the thousand, and inside the first six months of the war 20,000 came to the city, a number that grew throughout the conflict. Many of them worked twelve-hour shifts and lodged in various places. In some homes a night worker would occupy a bed in the daytime and a day worker use it at night, and sometimes three would share a double bed. The corporation opened hostels in Keresley and Willenhall where a small room could be rented and a cafeteria was provided. Workers were earning up to £10 a week and car ownership in Coventry became higher than anywhere else before petrol rationing put a stop to it.

177 *Hertford Street ablaze, 15 November 1940.*

178 *Eagle Street, 15 November 1940. (Les Fannon)*

The first air raid in the Coventry area took place on 25 June 1940 when five bombs were dropped on Ansty Aerodrome. In total, Coventry was to endure 41 actual raids and 373 siren alerts.[24] The first heavy raid was on 25 August, when the Rex Cinema was destroyed, and between then and the end of October the city suffered 16 more raids resulting in the deaths of 176 people. At the beginning of November several unco-ordinated raids took place leaving little damage and on 8 November the RAF bombed Munich, the birthplace of the Nazi Party, using Coventry-made Whitley bombers. Hitler was furious and ordered reprisals on the city. On the evening of 14 November 1940 around 500 bombers left their airfields in France; at their taking-off point a moulded concrete block embossed with the words 'Coventry Street' was placed.

Each squadron was given certain factories as targets but many were ordered simply to bomb the centre of Coventry and make it an example to the world. The force was led by a pathfinder squadron called Kampfgeschwader 100, which followed set radio beams called X-Gerat to their target. These beams were being jammed in England but on the wrong frequency. A large raid was expected at the time and Coventry was one of a number of possible targets. Many strange stories came out in later years regarding that night, including the suggestion that Churchill had sacrificed the city to protect the Enigma Code, but these have been proved untrue. Churchill had been led to believe the raid would be on London and went up on the Air Ministry roof to wait, as was his habit. When he found that Coventry was the target he spent much of the night on the telephone, apparently lambasting the commander of the city's air-raid defences in Radford Road because of their ineffectiveness.

The War Operations Rooms under the Post Office in Hertford Street and in Keresley were tracking a large force of planes heading for Coventry. At 7 o'clock the air-raid sirens sounded and at 7.20 p.m. the pathfinders began to drop parachute flares which hung in the sky like huge chandeliers. These were followed by incendiaries setting fires to mark the city centre for those that were to follow. As the main body of bombers arrived, mines and bombs were added to the incendiaries. By 7.40 Coventry's ancient cathedral was on fire after incendiaries burst into the roof space. Firefighters in the city were losing the battle as fires spread and falling bombs blasted the water mains. By 2 a.m. the Chief Fire Officer reported the centre of Coventry had 200 fires burning, which were being whipped up by a growing westerly breeze and merging into one great fire, which could be seen in neighbouring counties and by the enemy planes as they flew across the Channel.[25]

The bombing continued non-stop until 6.15 the following morning, when the few surviving sirens gave the all-clear and thousands slowly emerged from the overcrowded shelters to wander in shock amid the still burning, smoke-filled, damp destruction. During that long night the Luftwaffe had unloaded 500 tons of high explosives, 30,000 incendiaries and 50 land and oil mines. Amidst the

179 *Mass burial after November blitz.*

devastation, 554 lay dead and 865 were injured. It was recorded that 4,330 homes were destroyed and thousands more damaged; 75 per cent of the city's industrial buildings were also damaged. News of the bombing spread quickly around the world and the Germans coined a new word meaning complete destruction: 'Coventrated'.

Soldiers poured into the city to maintain order and commence the recovery, and all roads were covered by armed guards. Many people were homeless and Ministry of Information vans toured the streets giving out advice. The Women's Voluntary Service, Salvation Army and YMCA opened 29 relief stations handing out food and clothes, and numerous army field kitchens and mobile canteens toured the streets. The Royal Engineers laid a temporary water mains and within three days restored electricity to much of the city. Gas and water followed, and 100,000 people were inoculated against an outbreak of typhoid. One unforeseen problem was that 624 shops had been destroyed, so the ration book system had to be revised. The safe disposal of 527 unexploded bombs, 167 of which blew up before they could be safely dealt with, was a necessary task. Many of the city's industries were back into production within a few days and in full production again within several weeks.

180 *Coventry Cathedral, November 1940.*

Minor raids continued, then on the night of 8 April 1941 the city suffered another sustained attack lasting some eight hours. The Coventry and Warwickshire Hospital was badly damaged and patients, nurses and doctors were killed. The body of the rebuilt Christchurch was destroyed for the second time in its history. On the 10th the bombers returned for a long six-hour raid and the death toll in the city rose to 1,200. The last bombers to pass over Coventry came in August 1942. It took some time to clear the centre of Coventry of the rubble, much of which filled in old hollows and quarries in the surrounding countryside. Before the destruction was cleared, however, plans were already under way to rebuild the city.

REBUILDING THE CITY

The 20th century witnessed many rebuilding schemes in the city in the name of slum clearance and easier vehicular access. The earliest major scheme was in 1911, when many ancient properties were demolished in Earl Street to allow for the building of the Council House. In 1929 a huge swathe of buildings, including homes, factories and public houses, was cleared for the construction of Corporation Street, which was opened the following year. The year 1936 saw the destruction of a group of the city's finest timbered streets when Great and Little Butcher Row, Bull Ring and Trinity Lane were destroyed to create Trinity Street and easier vehicular access, an act of vandalism unequalled in the city's history of redevelopment.

In the years leading up to Second World War plans were already under way for road widening in Smithford Street, High Street and Cross Cheaping. Ancient buildings which blocked the schemes were torn down and more would have been removed had the bombs not completed the job. Other schemes put forward included the redevelopment of the ancient Broadgate, now minus most of its oldest buildings owing to 19th-century development. In 1938 the council appointed 29-year-old Donald Gibson as the city's first official architect. The role had previously been performed by City Engineer Ernest Ford, who was the first to suggest a traffic-free precinct.

181   *Area demolished for the laying of Corporation Street in 1929.*

182   *The King and Queen in bombed St Mary's Hall, looking at rebuilding plans, 1942.*

183   *The unveiling of the Phoenix Levelling Stone by Alderman George Biggs on 8 June 1946.*

184 *Gibson's revised 1945 plan for the precinct; traders pressured him to add a road along Market and Smithford Way. They also called for Hodgkinson's water feature down the centre to be removed.*

After Gibson's appointment Ford could get little backing for his own schemes, the council favouring the younger man. Within a short time of taking up his position, Gibson established an office of young architects and put forward plans for the demolition and rebuilding of much of the central area, including the Cathedral Quarter and Broadgate, where he envisaged civic buildings, libraries, museums and offices. Before the bulldozers moved in the bombs fell and Gibson and his team found themselves with a practically clean canvas.

In February 1941 both Gibson and Ford put forward plans for the redevelopment of the city centre and Gibson's were accepted. They incorporated a single-level development running down from Broadgate with a water feature in the centre, an addition suggested by ex-mayor and member of the Redevelopment Committee, George Hodgkinson. By 1945 the water feature was limited to the upper part of the development. A road was also added after traders insisted that customers would not come if they didn't have access. The first act was the laying of the Phoenix Stone to mark the symbolic rise of the city from the ashes. The stone doubled as a levelling stone, from which all computations for development could be made.[26] Work began on the construction of Broadgate Island, which was officially opened by the Princess Elizabeth in May 1948. The following year the Godiva statue was added, the idea for which went back to the 1920s, the statue already appearing on plans drawn up in 1944-5. The first building erected

185   *Coventry city centre cleared of rubble. Note the barrage balloons.*

in Broadgate, and replacing temporary shops, was Broadgate House in May 1953.
The *Hotel Leofric* and part of the Upper Precinct followed, built on a revised two-
tier level which Gibson based on the 'Rows' at Chester.

The Owen Owen building was opened in October 1954 (replacing one which
had been destroyed in the war), and was followed by the completion of the

Upper Precinct in 1955. While Broadgate was under construction, work had also begun on Market Way and its intersecting road. Gibson left in January 1955 and was replaced by Arthur Ling, who began by stopping the road through the development. He redesigned the Lower Precinct after it emerged that people disliked climbing the stairs to the Upper Precinct. The Lower Precinct's upper level was at the same height as the Upper Precinct and this appeared to have solved the problem. Ling believed the development needed more height and added Mercia House. He also built Smithford Way and the Locarno Ballroom to try to bring some nightlife to a city centre made up entirely of business premises. His Belgrade Theatre was opened in 1958, at a cost of £265,000,[27] and was followed by the Herbert Art Gallery and Museum in 1960 which was funded by the local industrialist.

Initially traders suffered, but by the time of its completion the precinct, built in what came to be called 'Festival of Britain' style, was a huge success. By 1964 shopowners were refusing offers of £25,000 for their leases.[28] By 1965 eight hundred other town councils had applied for traffic-free shopping centres and the trend has continued into the 21st century. In 1990 Cathedral Lanes was built over what was originally Broadgate Island, and the much criticised 'tent' was erected over the Godiva Statue. Part of Ling's Smithford Way was demolished and became the West Orchards Shopping Centre, which houses the largest typanteum in Europe. The Upper and Lower Precincts have undergone various alterations but retain their original concept, although the view up to the spire is now blocked and the Lower Precinct has a glass roof and arcade leading into the revamped market.

186   *Princess Elizabeth opens Broadgate in 1948.* (Coventry Evening Telegraph)

The 'Phoenix Initiative' has unearthed remains of the old Coventry Priory and created a garden and visitor centre. The nearby 19th-century ribbon factory has also been restored, part of the scheme involving the demolition of the old Coventry Theatre, which ended its days as a bingo hall. Its site is now a public square overlooked by the frontage of the Museum of British Road Transport. Building work and demolition continues in the city with varying degrees of success.

The building of the precinct after the war wasn't the only grand scheme, for Coventry sought also to restore its burnt-out cathedral. The Cathedral Church of St Michael had begun as the parish church attached to Coventry Castle. It grew to its present size following major building work in the 14th and 15th centuries, and the Perpendicular church said by Wren to be one of the glories of its age became a cathedral in 1918. On the night of 14 November 1940 fire took hold in the roof space of the north aisle, despite the efforts of Provost Howard and his men, which soon gripped other parts of the roof as no water was available to fire crews. Treasures inside were saved but the building had to be left to burn. The following day the church's stonemason Jock Forbes wired together two burned timbers and stood the cross in the rubble. This and the later cross of nails became symbolic of the cathedral and its work in world reconciliation.

187 *Building the Upper Precinct and* Hotel Leofric. *People still walk along the original Smithford Street past the* White Lion. (Coventry Evening Telegraph)

188 *The Upper Precinct nears completion in 1955. (Trevor Pring)*

189   *Market Way and Smithford Way in the 1960s.*

190   *Broadgate with the 'tent' in 2001. (John Ashby)*

Within a year of the building's destruction a commission sat to discuss ideas for rebuilding it. Many wanted the original building restored, but the commission invited Sir Giles Gilbert Scott to submit a new design. His proposal to build a new church on the site of the old with a central altar was approved by the Church Commissioners but not by the Royal Fine Arts Commission and Scott withdrew his design. In 1950 the council held an open competition and received 219 entries from all over the world, many of which proposed to demolish most of the old building. The winning entry, announced in August 1951, was tendered by Basil Spence, who would later be knighted for his work. Spence later said his design had come to him as a sort of vision when he visited the old cathedral with his wife in the summer of 1950. 'In the first five minutes I imagined the new

191 *The Godiva statue in Broadgate in 1978.* (Coventry Evening Telegraph)

building growing out of the side of the old Cathedral ... The new altar backed by a huge tapestry ... I imagined huge glass doors, twenty feet high ... Twenty-four hours later my first plan was finished.'[29] When Spence's plans were published he said that he received 700 letters. 'Eighty per cent were very, very rude and the remaining twenty per cent of them were rude.'[30] Because of the controversy, Spence found commissions beginning to dry up and he received no work for two years. He was on the verge of bankruptcy when he made his name with his new cathedral.

John Laing Construction built the huge edifice and Spence chose the best artists of the day to work on the building, including Graham Sutherland, who designed the tapestry which was then the largest in the world. It used 12,000 miles of wool and was made in Felletin in France. John Hutton created the glass West Screen carved with angels, apostles and saints using a small hand-tool. His work led to a premature death from breathing in the glass dust and Hutton's

192 *Coventry's new Cathedral.* *(Frank Scotland)*

193 *The consecration of Coventry Cathedral in 1962.* (Coventry Evening Telegraph)

194 *Cathedral interior with tapestry. (Joseph York)*

ashes now lie at the base of his last great work. John Piper and Patrick Reyntiens created the beautiful Baptistery Window, and Jacob Epstein's last great religious work was the huge bronze of St Michael defeating the Devil on the exterior east wall. Coventry's new cathedral of St Michael, which cost £1,385,000, was dedicated by Queen Elizabeth on 25 May 1962. Within its first year the cathedral had two and a half million visitors,[31] and although that has dropped drastically over the years it is still one of the most visited sites in England and was voted one of Britain's best-loved buildings in 1999.

Coventry city centre comprises 450 acres within a ring road which took 15 years to build and led to the demolition of hundreds of buildings. The first stage, between London Road and St Patrick's Road, was opened in December 1959, and after many hold-ups it was finally completed in 1973. The road has a remarkably good record regarding accidents and, although it is said to be strangling the centre, it also proves its worth by taking vehicles around the city instead of through it, making Coventry city centre one of the least congested in the land. Other developments outside the road, and the introduction of traffic lights at some roundabouts, have affected it in recent years, causing congestion where before there was none.

195   *Looking along the Upper Precinct in 2001. (John Ashby)*

The ring road was created for the motor car and for many Coventry is simply the place where cars were or are made. The motor car is however but a single feature of the city's long and illustrious past; Coventry is much greater than that. The walled city reached the zenith of its power in the 15th centry when it literally became the new capital of England. Since then it has had highs and lows, Dissolution, plague, unemployment, bombs and bulldozers, but it has always had the strength to re-invent itself and press forward. Few cities in England can claim a past as rich as Coventry's, and few have suffered as much. Described before the Second World War as one of the finest surviving medieval cities in Europe, Coventry has since been ripped apart. Redevelopment continues into the 21st century and Coventry – as it has always done – moves on.

NOTES

Chapter 1: Beginnings

1   F.W. Shotton, 'Geology', *The Coventry District, A Naturalist's Guide* (Coventry and District Natural History and Scientific Society, 1960), p.17.

2   Exhibition, Warwick Museum and *Coventry Evening Telegraph.*

3   F.W. Shotton, *Proceedings of the Prehistoric Society of East Anglia*, vol. VI, part III (1930), p.180.

4   *Coventry Standard*, 18/19 January 1935.

5   Iain Soden, *Excavations of St Anne's, Charterhouse, Coventry, 1968-87* (1995), p.128.

6   B. Stanley, 'Pre-Norman Archaeology', *The Coventry District, A Naturalist's Guide*, p.26.

7   W. M. Elliott, 'Two Stone Implements from Coventry', *Transactions of the Birmingham and District Archaeological Society* (1969).

8   Stanley, 'Pre-Norman Archaeology', p.26.

9   Ordnance Survey map *c.*1935 shows tumuli near the entrance to the Abbey and behind.

10   Bertram Windle, 'Some Prehistoric Implements of Warwickshire and Worcestershire', *Transactions of the Birmingham and District Archaeological Society* (1898), p.9.

11   *Coventry Standard*, 25 September 1936, from notes by 'Observer' dated 1910.

12   Thomas Sharp's Map of Coventry 1807, from *The Beauties of England and Wales.*

13   The photograph can be found in Coventry City Archives under 'War Damage'.

14   J.H. Gunstone (ed.), 'Bronze Age Implements in Coventry Museum', *Transactions of the Birmingham and District Archaeological Society*, vol. 19 (1882), p.92.

15   'Bronze Age axe found at Whitley', *Transactions of the Birmingham and District Archaeological Society*, vol. LIV (1929-30).

16   Charter of Edward the Confessor, British Museum; also facsimile in Birmingham Library. This charter is known to be a forgery from Westminster School, re-written to bias landownership, but this does not mean it was not based on a real document bearing the original spelling.

17   F.B. Burbidge, *Old Coventry and Lady Godiva* (1952), p.5.

18   Anglo-Saxon Chronicle Ms. 'C', one of many versions of the chronicle dating from 1060-66. Manuscript 'D' changes to 'Cofentreo'.

19   W.G. Searle, *Onomasticon Anglo-Saxonicum* (Cambridge, 1897) p.97.

20   Burbidge, *Old Coventry and Lady Godiva*, p.3.

21   John Bailey Shelton, *Austin's Monthly Magazine*, 1932-6 (Coventry and Warwickshire Local Studies Collection).

22   *Current Archaeology Magazine Directory* 2000, p.54.

23   *Coventry Mercury*, 4 January 1793, Coventry and Warwickshire Collection.

24   *The Gentleman's Magazine* 1793, p.83.

25   *The Gentleman's Magazine* 1793, p.86, letter of 30 July 1793, by 'Explorator'.

26   *The Victoria History of the County of Warwick*, vol. 1, p.248. William Hutton also confirms this find in *Highways and Byways of Shakespeare Country* (1915), p.394.

27   Andrews Newscuttings, Coventry and Warwickshire Collection.

28   Source: Iain Soden, Northampton Archaeological Unit.

29   *Transactions of the Birmingham and District Archaeological Society*, vol. 92 (1982), p.97.

30   *Transactions of the Birmingham and District Archaeological Society*, vol. LIV (1929-30), p.71.

31   Stanley, 'Pre-Norman Archaeology', p.28.

32   See also discovery of coin of Galinus in Cox Street.

33   Brian Hobley F.S.A., *Excavations at the Lunt Roman Fort, Final Report* (1972-3), p.4.

34   Lunt Fort leaflet by Margaret Rylatt.

35   Bodl. Ms. Bodley, 548, f.166v.

36   Joan Lancaster, *Godiva* (Coventry Corporation, 1967), endnote, p.15.

37   James Burkitt (ed.), *Oxford History of Britain* (Clarendon Press, 1984), p.41.

38   *Coventry Herald*, 28 August 1868, letter from Mr Moles.

39   Charles Macfarlane and Rev. Thomas Thomson, *Comprehensive History of England* vol. 1 (*c.*1880), p.112.

40   Crawford Charters, 111-12.

41   F.W. Humberstone, *Coventry's Story from Century to Century*, Section One, Part 9 (*c.*1920s).

42   Anglo-Saxon Chronicle and *Gesta Herewardi*.

43   Victor Head, *Hereward* (Sutton Publishing, 1995).

44   A.E.E. Cross, *Anglo-Saxon Worcester* (1958), p.149.

45   E. Barnard, 'The Evesham Chronicle', *Evesham and Shires, Notes & Queries* (1911), p.19.

46   H.O. Coxe (ed.), Roger of Wendover's *Flores Historiarum* (English Historical Society, 1841).

47   Matthew Paris, *Chronica Majora*, pp.526-7. Copy in Corpus Christi College library/early records.

48   *Coventry Mercury*, 26 May 1794.

49   Chambers Book of Days, 1863; see also Burbidge, *Old Coventry and Lady Godiva*.

50   Prof. R.H.C. Davis, *Early History of Coventry* (1976), p.7.

51   Burbidge, *Old Coventry and Lady Godiva*, p.76.

52   Quoted in Burbidge, *op.cit.* pp.77-8.

53   Additional Charter, no. 28,657.

54   Willis Browne, *A History of Mitred Parliamentary Abbies* [*sic*] *and Conventual Cathedral Churches*, 2 vols. (London, 1718), p.156

55   Suggested by Iain Soden, Northampton Archaeological Unit, at the Shelton Memorial Lecture 2000.

56   Burbidge, *Old Coventry and Lady Godiva*, p.126.

57   M. Hughes, *The Story of Staffordshire* (1925), p.115.

58   *The Antiquary*, July 1906, p.256.

59   Hughes, *The Story of Staffordshire*, p.104.

60   Prof. R.H.C. Davis, *An Unknown Coventry Charter* (1971), pp.533-45

61   The Laud Chronicle, E1137, p.263.

62   According to Walter of Newburgh and Roger of Wendover.

63   The Laud Chronicle, E1140, p[1141], p.266.

64   K.R. Potter (ed.), *Gesta Stephani* (1955), p.132.

65   Coventry Record Office, IA/C13/38.

66   P.R. Coss, *Early Records of Medieval Coventry* (Oxford University Press for Academy Press, 1986), p.xxii.

67   *Ibid.*, p.356.

68   Coventry Record Office, Ass.2/78.

69   Pittancer's Rental, 1410-11, The Register of the Cathedral Priory of St Mary's, Coventry (Birmingham University), p.22.

70   Corporation Deeds, 12 Ed. III and 14 Ed. III, C.R.O.

71   Coventry and District Archaeological Society, letter from Joan Lancaster re Castle.

72   *Midland Daily Telegraph*, 19 March 1914.

Chapter Two: Medieval Coventry

1   Coss, *Early Records of Medieval Coventry*, p.xxxv.
2   Davis, *Early History of Coventry*, p. 5.
3   Register of the Guild of the Holy Trinity, p.46.
4   *Coventry Herald*, 2 April 1915, article by Mary Dormer Harris.
5   Benjamin Poole, *Coventry: Its History and Antiquities* (1869), pp.5-6.
6   M. Dormer Harris, *Some Manors, Churches and Villages in Warks* (Coventry City Guild, 1937), p.228.
7   Frederick Woodhouse, *The Churches of Coventry* (1909), p.82.
8   Charles Nowell (ed.), William Reader Manuscript, Coventry Local Studies.
9   Sir William Dugdale, *History and Antiquities of Warwickshire* (Thomas Edition, 1730).
10 David McGrory, *Coventry, the Making of a City* (Coventry Evening Telegraph Millennium Supplements, 1999).
11 A.A. Dibben, 'Charter of Henry VI, 26 November 1451', *Coventry City Charters* (Coventry Papers, 2, 1969), p.27.
12 The Pittancer's Rental, 1410-11, p.4.
13 T.E. Freeman, *The Norman Conquest*, vol. 4, p.196.
14 M. Dormer Harris, *The Story of Coventry* (1911), p.96.
15 *The Antiquary*, January 1906, p.36.
16 R. Holinshed, *Holinshed's Chronicle* (1927), Richard II, Hiii, pp.494-5.
17 *Ibid.*
18 *Ibid.*
19 T.W. Whitley, *Parliamentary Representation of the City of Coventry* (1894), p.22.
20 David McGrory, *Coventry: History and Guide* (1993), p.41.
21 Joan Lancaster, *St. Mary's Hall, Coventry, A Guide to the Building and its History and Contents* (Coventry City Council, 1981), p.4.
22 Harleian Ms. no. 6466.
23 Coss, *Early Records of Medieval Coventry*, p.xlii.
24 Arthur Gooder, *The Black Death* (The Coventry Historical Association), p.22.
25 Humberstone, *Coventry's Story from Century to Century*, Section One, Part 19.
26 T. W. Whitley, *Humorous Reminiscences of Coventry Life* (1888), pp.14-15.

Chapter Three: Lancastrian Coventry and Henry VI

1   Bertram Woolfe, *Henry VI* (Methuen, 1981), p.251.
2   Mary Dormer Harris (trans.), *The Coventry Leet Book*, 20 June 1451, vol. 2, p.260.
3   Poole, *Coventry: Its History and Antiquities*, p.93.
4   H. Ellis (ed.), *Three Books of Polydore Vergil's English History* (1846), pp.97-8.
5   Alison Weir, *Lancaster and York, The Wars of the Roses* (Cape, 1995), p.211.
6   Register of the Guild of the Holy Trinity.
7   P.R.O., E.404/71/I/40.
8   Woolfe, *Henry VI*, p.308, from information supplied by Dr R. Jeffs.
9   Harris, *The Coventry Leet Book*, or *The Mayor's Register*, vol. 2, p.298, 14 March 1457. Most references to the Leet Book are from the edition published between 1907-13 in four volumes.
10 Fabyan's Chronicle, p.634.
11 J. S. Davies (ed.), *English Chronicle of the Reigns of Richard II, Henry IV, Henry V and Henry VI* (1856), p.79.
12 *Ibid.*, p.80.
13 G. and M. Harris (ed.), Benet's Chronicle for the years 1400-62, in *Camden's Miscellany* (Camden Society, 1972), p.221.
14 J. Strachey (ed.), Rotuli Parliamentorum (1767-7, 6 vols.), vol. 5, p.374.

15   Rotuli Parliamentorum, Coventry Parliament, 1459, vol. 5, pp.347-9.

16   Davies, *English Chronicle*, p.82.

17   According to Woolfe, *Henry VI*, p.371.

18   Coventry Leet Book, 6 February 1460, vol. 2, p.308.

19   M. Dormer Harris, *Life in an Old English Town* (1898), p.169.

20   Rotuli Parliamentorum, Reversal of Coventry Attainders, vol. 5, p.374.

21   Register of the Monastery of St Albans, Whethamstede, Rolls Series, p.393.

22   Weir, *Lancaster and York*, p.284.

23   Veronica Fiorato (West Berkshire Heritage Services), 'Towton, A.D. 1461, Excavation of a mass war grave', *Current Archaeology* 171, p.99.

24   McGrory, *Coventry: History and Guide*, p.46.

25   Charles Ross, *Edward IV* (Yale University Press, 1974), p.117.

26   *Ibid.*, pp.117-18.

27   Gila Falkus, *The Life and Times of Edward the Fourth* (1981), p.111.

28   Coventry Leet Book, July 1470, vol. 2, p.356.

29   G. Halliwell (ed.), Warkworth's Chronicle, p.11.

30   Weir, *Lancaster and York*, p.391.

31   Holinshed, p.682.

32   J. Bruce (ed.), *Historie of the Arrivall of King Edward IV in England and the final Recoverye of his Kingdomes from Henry VI, A.D. 1471* (Camden Society, 1838), p.126.

33   McGrory, *Coventry: History and Guide*, p.49.

34   Coventry Leet Book, 20 June 1472, vol. 2, pp.380-1.

35   Coventry Leet Book, 28 April 1474, vol. 2, pp.390-4.

36   Thomas Sharp, *Illustrative Papers on the History and Antiquities of the City of Coventry* (reprinted 1871 by William Fretton), pp.231-2.

37   Harl. Ms. 6,388, f.23.

38   Coventry Leet Book, 1477, vol. 2, p.420.

39   Rev. Canon J. Howard B. Masterman, M.A., *Coventry and Its Story* (Pitman & Sons, *c.*1900), pp.91-2.

40   Coventry Leet Book, 1424, vol. 1, p.96.

41   Proceedings of the Privy Council, IV. p.89. Also I. Ramsey, *Lancaster and York*, p.437.

42   Sharp, *Antiquities of Coventry*, p.207.

43   T. Green, *Town Life in the Fifteenth Century* (1928), p.127.

44   *Coventry Evening Telegraph*, report by Barbara Goulden, 1 January 2001, p.13.

45   Extract from the Reader Manuscript, ed. Charles Nowell.

46   Coventry Leet Book, Michaelmas Leet, 1423, vol. 1, p.59.

47   Coventry Leet Book, 4 October 1414, vol. 1, pp.19-20.

48   Coventry Leet Book, Measures 1474, vol. 2, p.400.

49   *Ibid.*, p.27.

50   *Ibid.*, p.28.

51   Harris, *Life in an Old English Town*, p.333.

52   *Ibid.*, pp.120-1.

53   Coventry Leet Book, Easter and Michaelmas Leets 1450, vol. 1, p.254.

54   Coventry Leet Book, 1434, vol. 1, p.151.

55   Harris, *Life in an Old English Town*, p.290, quoting from Coventry Leet Book.

56   Coventry Leet Book, John Leder's Proclamation, 1421, vol. 1, p.30.

57   Coventry Leet Book, 1461, vol. 1, p.312.

58   Thomas Sharp, *A Dissertation on the Coventry Mystery Plays* (Coventry, 1825), p.180.

59   *Ibid.*, p.242.

60   Coventry Leet Book, Easter and Michaelmas Leets, 1468, vol. 2, p.338.

61   Coventry Leet Book, The Priors Complaint, 1480, vol. 2, p.446.

62   Coventry Leet Book, Leets 1441, p.196.

Chapter Four: Tudor Coventry

1   T. W. Whitley, *The Parliamentary Representation of the City of Coventry* (1894), p.32.
2   Harl. MS. 6,388, f.24.
3   Neville Williams, *The Life and Times of Henry VII* (Weidenfeld & Nicolson, 1973), p.188.
4   Ronald C. Finucane, *Miracles and Pilgrims, Popular Beliefs in Medieval England* (London, 1977).
5   John Steane, *The Archaeology of the Medieval English Monarchy* (Routledge,1993), pp.174-5.
6   *Ibid.*, p.192 for comparisons in surviving pilgrim badges.
7   Woolfe, *Henry VI*, p.354.
8   *Ibid.*, p.350.
9   See the references to glass in Martin Biddle, *King Arthur's Round Table, An Archaeological Study* (of the Winchester Table), 2000.
10 All except Richard I that is; Henry's line went through Richard's brother John, but John had a poor reputation, and Henry preferred to have a 'Lionheart'.
11 The Duke of Portland's Manuscripts, six volumes (Welbeck), Letter to Lord Hartley, Coventry, 16 May 1719.
12 Sir George Scarf's paper on the tapestry is in *Archaeologia*, vol. 36, 1885.
13 Undated letter from J. H. Welch to unidentified Coventry newspaper, entitled 'The Tapestry in St. Mary's Hall: A New Description, *c.*1900'. Scrapbook in Coventry Local Studies.
14 Joan C. Lancaster, *Official Guide to St. Mary's Hall* (Coventry City Council, 1948), p.37.
15 Joan C. Lancaster, *St. Mary's Hall, Coventry, A Guide to the Building*, p.42.
16 Museum of Art, Toledo, Ohio, 'The Marriage of Henry VI and Margaret of Anjou', Flemish, early 16th-century. A copy also exists in the Radio Times Hulton Picture Library.
17 Similar chained swans and antelopes of Henry and Margaret can be found in Writhes Garter Memorial, British Library, Add. Ms. 37340, f.IV.
18 Woolfe records that the peak years of Henry's cult were 1484 to 1486, 1490, 1491 and 1499. *Henry VI*, p.345.
19 Coventry Leet Book, Leet 1493, vol. 2, p.556.
20 Coventry Leet Book, Easter Leet, vol. 2, p.564.
21 Harris, *Life in an Old English Town*, p.247.
22 Humberstone, *Coventry's Story from Century to Century*, Section Four, Part 3, 'Persecution'.
23 *Ibid.*, p.164.
24 McGrory, *Coventry: History and Guide*, p.56.
25 Rev. Frederick Colville, M.A., *The Worthies of Warwickshire* (1870), p.83.
26 Letter to John Bradford, Miscellaneous Cuttings, Local Studies, Coventry.
27 Thomas Sharp, *The History of Coventry* (1844), pp.162-3.
28 W.G. Fretton, *The Benedictine Monastery and Cathedral of Coventry* (Birmingham Archaeological Association,1876), p.33.
29 Abbot Gasquet, *Henry VIII and the English Monasteries* (London, 1902), vol. 2, p.427.
30 John Lisle, *Warwickshire* (Frederick Muller Ltd, 1936), p.222.
31 Fretton, *The Benedictine Monastery and Cathedral of Coventry*, p.32.
32 Cottonian Manuscripts (British Museum); see also Reader Manuscript.
33 Humberstone, *Coventry's Story from Century to Century*, Section Two, 'The Sixteenth Century'.
34 George Demidowicz (ed.), *Coventry's First Cathedral* (Watkins, 1994), p.7.
35 Whitley, *The Parliamentary Representation of the City of Coventry*, p.40.
36 Fretton, *The Benedictine Monastery*, p.32 footnote, from a book in the Corporation Treasury dated 16th Eliz.
37 Gasquet, *Henry VIII and the English Monasteries*, vol. 2, p.427.
38 The Trinity Deed of 1650, published by M.D. Harris in the *Coventry Herald*, 21 December 1914, states that Bryan built a house on the central tower of the Priory and he also made 'dwelling Houses on the Bottom of two Steeples' at the entrance, one of which later became Lych Gate House. Next to it stood an arched gateway which appears to have led to the dwelling on the central tower, probably 'Tower House'.

39   Postcard in David McGrory Collection.
40   Roy Strong, *Lost Treasures of Britain* (Guild Publishing, 1990), p.68.
41   See Bell's *Guide to Salisbury Cathedral*, p.81.
42   M.D. Harris, *A Selection of Pencil Drawings of Dr. Nathaniel Troughton* (The Fuller's Company/Batsford Press, *c.*1910), p.66.
43   Burbidge, *Old Coventry and Lady Godiva*, p.120.
44   L.T. Smith, *English Wayfaring Life in the Middle Ages* (T. Fisher Unwin, 1901), p.380.
45   The last reference to the building is in the Drapers Company Deeds, 7/437, Coventry Archives.
46   Calendar of Holy Trinity Church Deeds, no. 74, Coventry Archives.
47   L. Feasey, *Old England at Play* (Batsford, 1943), pp.14-15.
48   William Hone, *Ancient Mysteries Described* (W. Hone, 1823), p.139.
49   A.C. Ward, *Illustrated History of English Literature* (London, 1953), p.53.
50   Poole, *Coventry: Its History and Antiquities*, p.49.
51   Hone, *Ancient Mysteries Described*, p.218.
52   *The Victoria History of the County of Warwick*, vol. 8, p.213.
53   Coventry Leet Book, vol. 2, p.556.
54   H. Craig, *Two Coventry Corpus Christi Plays* (Oxford University Press, 1957), pp.31 and 70.
55   *The Victoria History of the County of Warwick*, vol. 8, p.213.
56   Thomas Sharp, *Dissertation on the Coventry Mystery Plays*, p.12.
57   *Ibid.*, p.38.
58   Alice Lynes, *Coventry Miracle Plays, A Short Account* (Coventry City Libraries, 1963), p.6.
59   McGrory, *Coventry, The Making of a City*, p.13. See also T.W. Whitley's paper, *Coventry Cross*, 1879.
60   Coventry Leet Book, vol. 1, p.57.
61   Treasurer's Accounts, p.26. See also Whitley, *Coventry Cross*, p.12.
62   Coventry Leet Book, vol. 3, p.775.
63   Simon Wilkin (ed.), Sir Thomas Browne's *Works* (1836), vol. 1, p.40.
64   C. Morris (ed.), *The Journeys of Celia Fiennes* (London, 1947), p.112.
65   Chambers Book of Days, 1886.
66   *Sketch of a Tour into Derbyshire and Yorkshire including part of Buckingham, Warwick, Leicester, Nottingham, Northampton, Bedford and Hertford...shires*, 1778, p.37.
67   The City Annals, 1565, Birmingham Reference Library. Also Whitley, *Parliamentary Representation of the City of Coventry*, p.54.
68   Arthur Heap Newscuttings, vol. 7, p.71, JN 080, article on Coventry Barracks Site, Local Studies.
69   *Ibid.*, p.124.
70   *Ibid.*, p.72.
71   Colville, *The Worthies of Warwickshire*, pp.364-5, taken from an 'ancient MS'.
72   Poole, *Coventry: Its History and Antiquities*, p.247.
73   Sharp, *Antiquities of Coventry*, p.162.
74   Poole, *Coventry: Its History and Antiquities*, Deed Tripartite Indenture, p.250.
75   Peter Burden, *The Lion and the Stars: A History of Bablake School, Coventry* (1990), p.2.
76   Humberstone, *Coventry's Story from Century to Century*, Section Five, 'Bablake School: The Foundation'.
77   Coventry Leet Book, vol. 4, pp.818-19.
78   Coventry City Annals, Ms. 'D', Coventry City Archives; the Leet Book confirms the year.
79   From a manuscript of the annals copied by Humphrey Wanley in 1690. See Burbidge, *Old Coventry and Lady Godiva*, p.226.
80   Coventry Leet Book, vol. 3, p.690.
81   Coventry Leet Book, vol. 3, p.653.
82   Coventry Leet Book, vol. 3, p.697.
83   W.G. Hoskins, *The Age of Plunder* (London, 1978), p.39.

84   John Hales, *Common Weal of the Realm* (*c*.1560s), p.128.
85   Coventry Leet Book, Easter Leet 1518, vol. 3, p.657.
86   Coventry Leet Book, Easter Leet 1518, vol. 3, p.698.
87   *The Victoria History of the County of Warwick*, vol. 8, p.156.
88   Hoskins, *The Age of Plunder*, p.96.
89   Poole, *Coventry: Its History and Antiquities*, p.292.
90   *Ibid.*, pp.297-8.
91   Coventry Leet Book, vol. 3, p.807.
92   Ostovich, H., *Records of Early English Drama*, vol. 21, no. 1 (Reed University, Toronto, 1996). All these dates are for when Shakespeare is known to have been a member of the groups playing the city. They do not include those times when the companies toured and Shakespeare stayed in London.
93   The Guildhall was first named as a venue for Shakespeare in David McGrory, *Coventry, The Making of a City* (1999), then in John Southworth, *Shakespeare the Player* (2000). Southworth believes that Shakespeare continued acting until his death, in which case he would have made two more visits with the King's Men.

Chapter Five: Seventeenth-Century Coventry

1   City Annals, 'B' Manuscript, Birmingham Reference Library. See also Burbidge, *Old Coventry and Lady Godiva*, pp. 236-7.
2   Whitley, *The Parliamentary Representation of the City of Coventry*, p.66.
3   McGrory, *Coventry, the Making of a City*.
4   City Annals, 'B' Manuscript, Birmingham Reference Library. See also Burbidge, *Old Coventry and Lady Godiva*, p. 339.
5   Translation of charter granted by James I to the City of Coventry, pp. 18-19; unsourced 19th-century document in author's collection.
6   Humberstone, *Coventry Century by Century*, Section Seven, Part 12.
7   Coventry City Archives, Ass. W987, 1640.
8   Common Council Book. See also William Reader, *The New Coventry Guide*, p.25.
9   Extracts from the Reader Manuscript, ed. Charles Nowell, August 1642.
10   'Warwickshire in August 1642, before the raising of the Royal Standard at Nottingham', paper read by Matthew Bloxham before the Warwickshire Natural History Society, 1872, p.12.
11   'Letters from a Subaltern Officer in the Earl of Essex's Army, written in the summer and autumn of 1642', *Archaeologia Tracts* relating to *Antiquity*, vol. XXXV, Society of Antiquaries, 1853.
12   Charles Nowell, F.L.A., *Some Account of the Gates, Towers and Wall of the City of Coventry* (Coventry City Guild, 1924), p.10.
13   *Ibid.*
14   J. Featherstone F.S.A. (ed.), 'The Battlefields of Warwickshire during the Civil War, 1642-3', *Warwickshire Antiquarian Magazine*, 1859-77.
15   *Ibid.*, pp.24-5, from a tract entitled, 'A true Relation of Prince Rupert's barbarous Cruelty against the Towne of Brumingham'.
16   City Annals, 'W' Manuscript, prepared by Humphrey Wanley. See also Burbidge, *Old Coventry and Lady Godiva*, p.247.
17   Trevor John, *Coventry's Civil War, 1642-1660* (Coventry Historical Association, 1994), p. 25, extract from *Reliquiae Baxterianae*. See also J. Adair, *By the Sword Divided* (Century Publishing, 1983), p.210.
18   Antonia Fraser, *Cromwell our Chief of Men* (Weidenfeld and Nicolson, 1973), p.152.
19   Whitley, *The Parliamentary Representation of the City of Coventry*, p.91.
20   M.D. Harris, 'Catalogue of Trinity Deeds', *Midland Daily Telegraph*, 31 March 1914.
21   See letters of Nehemiah Wharton, 26 August 1642.

22　Diary of William Hinton, Birmingham Reference Library.

23　Coventry Leet Book, vol. 4, p.835.

24　Burbidge, *Old Coventry and Lady Godiva*, p.244.

25　Humberstone, *Coventry from Century to Century*, Section Six, Part 18.

26　John, *Coventry's Civil War*, pp.28-9.

27　Adair, *By the Sword Divided*, p.210-11, quoting from *Reliquiae Baxterianae*.

28　Sharp, *Antiquities of Coventry*, p.103.

29　City Annals, 'B' Manuscript, Birmingham Reference Library.

30　City Annals, 'W' Manuscript, begun by Humphrey Wanley. See also Burbidge, *Old Coventry and Lady Godiva*, p.249.

31　City Annals, 'B' Manuscript, Birmingham Reference Library.

32　Robert Beake's diary extracts from Dugdale Society 'Miscellany'.

33　Levi Fox (ed.), 'Coventry Constables Presentments 1629-1742' (Dugdale Society, 1986), p.52.

34　*Nugae Antiquae*, vol. 3, p.158.

35　Extracts from Charles Nowell (ed.), the Reader Manuscript: 'The Free School, Coventry', 1929.

36　Sharp, *Antiquities of Coventry*, p.180.

37　Cottonian Manuscript (British Museum), Julius CV, folio 58.

38　Sharp, *Antiquities of Coventry*, p.182.

39　Poole, *Coventry: Its History and Antiquities*, pp.257-8.

40　Common Council Book, p.568, Coventry City Archives.

41　Humphrey Wanley's Diary, Harl. MS. 7017, British Museum.

42　Extracts from Reader Manuscript.

43　Poole, *Coventry: Its History and Antiquities*, p.267.

44　'A True Catalogue of the several places and persons by whom Richard Cromwell was proclaimed Lord Protector', Ashmolean Museum, No. 531.

45　Camden's *Britannia* translated by Philemon Holand, 1610, originally belonging to John Warren, p.568. See also the *Antiquarian Magazine and Bibliographer*, vol. 3. (1883), p.85.

Chapter Six: Everyday Life in Eighteenth-Century Coventry

1　According to Samuel Bradford's plan of Coventry 1748-9 (published 1750).

2　Thomas Pennant, *A Journey from Chester to London* (1782).

3　P.T. Priestley, 'Watch Case Makers of England 1720-1920', *NAWWC Bulletin*, Supplement 20 (Spring 1994), pp.38-9.

4　*Coventry Apprentices and their Masters, 1781-1806*, Dugdale Society, vol. XXXIII (1983).

5　*Coventry Mercury*, 17 May 1779.

6　*Coventry Mercury*, 23 June 1760.

7　*Coventry Mercury*, 18 April 1757.

8　*Coventry Mercury*, 27 June 1757.

9　Peter Burden, *The Lion and the Stars, A History of Bablake School, Coventry* (1990), p.10.

10　Humberstone, *Coventry's Story from Century to Century*, The Eighteenth Century, Section 25, 'Education'.

11　Irene Morris, *Three Hundred Years of Baptist Life in Coventry* (1926), p.14.

12　*Ibid.*, pp.32-3.

13　Albert Peck, *Two Hundred Years of Methodism in Coventry* (A. Peck, 1979), p.15.

14　John Hewitt, *A Journal of the Proceedings of J. Hewitt, senior alderman of the City of Coventry, and one of His Majesty's justices of the peace for the said city and county, in his duty as a Magistrate, during a period of thirty years and upwards, in cases of riots, coiners, murder, highway robberies, burglaries, returned transports and other matters* (2nd edition, 1790).

15　David McGrory, *Swing 'em Fair. Coventry's Darker Side* (Jones/Sands Publishing, 1999), pp.85-9.

16　*Coventry Mercury*, 17 September 1783.

17　'Plays and Players', *Coventry Herald*, 27 August 1915.

Chapter Seven: Nineteenth-Century Coventry

1   *The Story of Whitefriars* (City of Coventry Leisure Services, n.d.).
2   *The Victoria History for the County of Warwick*, vol. 8, 1969.
3   Frederick Smith, *Coventry: Six Hundred Years of Municipal Life* (1945), p.127.
4   *Ibid.*, pp. 128-9.
5   Report in the *Coventry Times*, 1870. The report appears to refer to the situation pre-1863.
6   Poole, *Coventry. Its History and Antiquities*, p.345.
7   J. Howard Masterman, *Coventry and Its Story* (Coventry Education Committee, *c.*1910), p.179.
8   Letter from Peter Moore to Colonel Brownrigg, 1802; see also 'Political Literature', *Coventry Herald*, 1915.
9   Whitley, *The Parliamentary Representation of the City of Coventry*, p.225.
10 *Ibid.*, p.305.
11 Smith, *Coventry: Six Hundred Years of Municipal Life*, pp.145-6.
12 McGrory, *Coventry, The Making of a City*, part four, p.5
13 Levi Fox, *Coventry's Heritage* (Coventry Evening Telegraph, 1947), p.70.
14 Peter Searby, *Coventry in Crisis 1858-1863* (Coventry and North Warwickshire History Pamphlets, No. 10), p.1.
15 *Coventry Herald*, 24 August 1860.
16 Masterman, *Coventry and Its Story*, p.172.
17 Searby, *Coventry in Crisis*, p.12.
18 Priestley, 'Watch Case Makers of England', pp.66-7.
19 *Coventry Herald*, 30 November 1923.
20 John Kemp Starley gives the date of the Rover as 1885 in the *Temple Magazine*.
21 McGrory, *Coventry: History and Guide*, p.91.
22 'The Evolution of the Bicycle', *Alfred Herbert News*, vol. 28, no. 2 (1954), p.43.
23 According to H.O. Duncan, Lawson's assistant, in an article in the *Coventry Herald*, 12 October 1929.
24 *Midland Daily Telegraph*, 6 May 1929.
25 The letter appeared in the *Evening News*, 9 August 1928.
26 Fox, *Coventry's Heritage*, p.146.
27 *The Victoria History of the County of Warwick*, vol. 8, 1969, p.300.
28 Local Studies, Education: 7/127/19; 16/218/2.
29 J.W. Docking, *Victorian Schools and Scholars* (Coventry and North Warwickshire History Pamphlets no.3, 1967), p.16. See also the *Coventry Herald*, 28 June 1901.
30 *Coventry Mercury*, 21 June 1824.
31 Newscuttings of the 19th century, Local Studies, Godiva Procession, JNo80.
32 *Coventry Herald*, 25 April 1845.
33 *Ibid.*
34 Burbidge, *Old Coventry and Lady Godiva*. See also R. Clarke and P. Day, *Lady Godiva: Images of a Legend in Art and Society* (Coventry Leisure Services, 1982), p.27.
35 *Coventry Herald*, 7 March 1834.
36 *Coventry Standard*, 4 April 1851.
37 *Coventry Herald*, 8 October 1915, reprinted from the 1814 press report in the *Herald*.
38 *Coventry Herald*, 26 June 1825.
39 'Coventry as an Assize Town', a paper by F.W. Humberstone, undated.
40 *Coventry Herald*, 13 March 1829.
41 McGrory, *Swing'em Fair*, p.87.
42 *Ibid.*, p.79.
43 Report from the Watch Committee, reprinted in *Coventry Standard*, 19 April 1935.
44 *Coventry Standard*, 23 June 1858. See also Karen Sheppard, *True as Coventry Blue, the History of Coventry Police 1836-1914* (n.d. but *c.*2000).
45 S.L. Ollard, *Dictionary of English Church History* (1912), p.323.

46	*The Victoria History of the County of Warwick*, vol. 8, p.319-20.

47	Coventry Evening Telegraph, *Story of Two Centuries of Catholic Progress in Coventry*, 31 August 1945.

48	H.O. 129/400; Kiernan, Archdiocese, Birmingham, p.37.

49	*The Victoria History of the County of Warwick*, vol. 8, p.394.

50	*The Victoria History of the County of Warwick*, vol. 8, p.389.

51	*The Jewish Chronicle*, 5 June 1936.

52	Henry Wilkins, *Unorthodox Coventry or Wanderings Beyond the Church* (1889). Originally printed in the *Coventry Standard*.

53	Joseph Gutteridge, *Light and Shadows in the Life of an Artisan*, pp.126-38.

Chapter Eight: Coventry in the Twentieth Century

1	Newspaper article *c*.1916, 'The Central City; A Miniature England; Coventry, Past and Present', by Harold Begbie.

2	Population figures derived from the city's official guide of 1912 and the *Coventry Herald*, 3 May 1935.

3	E. Castle and C. Kennedy, *Coventry Through Time* (Coventry Archives Educational Service, 1989).

4	According to A.F. Underhill, Housing Director, *Coventry: Official Handbook*, 1937.

5	Smith, *Coventry: Six Hundred Years of Municipal Life* (1945), p.163.

6	*Midland Daily Telegraph*, 23 May 1930.

7	David McGrory, *Coventry at War* (Alan Sutton Publishing, 1997), p.148.

8	*Coventry: The Modern Developments of an Ancient City* (1909), p.28.

9	'City's Health Record', *Coventry Herald*, 1 October 1938.

10	Kathleen Adams, *The Chronicles of Barr's Hill house, 1850-1982*, (1983), pp.8-9.

11	A. Denton and F. Groves, *Coventry Transport, 1884-1940* (BTHG Publication, 1985), p.65.

12	E.B. Newbold, *Portrait of Coventry* (Hale, 1972), p.125.

13	*Ibid.*, p.129.

14	Advert in *Coventry Evening Telegraph* supplement, 18 May 1962.

15	A complete list of manufacturers is in Brian Long, *The Marques of Coventry* (Warwickshire Books, 1990), p.96.

16	McGrory, *A Century of Coventry*, p.55.

17	Newbold, *Portrait of Coventry*, p.137.

18	*Ibid.*, p.138.

19	*Ibid.*, pp.139-40.

20	H. Wilkins, 'Coventry in the Great War', *City of Coventry: Celebration of Peace* (1919), p.14.

21	Letter supplied by Bob Ashmore written by his mother in 1917.

22	McGrory, *A Century of Coventry*, p.49.

23	'Poor Evacuation Response', *Coventry Herald*, 16 September 1938.

24	McGrory, *Coventry at War*, p.7.

25	Report of the Chief Officer of the Fire Brigade, W.H. Cartwright, on an enemy air attack at Coventry on 14/15 November 1940.

26	*Coventry Evening Telegraph*, 31 May 1946.

27	Newbold, *Portrait of Coventry*, p.48.

28	'Trade Fantastic in Car Free Precincts', *The Times*, 31 June 1964.

29	*Birmingham Post*, Commemorative Supplement, May 1962, p.V.

30	*Coventry Evening Telegraph*, Consecration Supplement, 18 May 1962.

31	Newbold, *Portrait of Coventry*, p.73.

SELECT BIBLIOGRAPHY

An Account of the Many and Great Loans, Benefactions and Charities belonging to the City of Coventry, Coventry, 1802

Andrews Cuttings, Coventry Local Studies, Central Library

Anglo, S., *Images of Tudor Kingship*, Seaby, 1992

Anglo-Saxon Chronicle, translated by G.N. Garmonsway, Dent, 1972

Antiquary, 1906

Ashby, J., *The Character of Coventry*, Coventry, 1984

Barnard, E., *Evesham and Shires, Notes & Queries*, W.H. Smith, 1911

Bassett, S., *Anglo-Saxon Coventry and its Churches*, Dugdale Society, 2001

Blyth, Rev. T.A., *The History of Stoke*, Birmingham, 1897

Bloom, J., *English Tracts, 1473-1660*, 1923

Bloxham, H., *The Civil War in Warwickshire*, Warwickshire Natural History & Archaeological Society, 1867-1872

Bloxham, H., 'Warwickshire in August 1642', *Warwickshire Antiquarian Magazine*, 1859-77

Burbidge, F.B., *Old Coventry and Lady Godiva*, Birmingham, 1952

Burden, P., *The Lion and the Stars: A History of Bablake School, Coventry*, Coventry, 1990

Calendar of Patent Rolls, London, 1897-1901

Cassell's Illustrated History of England, c.1850

Chatwin, P., 'Some Aspects of Ancient Coventry', paper, Coventry, 1944

Chatwin, P., 'Coventry's City Wall', paper, Coventry, 1928

Christie, M., *Henry VI*, Constable, 1922

City Annals, various dates

Clitheroe, Rev. G.W., *Coventry Under Fire*, Coventry, 1941

Coventry: Up to Date, Coventry, 1896

Coventry Evening Telegraph, various dates

Coventry Herald, Coventry Local Studies

Coventry Mercury 1745-1830, Coventry Local Studies

Coventry Standard, Coventry Local Studies

Coss, P.R., *Early Records of Medieval Coventry*

Cross, A., *Anglo-Saxon Worcester*, Baylis, 1958

Cross, G.W., *George Eliot's Life*, Blackwood, 1885

Davis, R.H.C., *The Early History of Coventry*, Dugdale Society, 1976

Dibben, A.A., *Coventry City Charters*, Coventry Papers, 1969

Dugdale, W., *The Antiquities of Coventre*, Coventry, 1765

Ellis, H., *Polydore Vergil's English History*, Camden Society, 1846

Erlanger, P., *Margaret of Anjou, Queen of England*, translated by Hyams, Elek Books, 1970

Fenn, J., *Paston Letters*, London, 1841

Fetherston, J., 'Battlefields in Warwickshire', *Warwickshire Antiquarian Magazine*, 1859-77

Fox, L., *Coventry's Heritage* (Coventry Evening Telegraph), 1947

Foxe, J., *Book of Martyrs*, New York, n.d.

Fretton, W.G., Papers on Coventry's History, 1865-1880

Fretton, W.G., Papers on Coventry Antiquities, Coventry, 1872-1891

Gairdner, J., *History of the Life of Richard the Third*, Bath, 1898

Gentleman's Magazine, 1790-1820, private collection

Geoffrey of Monmouth, *Histories of the King's of England*, Everyman, 1944

Gooder, E., *Coventry's Town Wall*, Coventry & Warwickshire History Pamphlet, 1971

Gutteridge, J., *Light and Shadows in the Life of an Artisan*, Coventry, 1893

Hallam, E., *The Chronicles of the Wars of the Roses*, Bramley Books, 1988

Harris, M.D., *Catalogue of the Trinity Deeds*, Coventry Herald, 1913-14

Harris, M.D., *The Coventry Leet Book*, Early English Text Society, 1907-13

Harris, M.D., *Life in an Old English Town*, London, 1898

Harris, M.D., *The Story of Coventry*, London, 1911

Haswell, J., *The Ardent Queen*, London, 1976

Head, V., *Hereward*, Sutton Publishing, 1995

Heap, A., *Plays, Players and Playbills in Coventry*, Coventry Herald, 1915-16

Hewitt, J., Two Journals, Coventry, 1790

Historie of the Arrivall of Edward IV in England (J. Bruce ed.), Camden Society, 1838

Hobley, B., 'Excavations of St. Mary's, Coventry', *Birmingham and Warwickshire Archaeological Society*, 1971

Holinshed, R., *Holinshed's Chronicle*, Dent, 1927

Humberstone, F.W., *Coventry's Story from Century to Century*, newspaper articles, 1910-14

Jeaffreson, C., *A Calendar of the Books, Charters, Letters Patent, Deed Rolls, Writs and other Writings, in the Cases and Drawers of the New Muniment Room of St. Mary's Hall, Coventry, 1896*

Kimball, E.G., *Rolls of the Warwickshire and Coventry Sessions of the Peace, 1377-97*, Dugdale Society, 1939

Lane, J., *Coventry Apprentices and their Masters*, Dugdale Society, 1983

Lewis, T., *Moonlight Sonata*, Coventry, 1990

Long, J., *Marques of Coventry*, Warwickshire Books, 1990

Longmate, N., *Air Raid: The Bombing of Coventry, 1940*, Hutchinson, 1976

Lowe, A., Newscuttings, Local Studies

McGrory, D., *Around Coventry in Old Photographs*, Alan Sutton, 1991

McGrory, D., *City of Coventry: Images from the Past*, Jones-Sands, 1996

McGrory, D., *Coventry: History & Guide*, Alan Sutton, 1992

McGrory, D., *Swing'em Fair: Coventry's Darker Side*, Jones-Sands, 1999

Masterman, Rev. J., *Coventry and its Story*, Coventry Education Committee, *c.*1910

Medieval Coventry: A City Divided?, various authors, 1981

Midland Daily Telegraph (various articles)

Morris, I., *Three Hundred Years of Baptist Life in Coventry*, Kingsgate Press, 1926

Ollard, S.M., *Dictionary of English Church History*, London, 1912

Ostovich, H., *Records of Early English Drama*, Reed University, Toronto, 1996

Paris, M., *Chronica Majora*, Corpus Christi College

Phythian-Adams, C., *Desolation of a City*, Cambridge University Press, 1979

Pollard, A., *English Miracle Plays*, Oxford, 1923

Poole, B., *Coventry: Its History and Antiquities*, Coventry, 1869

Potter, K.R., *Gesta Stephani*, 1955

Priestley, P.,'Watch Case Makers of England', NAWCC, 1994

Reader, W., Manuscripts (C. Nowell ed.), Coventry Local Studies

Reader, W., *New Coventry Guide*, Coventry, 1836

Register of the Cathedral Priory of St Mary, Coventry: The Pittancer's Rental, 1410-11, Birmingham University, 1973

Richardson, K., *Twentieth Century Coventry*, Coventry, 1972

Rylatt, M. and Adams, A., *A Harvest of History*, Coventry, 1983

Rylatt, M. and Gooder, E., *Coventry: Archaeology and Development*, Coventry Museums, 1977

'Scenes in Warwickshire during the Civil War', *Westminster Review*, 1858

Sharp, T., *History of Coventry*, Coventry, 1844

Sharp, T., *Illustrative Papers on the History and Antiquities of the City of Coventry*, Coventry, 1871

Shelton, J.B., *Austin Monthly Magazine*, 1932-36

Shotton, F. W., 'The Distribution of Neolithic Bronze Age and Iron Age Relics Around Coventry', *Coventry Natural History and Scientific Society*, 1937

Shotton, F. W., 'Flint implements from Fields around Coventry', *Coventry Natural History and Scientific Society*, 1953

Smith, F., *Coventry: Six Hundred Years of Municipal Life*, Coventry Corporation, 1945

Soden, I., *Excavations at St Anne's Charterhouse, Coventry, 1968-87*, Coventry Museums, 1995

Steane, J., *The Archaeology of the Medieval English Monarchy*, Routledge, 1993

Talbot, H., *The English Achilles*, Chatto & Windus, 1980

Templeman, G., *The Records of the Guild of the Holy Trinity, St Mary, St John the Baptist and St Katherine*, Dugdale Society, 1935-44, two vols.

The Victoria History of the County of Warwick, Volume VIII, London, 1969

Walford, E., *The Antiquarian Magazine and Biographer*, Redway, 1883

Warkworth, J., *A Chronicle of the First Years of the Reign of Edward IV* (G. Halliwell ed.), Camden Society, 1839

Weir, A., *Lancaster and York, The Wars of the Roses*, Cape, 1995

Whitley, T.W., *Humorous Reminiscences of Coventry Life*, Coventry, 1888

Whitley, T.W., *The Parliamentary Representation of the City of Coventry*, Coventry, 1894

Woodhouse, F., *Churches of Coventry*, London, 1909

Woolfe, B., *Henry VI*, Methuen, 1981

Yates, J., *Pioneers of Power*, Coventry, 1950

INDEX

Samuel Bradford's map of Coventry 1748-9 published 1750 by Thomas Jeffreys.